D0794241

PLAY AS EXPLORATORY LEARNING

PLAY AS EXPLORATORY LEARNING
Studies of Curiosity Behavior

MARY REILLY, EDITOR

Professor, Department of Occupational Therapy
University of Southern California
Los Angeles, California

 SAGE PUBLICATIONS   Beverly Hills / London

For information address:

SAGE PUBLICATIONS, INC.
275 South Beverly Drive
Beverly Hills, California 90212

SAGE PUBLICATIONS LTD
St George's House / 44 Hatton Garden
London EC1N 8ER

Printed in the United States of America

ISBN No. 0-8039-0159-3 (cloth)

ISBN No. 0-8039-0668-4 (paper)

Library of Congress Catalog Card No. 72-98044

SECOND PRINTING

FOREWORD

Play, whether serious or lighthearted, is a serious topic. Psychologists and other social scientists generally acknowledge its importance, as well they must in view of its human universality, its salience in the long developmental sequence of human immaturity, and its polar opposition to "work" in the coordinates of the meaningful adult world. Having paid their respects, however, they have mostly lapsed into inarticulateness. Since the grand speculative syntheses of Groos and Huizinga went out of fashion, the topic has eluded satisfactory treatment. Only now does it promise to come into its own as a focal concern in "the proper study of mankind"—and in the formulation of appropriate strategies for the realization of human potentialities and the remediation of damages and deficits in the course of human life.

Just before reading the manuscript of Dr. Reilly's book, I encountered a major sign of the renaissance of scientific interest in play in Jerome Bruner's (1972) magisterial treatment of the "nature and uses of immaturity." Himself a path-setting contributor to our understanding of thinking, teaching, and cognitive development, Bruner reflects and partially synthesizes, in this essay, the broadened perspective within which we are now able to come to grips with human developmental processes in childhood. The seminal discoveries and lines of evidence that have emerged in recent years once more permit speculative synthesis on a scale that is compatible with human significance—synthesis that in this round is informed and constrained by evidence to a much larger extent than before, and therefore promises to be productive of cumulative understanding and cogent guidance to the human service professions. The new lines of evidence, of course, concern such matters as man's immensely long prehistory as a tool user, in which his biology and his culture evolved in tandem; his resemblances to and his differences from his close cousins the higher primates, which are now being closely studied under natural conditions; the nature of his language competence as revealed by Chomsky and his successors; the steps by which the emerging human mind actively (better, *inter*actively) constructs its world, as clarified especially by Piaget. In this new context, Bruner's speculations about the adaptive functions of play have a degree of substance and authority that was notably lacking in earlier formulations. Play becomes an indispensable context that helps to account for the distinctive human pre-eminence in tool use, in observational learning, and in symbolic transformations, not an anomaly or embarrassment to prevailing theoretical conceptions.

There has recently been a revolution in scientific ways of thinking about human development and adaptation. The traditional behavioristic model of a mechanically reactive organism shaped by its environmental encounters (a model that was incidentally given decisive criticism by the psychologist-philosopher-educator John Dewey before it was properly born) did indeed find play a theoretical embarrassment. Playfulness, curiosity and exploratory behavior, and tension-*seeking* activities in dooryard or playground seemed anomalous from a view of man as *re-actor* preoccupied with the reduction of drives. Neither did they mesh well with the abstract formulations of psychoanalysis, which sought to distill the clinical richness of psychoanalytic observation into formulae about the economy of "psychic energy" that converged with behaviorism on tension-reduction as the underlying theme. Play just does not fit a model of man misconstrued in terms of analogies with the laws of thermodynamics!

No wonder, then, that the incontrovertable facts of human playfulness have figured importantly in the reconstruction (by Robert W. White and others) of a view of developing man as *actor* or agent. From many quarters, behavioral and social scientists and allied professionals are contributing to this emerging view, in which a fuller understanding of play becomes a proper and central concern. Dr. Reilly's book fits squarely into this development.

The contest between mechanistic-reactive and active-playful views of human development is far from concluded. Skinner's (1971) version of behaviorism and the behavior modification movement with which it is loosely linked represents a vigorous contemporary thrust according to which the view of man (and child) as actor is rejected as unscientific—on what I think are dogmatic philosophical grounds, not scientific ones. Skinner and the behavior modifiers are far more sophisticated than the old behaviorists (and than some of their critics). They have made enduring theoretical and clinical contributions. But they have little to say about play, and rightly gain no notice in Dr. Reilly's wide sweep of reference. The value of their contribution lies in aspects of their technology, not in their restrictive view of human functioning.

It is altogether appropriate, then, that occupational therapists should become concerned with "play as exploratory learning." Occupational therapy deals with activities by which the physically or psychologically maimed or deficient may gain or regain *competence,* as actors or agents managing their own lives insofar as possible. As a profession, it is committed to the transformation of "patients" into agents. Playful activity, engaged in for its own sake ("intrinsic motivation"), is perhaps the purest case of agenthood: creating interesting effects, testing possibilities, measuring one's growing skills, all protected by the spirit of "as-if" from the preemptive urgencies of drives and reality demands and from the harsh consequences of failure. If we understand it, play is obviously a crucial medium of therapeutic activity. When the child—or adult—lacks the capacity to play, a first challenge may well be to discover contexts and levels at which the playful spark can be ignited and fanned.

Dr. Reilly's substantial theoretical contribution to the book begins by placing the topic of play in the broadest setting of contemporary utopian thought about our cultural crisis. To the extent that alienation and apathy reflect pathologies of modern postindustrial society, it seems reasonable to think that man's involvements in both work and play—including the sharp demarcation drawn between them in the modern world—require reconsideration.

In the course of the wide-ranging review of previous thought about play that follows, Dr. Reilly not only acquaints the reader with the major existing treatments of the topic, but, along the way, she also provides brief guides to the central theoretical ideas that have guided recent thought about human development. The perspectives of major figures including Freud, Erikson, G. H. Mead, and Piaget get expounded in the natural course of her exposition.

Her own major account of play in Chapter 3 is cast in the framework of "systems theory," a relevant approach that she also makes meaningful in discussing the contributions of Boulding and von Bertalanffy. Although she labels the chapter "an explanation of play," I would rather regard it as a cogent interpretative perspective. The clinical reader of this chapter will share in a way of thinking about play that is in accord with what we presently know, and, perhaps more important, in tune with conceptual strategies that presently seem appropriate to man and his problems. The explanatory task in the stricter sense remains largely before us, as research and theory that in the past has brushed lightly against play can be brought focally to bear upon it, unencumbered by the previous awkwardness produced by discrepant theoretical models.

The last five chapters of the book contributed by Dr. Reilly's student-collaborators are promising applications to the realm of occupational therapy. As a psychologist outsider, I found them provocative and likely to be sensitizing to the reader, though I wished for normative data where developmental scales or inventories are involved. This is early in an ambitious undertaking, however, and there is room for much good clinical research to build on these beginnings.

I heartily concur in the underlying premises of this ambitious book: the occupational therapist's professional rejection of the fatalistic view that "the incompetent are always with us," and the assumption that in human capacities for play lie the developmental roots of competence, and therefore a major resource for endeavors to remedy human deficits. I hope that the efforts of Dr. Reilly and her collaborators will turn out to be part of a new stream of interest in play as a scientific problem and as a therapeutic and educational strategy.

—M. Brewster Smith
Division of Social Sciences
University of California
Santa Cruz 95060

REFERENCES

BRUNER, J. S. (1972) "Nature and uses of immaturity," Amer. Psychologist 27 (August): 687-708.
SKINNER, B. F. (1971) Beyond Freedom and Dignity. New York: Alfred A. Knopf.

PREFACE

For the past half century, occupational therapy has had a natural laboratory in hospitals to observe and help disabled people who are struggling to master their environment. The mastery struggle appeared to us to be a competency process from which skills emerge as the product. From the earliest record of therapeutic intervention, the struggling process has been intermeshed with playful behavior. The content of pure play, competitive games, arts, and crafts permeated both ancient and modern treatment strategies.

The practical partnership of treatment and play was based on the clinical impression that play had an organizing effect upon patients who were obviously incompetent or behaviorally disorganized. The association, born of necessity, continued in occupational therapy because the mediating or midwifery role that play assumes for mastery was recognized as a fundamental truth in the world of disability. The difficulty lies in the explanation of this conviction. Why playful behavior generates the tools of mastery, or how this methodology functions, is an enigma. Leaving play as an assumed 'good' abandons the exploitation of this phenomenon to intuition.

Occupational therapy searched for the understanding of this process in the medical sciences and found that medicine explains pathology and the control of disease—but not the reorganization of behavior. Studying pathology led to much useful knowledge about sensory motor and perceptual deficits, neuromuscular patterning, and the engineering of mechanical aids for movement. Medically derived theories suggested insights by offering clues about the reciprocal relationship between the skills of daily living and the psychological mechanisms of defensing and coping. What we learned from the medical sciences is that there are conditions internal to the functioning of the body and mind that are preconditions for competency. What we have yet to learn is why, when these preconditions have been modified, competency is not a natural sequel.

As the power in rehabilitation to control pathology and retrain residual behavior enlarged over the years, an underlying form of incompetency moved into visability. Chronically disabled patients, we have come to realize, share few characteristics with their fellow patients suffering from short time illnesses. Instead, their most common characteristics are shared with the school dropout and the economically deprived member of the welfare society. We now conclude that individuals whose biological structures are impaired by disease or injury are vulnerable to cultural deprivation. Chronic disability, in this sense, becomes a special case of deprivation. This book develops the theme that play contains the answer to problems of biocultural adaptation and is a natural modifier of deprivation. The issue, however, is what questions about behavioral organization and adaptation play answers. The intent is heuristic, focusing on determining the questions that ought to be asked of play.

The book is divided into two parts. Each part is an aspect of an heuristic approach to the phenomenon of play. Part One searches for the most general questions about external and internal reality that play can answer; Part Two applies specific play questions to the behavior of disabled people. What the reader should realize is that the theoretical approach of Part One is not applied in Part Two. All the authors were free to ask questions without reference to each other. The heuristic strategies, it needs also to be said, grew from the remedial setting in which occupational therapists use play. As an applied field, occupational therapy is not obliged to hold any allegiance to a specific science or theoretical methodology. The graduate student contributors in Part Two used play as a masters thesis theme at the University of Southern California, and drew upon their abundant clinical experiences acquired in rehabilitation clinics. Both the strengths and weaknesses of the contributors are that they were under no compulsion to make their data fit a particular scientific methodology or theoretical foundation.

As a teacher, I am grateful for the opportunity to collaborate with student authors like Shirley Michelman, Nancy Takata, Janith Hurff, Susan Knox, and Phillip Shannon. For financial support involved in publishing this book, we owe thanks to the Maternal and Child Health Service in the Department of Health, Education, and Welfare, and particularly to the Occupational Therapy Consultant in HEW, Wilma West, who encouraged the venture.

—Mary Reilly

September 1973
Department of Occupational Therapy
University of Southern California
Los Angeles

CONTENTS

PLAY AS EXPLORATORY LEARNING

PART ONE

INTRODUCTION

The first three chapters of this book accept a foundation assumption that play is a "connectivity" phenomenon. In Chapter 1, Mary Reilly sets before the reader the broad themes of social progress and the threats that interrupt, or break into, the continuity of reality. An extensive dialogue with social theorists describes the many problems of socialization imposed upon the adaptation of man whenever society changes so rapidly that reality no longer fits his expectation. Human adaptation falters when meaning cannot be derived from environmental interactions. Man becomes a stranger in his world when his senses cannot decode the social order. Play, or the oxymoronous approach to puzzling reality, is traced as a persistent strategy used by man to apprehend the unknown. The playful approach, social theorists agree, could be a critical vehicle for social transformation and a rational strategy for strengthening the adaptation of marginal man.

Chapter 2 attempts to define the ubiquitous, cobwebby nature of play. The behavior was found embedded—indeed hidden—in the knowledge bodies of evolution, anthropology, psychology, and sociology. The task becomes one of rescuing the phenomenon of play from the pre-emptive efforts of the single disciplines and to free play so that it can have an identity and explanation of its own.

Chapter 3 searches for an explanatory structure appropriate for theorizing about play. The multiple dimension of the behavior suggests the systems approach. The critical service play offers man for processing meanings suggests a theory designed to explain the process of evaluation. The appreciative system of the British theorist

Vickers was accepted as an appropriate vehicle for explaining play because the theory addressed itself primarily to the complex ways man uses his unique capacity to symbolize or to internalize reality by evaluating it. Play, as an appreciative construct, is conceptualized as a curiosity-based phenomenon that explores outer reality through playful interaction with the environment and, in this process, the rules or the tools of mastery are fashioned. Man begins his adventurous response into the unknown by searching for the rules of sensory motor mastery in the play of his childhood. He incorporates the rules of role behavior in the symbolic play of pre-adolescence. The rules of profit and loss are absorbed in the competitive and cooperative games of adolescence. The rules learned in the pure play of childhood are exercised in the risk-taking behavior of craftsmanship and sportsmanship. These latter behavioral configurations can then be proposed as the necessary preconditions for the transformational process of adult workmanship.

The appreciative system theory permits and even requires play to be investigated as a rule processing form of behavior. The possibility of examining the relationship between play and competency emerges in a new form and sets the stage for another order of questions. To be competent, man must know what he is doing and knowing can be defined as knowing the rules. Chapter 3 concludes that if rule processing is the common denominator of playful behavior, then man internalizing the rules of his world is man constructing his own competency.

CHAPTER 1

UTOPIAN MYTHS OF PROGRESS

Mary Reilly

It is paradoxical that when man through scientific knowledge has become too efficient in securing with little effort his basic necessities of life, he becomes deadly serious and looks nostalgically at the creative centuries of the past when he still had time and detachment for play and creativity. In this paradox lies the secret of understanding the crisis of Western civilization.

—Franz Alexander

KNOWLEDGE-ACTION DISCONTINUITY

Utopian Form of Social Design

There have always been times, history and common sense tell us, when certain classes of people and certain kinds of societies failed to be caught up and swept along in the mainstream of progress. In the United States we know this to be true of the disabled, the school dropout, and the hardcore unemployable. Internationally it is true of nations that are underdeveloped. When socialization fails to occur for the individual or society, life tends to sink into a paralysis of inertia or explode into the chaos of violence.

Anthropology claims that every civilization contains a ground plan, an image of the future which supplies the energy to shape social progress. The guiding image is energized by hope disguised in the many costumes and speaking the many tongues of progress. It is one of the great ironies of fate, however, that as the image converges with reality, hope disappears, progress becomes paralyzed, and the civilization declines. The thrust of progress narrows, slows down, and eventually disappears. So far, few civilizations have had the wit or flexibility to keep an old image alive for long periods or reconstitute new ones that provide an alternative source for continuing social progress.

The oldest hope of mankind, the ultimate abstraction of progress, has been described as a "time of milk and honey, and economy of abundance." Aristotle rhapsodized this mythical future as a time when the shuttle would weave by itself, the lyre would play without player, and the loaves of bread would spring forth from the oven untouched by human hands. The specifications proposed by Aristotle have been met, and even surpassed, in the United States by the democratic capitalistic system. With the arrival of automation, bread untouched by human hands is springing from the oven faster than it can be consumed. Plastic recorded music plays on without the player. Clothes no longer need either the weaver or the natural fibers of cotton and wool. But as the myth and reality converge in our time, we are reminded anew of the ancient warning to be aware of the Greeks bearing gifts. For as abundance increased, the quality of life in the United States has tarnished.

The American society, as well as most of the Western civilization, admit to being in a social adaptation crisis. Everywhere mankind would welcome a revitalizing vision. Visionary ground plans for social progress are nothing new, they have been around as long as society itself. Robert Boguslaw (1965), a social systems engineer, suggests that what we have always called "utopia" is the driving force and the ground plan for societal structure. He uses the concept utopia within the system design context and sees those who analyze and design social changes as the new utopians.

Contemporary utopians, that is systems engineers, computer programmers, operations researchers, are people who link the peoples of the world together in communication networks. They ensure the timely production, transportation, and distribution of bananas, beeswax, and bombs. Increasingly in the process of social designing, the modern social scientist makes use of high speed computers. While proposals for social changes are usually disguised in the language of systems technology, the designs are borrowed and adapted utopias from the ancient past. In an archetypical sense utopia is an idealized or mythical society that seems to belong either to the present or to the future. David Riesman once described utopia as a plan that is now nowhere but that someday may be somewhere. In the contemporary world the utopian plan is known as the process of system design.

Utopians are builders who reject the contemporary status quo and reach out for new forms within their society to shape their wished-for worlds. Both ancient and modern utopians attempt to come to grips with the highly visible global and unresolved problems of their society. New forms that are proposed stem from a methodology which is a blend of the ancient art of vigorous philosophical criticism and systems analysis technology. Utopian thinking embraces more than a plan for the total venture, contains the implicit notion that societies can and must be improved. A utopia is a statement of society built free from imperfections, and specifies the human error to be reduced.

The classical utopians tried to achieve their purpose by populating the social system with perfect human beings, perfect social structures, perfect situations, or perfect principles. They were the do-gooders in the finer sense of the word. They wanted to escape from the melancholy world in which they lived into a happier, more moral, more just or more prosperous one. Their primary concern was people, and although some focused their efforts on saving souls, others focused on filling stomachs. What classical utopians and systems engineer-type utopians have in common is that they receive their impetus from a dissatisfaction with existing reality. They both represent attempts to design a society more consistent with notions about what was "good" for the mankinds they knew or dreamed about. Utopians range from Plato and George Orwell to those who are proposing now the new post-industrial man. When their utopias are unsuccessful, it is because their visionary plans, despite the highly technical analysis, do not take into consideration the nature of the situation within which the utopia is to operate. Designs are the most successful when this brave new system promises to increase the power of man over his world and promotes a new universal hope for progress.

For centuries the universal vision of progress has been the myth of the golden age, recorded by Hesiod in the eighth century B.C. This classical utopia foretold of "a golden race of moral men who would dwell on the earth and who would live like gods without sorrow of heart, remote and free from toil and grief. Miserable age would rest not upon them, but with legs and arms never failing they would make merry, feasting beyond the reach of all evil. When they died, it would be as though they were overcome with sleep, and they would have had all good things; for the fruitful earth bore them fruit abundantly without stint. They would dwell in ease and peace upon their lands with many good things, rich in flocks and loved by the blessed gods. The golden age, according to Hesiod, came to an end when Pandora lifted the lid of her box and allowed the escape and spread of previously unseen evils."

The difference between this ancient universal myth and Western ones is that contemporary utopians are concerned with issues rather than people. The planning is done with computer hardware, systems procedures and functional analysis. The new breed seek to identify and reduce the social disorder created by human error. The theoretical and practical solutions they propose call for refinement of responsibility of human beings within the operating structures of their new machine systems. They begin with the acceptance of the status quo in such areas as the facts of our physical environment, human physiology, and the state or projected state of machine technology. They consider the requirements for food, shelter, reproduction, and recreation in the light of this status quo and then proceed to explain how human groups can or do adapt to the world in which they find themselves. Principles, empirical conclusions, theories, and hypothesis emerge from this analysis. Their recommendations take the form of a concern with the consequences that advances in automation will have for such things as family life, employment, juvenile delinquency, community organization, leisure, and educational practices. Utopia and utopians are proliferating because there is a general recognition in our society that supports to old utopias are being exhausted. To maintain the sophisticated state of progress in a highly technical society, new utopias are required that will repropose what technology will do to improve, not destroy, the quality of our lives.

Specifications for contemporary utopias have been proposed most ably by Dennis Gabor (1964, 1972), a British physicist and Nobel Laureate. The Gabor specifications not only identify the real issues of our time but they reconceptualize the problems of social change in such a way that the issues he proposes are fermenting an international dialogue of social restructuring. His major thesis is that in Western civilization exponential growth cannot be continued indefinitely. While recognizing that growth has become synonymous with hope and man cannot live without hope, he maintains that the growth is self-limiting. The growth of technology has not only mastered but defeated nature which fights back only as a rotting corpse does—by pollution.

Gabor's assertion is that "until now man has been up against nature, from now on he will be up against his own nature." The age-old enemy, poverty, is defeated in one-quarter of the world; almost all the ailments that used to kill half the people in childhood, are eliminated. There is no enemy left but man. We have every right to be proud when we look back, none at all for pride when looking forward. The tragic situation has arisen that the very talents that have made the naked ape the master of the earth are now turning against him—his fighting temper, his restless quest for novelty, his craving for excitement and adventure, even his virtues, such as the love and care for his progeny, and his willingness to sacrifice himself for his tribe or for his nation.

Science in combination with nationalism has created a situation in which a total war could wipe out all civilization. Science in combination with love for progeny has created overpopulation. Science in combination with the old economic virtues has created techniques that can virtually eliminate work, the most harmless occupation of men, and have brought us face to face with an age of leisure for which we are psychologically unprepared.

The Gabor analysis concludes that leisure is one of the main concerns for the maturation of a post-industrialized society. Because this problem is new in history it urgently needs the involvement of utopians. The old myth of the golden age is ready to be replaced with a new vision of men and women living in peaceful and contented life at a high level of material comfort and security. The key concept now for emerging man is that he must learn to live without a daily struggle against nature. The key problem for an emergent society is to learn that social institutions must serve leisure in much the same way they learned how to support work.

Leisure and the underlying phenomenon, play, unfortunately, is a missing link in our chain of knowledge about man and his behavior. We may suspect, as some theorists have, that play is a way of learning and leisure is a social structure for the transformation of learning. But despite its universality, this behavior has little representation in organized knowledge. The great question to be raised is: can play really be considered a serious form of human behavior and subjected to serious study?

An understanding of this ancient commonplace activity might be served well by techniques drawn from the utopian tradition. The design orientation of this tradition would require a functional analysis based upon such questions as: what does a post-industrial society require of play? What functions for man does play serve? What components will it include? What tasks will be assigned to these components? Like any good utopian, let us begin by attempting to identify in our emerging society those undesirable characteristics which stem from human error. For impatience with human error, it seems, is a unifying imperative among utopians.

Science and Specialization

The American social critic, Max Ways (1971), blames the exploding knowledge generated by narrow specialists in the many scientific fields as the ultimate source of pollution. The most biting and perilous irony of modern civilization turns upon knowledge because people today believe they can do more because they know more. While science keeps adding to the store of truth, educational and other communication systems have speeded up the distribution of knowledge. Our great industrial complexes are transforming knowledge into technology and producing a higher level of material affluence. But as knowledge mounts, ignorance increases. The real confusion in contemporary life is the way knowledge and action are related. Modern society pushed on by the fast pace of its technology is in danger of rattling apart because what we know is so unevenly applied to what we do.

While we are growing exponentially, we Americans oscillate between expecting either too much or too little from a unique civilization that learns so fast and yet blunders so horribly, that achieves so magnificently and yet leaves more and more undone. At a time when our knowledge exceeds our dreams we are in a crisis of incompetence. Quantitatively and qualitatively we are disappointed in our efforts to come to grips with the good life. As knowledge grows the interlocking problems of unemployment, technological illiteracy, physical and mental disability, and civil disorder become more visible. The computer spews forth an overabundance of information on the issues of race, poverty, crime and urban decay. The unpleasant disorder of our progress is everywhere and threatens to overwhelm us. Contemporary times reverberate the conditions of "illo tempore" the other times of which the Greek myths spoke.

The ancient Hittites, for instance, left records of the myth of a missing god whose disappearance precipitated a decline in their progress. According to the myth, the god of progress leaves when beliefs have no expression in empiricism or when empiricism has no supporting beliefs. Progress, the Hittite myth recounts, returns, when man looks to himself and his experience for new ways to unite his world of action and though. The British physicist Whyte (1954) repeats the Hittites' myth when he calls today's state of affairs a present "wrongheadedness" in which no analogies from the past are valid. It is, he says, a totally novel situation which calls for unusual measures. The progressive changes in the condition of the race and the changed interrelatedness of things require a new coherence. Contemporary thought, says Whyte, has no direct relation to the immediate experience of life; thought is deeply and essentially frustrated and does not flow unchecked into action.

Whenever action contains the same beliefs that guide the invention of knowledge, the mind comes to perceive thought and action as being the same. The philosopher Aeschylus warned against the tendency of man to imitate gods by acting as if thought, word, and deed were one and the same. Thinking, feeling, and doing are discrete but interdependent streams of behavior through which reality is processed. Contemporary man adds to his confusion and frustration when he assumes that some day knowledge will become so complete that all problems will have answers and everything will be accomplished. All man has to do, this belief purports, is to continue to do in the future what has worked in the past and any present storm of ignorance will be ridden out. If modern man confuses words with deeds or thought with feeling and fails to integrate thought, feeling, and word, he will indeed be dinosaured out of existence.

Poisoned Expectancies

The utopian view of progress through scientific knowledge is the hope underlying our hidden perception of the actions of our times. But when expectations consistently outdistance performance, it is time to reexamine our notions of how much practical improvement should reasonably be anticipated from what has been called scientifit progress. Echoing the Karen Horney principle that the tendency to overidealize leads to the despised, we should suspect that the unlimited expectancy from scientific knowledge may be responsible for much of the cynicism and bitterness that now discolor public life in the United States. For more than two centuries Western culture has been subject to an accelerated enlightenment. We have acquired a blissful optimism that the linked agencies of science and education would gradually solve all practical problems.

More than any other people we Americans are deeply involved in the knowledge-action nexus and therefore more bewildered and frustrated by the disappointments it generates. Without the knowledge expansion, we would not be able to foul up the physical environment. Yet, when we turn to straighten out the mess, we never seem to know enough. Public criticism is mounting against an educational system in which students do not learn, a medical system that ignores health, an economic system that increases our wealth while it destroys our air and water.

As utopian visions move underground through the contemporary psyche they poison our expectancies and give rise to such metaphors of frustration as: if man can reach the moon, he ought to be able to solve the commonplace problems on this earth. Utopian visions such as those that man is a rational scientific thinker bear within them the dangerous poison of all kinds of expectations for scientific knowledge. They tell us what we want to hear: that salvation is at hand and scientific knowledge made it possible. The good life is just around the corner, and all that is required is momentum of progress. Yet, why are scientific knowledge, our social institutions and our leaders not moving us closer to affluence? The magnitude of the promise and the disappointment in its delay extend to every sector of contemporary life. For disappointment is sharpened everywhere when knowledge cannot master events.

The finite nature of psychological knowledge is a prime example of "wrongheadedness." The attention that psychology has given to learning has been neither deep nor fruitful for society. American psychology, following policy internal to itself, has been interested primarily in motivation as it occurs in the bedroom, crib, and rat cage. The limited themes pursued during this century were tension reduction and stimulus response. The reality data of actual experience have been screened out by the experimental method that dominates psychology. The models that psychology has chosen for its theories do not permit the more complex—but commonplace— behavior of daily living to fit easily within them.

Psychology has succeeded in making us aware of our ignorance about learning while at the same time leaving us discouraged as to whether there will be any breakthrough by the present method. The answerable questions put to the development of intelligence and motivation have caused an avalanche of knowledge, while avoiding any coherent explanation of learning. Knowledge of how man learns remains fragmented and incoherent. Common sense about learning and behavior appears to have been brutalized while theorists pursue their answerable questions as dictated by some limiting frame of reference.

There is another damaging myth internalized in our culture and dangerously poisoning our child-rearing practices. We all know that child care is influenced by the considerable knowledge generated this century. The works of Freud, Dewey, Spock, and Gesell on child development are generalized public information. Parents who rear an aberrant child are automatically blamed and blame themselves, just as if our organized folklore had ready recipes on how failure and incompetence can be averted. A high level of expectation leads many parents to approach child-rearing with such trepidation or hopes that it would have been better if nothing new had been learned in the last century. Never, it would seem, have our child-rearing practices been so inept.

American medicine is yet another example of disenchantment. Our admiration for advances turns into bitter recrimination whenever patients die of causes beyond the reach of medical science. Public anger mounts as the physician service for health grows less available and as costs rise extravagantly for treatment of illness. We might expect that such pressure would spur medicine on to further discovery and better performance. Its more potent effect, unfortunately, is to create distrust where there should be trust and to demoralize a profession which cannot meet the expectations of those it serves.

Intimately related to the crisis in medicine is the strong affinity that American medical practice holds for scientific methods. The laboratory sciences of biophysics and biochemistry have enabled the successful control of many diseases. But as enormously successful as medical science has been for developing knowledge of pathology, it has been equally ineffectual in generating understanding of health. A patient expects a physician to have on tap not only the drugs and surgical procedures necessary to relieve pain and save life, but also have the ability to teach him how to optimize his health and extend his life span.

Perhaps the greatest example of medicine's mixed triumph and disaster is illustrated by the plight of the chronically disabled. This segment of population exists in an all-too-obvious state of health deterioration and social incompetency. Their lives have been salvaged by the scientific medical technology, but they are left to eke out a marginal existence handicapped by the residual dysfunction. A disabled patient has been led to expect medicine to restore both his physical and social functioning. Those with chronic mental and physical disabilities expect medicine or society to fulfill an implied contract by helping them attain at least a beginning level of social adaptation. Unfortunately, scientific method linked as it is to biological and psychological scientific frames of reference contain little in their bodies of scientific knowledge which might fulfill the social expectancies of rehabilitation.

Simplicity and Complexity

The mystery of why we are ignorant in the presence of so much knowledge is now shaping into a crisis of confidence in America. It is substantially affecting the vigor of democratic progress at many levels. The Swiss historian, Jacob Burckhardt, foresaw the twentieth century as the age of the great analyzers and hence simplifiers, and that "the essence of tyranny would be the denial of complexity." The sociologist, Daniel Moynihan, in 1970 made the Burckhardt warning the springboard of his farewell speech upon quitting his service to President Nixon. He called the tendency to oversimplify the single greatest temptation of our time and the "great corrupter." We need, he urged, great complexifiers—men who would not only seek to understand what it is that society is concerned about but who will also dare to share that understanding with those for whom they act. The intellectual refusal to admit the genuine difficulties of our times institutionalizes the denial of complexity. Perhaps what it comes down to is a willingness to examine and live with complexity. Our present problem is asking for the development of thinking models which acknowledge complexity and make coherent the partial information bits being spewed at us from the data processing machines. In essence we are caught up in a challenge to unite what we know with what we do.

The scientific method of problem-solving with its pursuit of narrow truths and its devotion to minute abstracts like the atom, cell, id, or virus has been blamed for the fragmentation of action. The disdain for the study of the obvious and visible is an attitude derived from the scientific method. Alfred North Whitehead once said that it requires an unusual mind to undertake the analysis of the obvious. But he did not confuse the obvious with the simple, because he added the injunction to seek simplicity and upon finding it, distrust it. Scientific method exercises the simplest approach frequently at the expense of both the mind that used it and the events being investigated. The myths and rituals of pure science require that only answerable questions be put to the world of raw and total phenomena. The answerable questions, once the province of scientists, are now generalized modes of thinking and have resulted in the accumulation of the considerable answers we now have on hand.

Using again the physicist Whyte's apt label, the "wrongheadedness" of the situation is that much of what the answerable question is shaped to "know" ignores other things in the context which later emerge and distort the application of scientific findings. Reality is further confounded by the very effectiveness of the answerable questions. The complete commitment to this method has succeeded in moving the unanswerable questions into uncomfortable, insistent visibility. What we should suspect is that most of the easy questions have already been raised. We are now left with those that are harder to ask and more difficult to answer.

While few scientists think they may be running out of questions, they would agree that society faces more problems now that it did fifty years ago. Nobody can be sure that the emergence of new questions and new problems is not going to continue to accelerate knowledge. Nor can we foretell the limits which the multiplications of methods and problems must reach. The glaring truth beginning to seep into our awareness is that, as knowledge advances, ignorance does not diminish. The hippy phenomenon and the dropout fad are dramatically suggesting that if contemporary man does not learn to live with this paradox, he will come to despise both knowledge and the practical achievements made possible by knowledge. Any need for future knowledge, any field of ignorance of which we are made aware, may contain more difficulties than did vanquished ignorance. We are now facing the hard questions which the answerable ones avoided. Emerging man is destined to require multiple and flexible ways of knowing rather than fewer and simpler.

OCCUPATION-EDUCATION DISCONTINUITY

The Metaphors of Knowledge Production

The pursuit of knowledge, as it is going on now, is bound to broaden its methodology. Whether this change will come about fast and easily or with painful slowness, cannot be said. A critical first step in shifting to other ways of knowing lies in the willingness of the contemporary mind to accept the limitation of scientific method. Are we uncomfortable enough to acknowledge the finite nature of scientific knowledge? The idealized expectancy that we have for the continuous progress of science and the determined habit of simplification that is the root of this method have disarmed us in many ways from dealing with complexity. Dependence upon science as the only way of knowing is probably at the foundation of our frustrated sense of paralysis. For modern man it is a dangerously narrow form of specialization. How else could we explain our apparent refusal to explore new ways of knowing and hence discovering alternative learning technology?

One cannot belong to the twentieth century without believing deeply in the very oversimplifications upon which scientific method is based and which yielded our present knowledge explosion. Without scientific methodology we would not have been bogged down as we are in technological complexities and the post-industrial society of the seventies could hardly have managed to get off the ground. Yet to prevent modern man from moving toward the fate of the dinosaurs, we need to be aware of limitations of scientific methodology. An examination of the constraints of this method may suggest new directions to be explored.

Semanticists and epistomologists have studied the ways man uses metaphors to analyze his reality. The metaphorical approach to thinking is based on Hayakawa's principle that "our thoughts do not select words we use; instead words determine the thoughts we have." The physical, biological and social sciences use quite different forms of conceptualization to apprehend the problems they work on and each discipline tends to be identified readily by the metaphors it uses.

The physical or natural sciences use the metaphors of Newtonian mechanics. As a consequence, physical sciences see the reality as processes directed into given paths by the action of impersonal, external forces. The motion (behavior) of bodies (in human beings) are preset. Their events are controlled by the laws of nature which are the laws of balance or homeostasis. The metaphors of biology shift thinking from the world of non-living thing of machines to living organisms which are subject to growth, development, change, adaptation or alteration.

Some time in the mid-twentieth century a new methaphor, the systems approach, emerged. The language of systems speaks to a reality which was not made up of living and non-living material. The reality of systems is the world of organizations. Its focus is on the process of change from which it derives principles of connectivity. The language of systems describes change as a series of successive stages, in which any present performance is dependent upon performance in other stages. The metaphors include such concepts as boundaries, tension, equilibrium, feedback, input, throughout, output, and hierarchy.

Metaphorical analysis of thinking assumes that both a society and man pursues an evolutionary course to contemporary problem-solving. Evolution, unfortunately, guarantees no promise of progressive continuity. There has been, therefore, no sequential learning or flexible use of metaphors. Of all metaphorical forms used, the physical science metaphor is the most common. The scientific discoveries of the chemist, physicist, and biologist using Newtonian ways of thinking have been picked up by industry and processed into technology that produces goods. The "goods" section of the American economic system and the resulting affluent society owes its productivity to physical science metaphors. The biological metaphor based upon the evolutionary species and developmental life cycles remain fairly undeveloped. Its body of knowledge is dominated by the physical science of biochemistry and biophysics. The weak state of organismic knowledge is a critical loss to progress since it delimits the understanding of environmental influences upon inherited behavioral systems.

The emerging metaphors of the social sciences describe the modes of thinking that dominate the service in contrast to the goods sector of the economic system. In the post-industrial society, systems analysis is expected to define the problems of the service sector of the economy; that is, education, governmental services, and medical care. This sector will rapidly outpace the goods-producing sector which includes agriculture, industry, and mining, and which is the consumer of the physical science Newtonian methodology.

The wrongheadedness, as Whyte would say, is that the dominant metaphor for the prehension of reality, regardless of appropriateness, is that of the physical and natural sciences. The exclusive use of this method is the driving force behind specialization and compounds technological fragmentation. It obscures and delays the understanding that the goods sector may be in need of declaration while the service sector requires acceleration. The power to reorder muddled or distorting modes of thinking lies in the education institutions within a society. Fortunately there is continuous dialogue in the United States about education methodologies and goals. Pouncing upon and speculating on educational errors is one of the popular sports in American life. There is no lack of utopian propositions, the problem is one of selection.

Education System Errors

A new and unexpected symptom which reveals a critical discontinuity of social needs and the educational system which serves it, is the decreasing demand for doctoral trained manpower. Herbert Carter, Chairman of the National Science Board, maintains that doctoral personnel are no longer needed to staff the expansion of the educational system nor for the industrial production complex. The reorganization of higher education is required by the approaching end of exponential expansion of the educational system and the shift of science away from the pure research of the physical sciences to pure research in the social sciences.

It is clear that the educational system is approaching the end of an exponential phase of growth because there can be no more doubling of the school population. In 1870, only 7 percent received education beyond the sixth grade; currently 96 percent do and about 80 percent complete high school. In 1900, about 4 percent of the college age entered college and that percent has doubled about every twenty years and now stands at over 50 percent. The number of doctorates produced in the United States has doubled every ten years since 1880, and up to two or three years ago a further doubling was projected for the 1980s. Carter doubts that there are many, if any, factors of two left in high school, bachelor's or doctoral degree populations. Any future change, he predicted, will be qualitative rather than quantitative. Doctoral personnel anticipated for the education system will be for maintenance rather than for expansion.

The real issue in the next decades will be the research and development required for the service sector of the American economic system. The major part of this need Carter associated in one way or another with information, its acquisition, transmission, and interpretation. Computers, communication, data storage and retrieval necessarily will play central roles in educational technology. Universities must play a major role in providing an innovative program as the error in the system is not due to an overproduction of doctoral graduates. The error lies in the way the higher education system prepares doctoral personnel for public service.

Graduate education, it is abundantly clear, must take a less passive part in helping society resolve contemporary problems that exist in the housing, health care, transportation, crime, legitimacy of government, race, and minorities. These are problems of large complex systems involving man and his environment. Few if any such problems can be effectively attacked by an individual scientist or indeed by a single science.

Carter warned the deans of American universities that future employment of doctoral manpower is not totally dependent upon the changes made within the university structure. Most of the social problems today do not have adequate agencies waiting to put new knowledge and understanding to work for the benefit of society. The error in education, Herbert Carter of the National Science Board would say, lies in the discontinuity between the public service preparation of the Ph.D. and the needs of society for a new approach to the problems contemporary man is experiencing in adapting to his environment.

Not so, says James Conant (1967) in his survey of the American high school; the error in educational practices is the most glaring at the high school level. There is a dangerous discontinuity between the expectancies of a technically knowledgeable society and the high school student. Young people entering a technically demanding market have the following choices: they can stay in school, for which they might be unsuited either by motivation or by intelligence; they can seek training that might raise them out of the untrained work force; they can compete in the growing manpower pool for those seeking relatively unskilled jobs; or they could loaf.

If they choose to loaf, the historical experience of society is that the idle are the deviants. Social disruption emerges as a natural consequence when unemployment is the only choice of life occupation. The vacuum created by loss of occupational identity and purpose and the disorganizing effects of an absent work-leisure schedule will demand eventually some form of public intervention as a necessary means of controlling civil disorder. The Roman Empire experienced a similar crisis when numerous conquered slaves replaced the worker-class Roman citizens and large numbers of soldiers were demobilized following military conquests. The American democratic system, like the Roman Empire, may be forced to turn its attention to the work idle. What answers can capitalistic democracy propose that might improve upon the emperor's grainery or the Roman Circa Maxima? The descriptions of the life style of the young dropouts suggests that the Roman grainery could be equated with public welfare and the circus with drugs.

The systems error that Conant located was occurring at the junction between education and society at the point of the market place. A highly specialized technological society required a technologized man. If there is no economic utility, there could be no social utility for members of this society. The educational error was a structural one at the level of the high school. The implied solution was a dual one of vocationalizing the high school and resocializing the technical society.

But it is not the high school structural dysfunctioning that worries James Coleman (1972) in his study of education in the age of computers and mass communication. Coleman claims the error lies in the failure of the total educational structure to recognize an emerging social reality that set new conditions for learning. The changed condition he identifies as the reversal in the traditional relationship between vicarious experience and direct experience.

Not many years ago, explains Coleman, a child obtained most of his information from direct experience. It was information restricted largely to his family, neighborhood, and community. Personal experience was supplemented by a few windows to the outside world that the child opened by reading at home or in school. The reading material provided vicarious experiences that extended his horizons beyond direct knowledge, and gave him a broader base from which to act because it drew upon other experiences as well as his own.

Schools throughout history, Coleman reminds us, have been the communities' gateway for information. They have been a source of and a guide to books which were the principal information door to the world beyond personal experience. The traditional purpose of schools has been to use vicarious experience of reading as a supplement to direct personal experience. The great contemporary educational issue is that there has been a critical change in the ratio. For those who read widely, the ratio of vicarious experience to direct experience grew as their range of reading increased. But the rate of shift was limited by the rate of frequency of reading which for most persons was not high. But with the emergence of electronic methods of communication such as television and radio, the shift has favored the vicarious aspects of the ratio. While this is true for all members of Western society, it is crucially true for the young. Instead of information poverty, contemporary young people are confronted with information richness. Schools, as they are structured now, are designed for an information-poor society. Their purpose was to give a child vicarious experience through books and contact with a teacher. Obviously, that function has been altered radically. The educational error is this system's failure to recognize the changed conditions.

Vicarious experience, which was formerly a slowly developing supplement to direct experience, is now an early and large component of a child's total experience. If schools are to continue their critical socializing function, these are inescapable conditions to be acknowledged. Any school structure of the future must include the behavior that in the past was accomplished outside the school. This would mean first, a curriculum made up of productive action with responsibilities that affect the welfare of others and develop the child's ability to function as a responsible and a productive adult, and second, a learning strategy that makes use of the information richness and the information processing capabilities of the contemporary environment.

The Coleman utopian design specifies that activities central to a school's functioning, such as the expansion of factual knowledge and cognitive skills, must play a decreasing role. From the upper elementary grades on, a school would become a productive community in which the young carry out responsible activities in service to a larger community. The teaching would center on general strategies for learning, especially how to employ the information resources of a complex social environment. The key concept is that the principal orientation of the school would be toward action or services.

The intent of the new school-community would be far broader than that of the present schools, because its mission would be to make responsible productive human beings who can lead in a task, or follow, and who are able to live with the consequences of their actions. Such socialization requires a shift of attention, away from the narcissistic goal of self-improvement currently imposed on the students through interacting with books. The new learning strategies would focus on action, and learning would be a by-product of the productive activity.

A second more radical reorganizational proposal was economic rather than educational in that it was directed at the market place. The proposal was to modify work places so that they might incorporate students. Older children would be partly integrated into work activities with some time reserved for learning and some for productive work. The separation between economic and educational institutions would vanish, as a work place served education's purposes and schools served a production purpose. The reorganization has implications for adults as well, because full-time education up to a given age, followed by full-time work would be replaced by a continuing mix that would begin at an early age and run through adulthood.

The educational reform proposed by Coleman is a legitimate system design and is what a systems engineer like Boguslaw (1961) would call an emergent-established design. An established situation is one in which all action-relevant environmental conditions are specifiable and predictable. A book, multiplication table, a learned skill, or any routinized problem-solving action pattern are examples of an established situation. Any new unknown or partially known experience is an emergent situation. An example would be any participation in an environment subject to unpredictable change or in an environment of such complexity that available analytical techniques cannot provide probability statements. An established situation is known a priori, is specifiable and predictable. In contrast, an emergent situation is one in which some of these conditions do not prevail and is known through participatory action. It is the distinction between those two kinds of situations that enables the examination of the relative virtues of book learning as the established situation and responsible activity as the emerging situation. The specialization of learning established situations is a worthless strategy for dealing with problems of everyday life; while an emerging situation in which a student has responsibility for action produces learning that unites thought and action. Systems analysis defines the established situation as the pool of old learnings which supplies the older elements of strategizing. The emergent situation both creates new elements and dominates the integration of the new and old elements in a new organization or strategy. In this way systems describe action shaping thought which says one of the oldest beliefs in education, is the way education ought to be.

The Oxymoron-Learning Strategy

What all utopian designs share is a common interest in massive global restructuring of society. Because the utopians do not address themselves to an isolated facet of society, much of their designs overlap and illuminate each other. Robert Abt (1970), a systems engineer, sensed the thought-action discontinuity and conceptualized a utopia that has much in common with the Coleman education reform. The error of education Abt defined was the perspective from which students were trained to look at complex social reality. His design of play as an "oxymoron-learning strategy" suggested a new metaphor for analyzing complex social problems. He proposed that games could be designed to simulate or to model complex social problems and that student players could learn in this abstracted form of reality the strategies of complex problem-solving. In the course of this learning, a commitment could be built to social problem-solving.

Oxymoron in the Abt design means the act of thinking in contradictions and in conjuction with the incongruous. The word is made up of "oxy" meaning sharp and "moron" meaning stupid, foolish. As a metaphor its language addresses itself to a complex changing situation and requires that problem-solving behavior operate according to the rules of strategizing. It allows for the manipulation of ends and means; the open consideration of win, lose, and draw alternatives; the short range ad hoc style of decision-making; the disguised trial and error of the make-believe; the practice afforded by imitation; and the generalized modes of behavior constructed for puzzling and teasing.

Because the oxymoronous form of thinking welcomes the incongruous and contradictory, it does not oversimplify a complexity nor exclude information selectively. The very perspective of playful strategizing protects incomplete information from further fragmentation. By contrast, scientific thinking is clear and direct. Its stock-in-trade is based upon simplification of a problem situation and single-minded pursuit of a question. The new metaphor was defined as a new form of scientific logic designed specifically to increase the flexibility of the older mode.

Taking a systems analysis approach to gaming, Abt hypothesizes combines the analytical and questioning concentration of the scientific viewpoint with the intuitive freedom and rewards of imaginative play. Although borrowed from an earlier form of learning used in childhood, game-playing is essentially scientific in that it is based objectively on systems analysis, quantitative model-building, and reality-testing. Game strategizing provides for human action, problem-solving, and dramatization. It offers a rich field for a risk-free active exploration of serious intellectual and social problems. In the course of this exploration learning-strategies are developed and man returns to a classical idea of life in which thought and action, individualization, and participation are combined in the same activity.

Reduced to its formal essence, a game is an activity between two or more independent decision makers, seeking to achieve their objectives in some limiting context. A more conventional definition would say, a game is a contest with rules among adversaries trying to win objectives. The trouble with this definition is that not all games are contests among adversaries. In some games, players cooperate to achieve a common goal against an obstructing force or natural situation which is itself not really a player because it does not have objectives. Most real-life activities, however, involve independent decision makers seeking to achieve objectives in some limiting context. The autonomy of human wills, the diversity of human motives, result in gamelike forms in all human interaction. In this sense all human history can be regarded as oxymoronous or gamelike in nature.

The interest that Abt developed in this oxymoron way of thinking grew from his experience as a systems engineer with games in warfare. Wars are obviously costly and learning warfare precludes experimentation. War games involve competitive activities on a large scale in which adversary decision makers struggle for objectives within limits of their will and resources and towards outcomes whose processes are uncertain. Strategic game technology grew from the fact that generals could not afford to plan strategies and tactics without considering what the adversary might do to counter the plan, and what the general might do to counter the countermeasures. Thus, a working model of these reciprocal processes became an essential element in military planning and training. There was no reason that Abt could see why the learning, analysis, and planning of such processes in the form of games should be limited to military problems. From an extensive analysis of problems in both social and educational systems, he designed a set of learning games which required a player to use the oxymoron problem-solving strategies.

In addition to the ease with which this playful mode of thinking acquires learning, it has one other advantage. It is peculiarly sensitive to internalizing the logic of abstractions. The mass of abstractions that contemporary man accumulates is one of the constraints of his social adaptation. As civilization evolves toward higher technological societies, the ability to use abstractions becomes more necessary for effective functioning. Only a few generations ago, most men could manage their personal affairs without any knowledge of the abstractions of the written word or numbers. Today in Western society it is difficult for an illiterate person to function at even the simplest level, when he cannot internalize a required set of abstractions.

The increased emphasis on abstract knowledge is reflected in the education system because educational goals always rise to meet the demands of society. Unfortunately, the demands define one generation's conception of what a younger generation must know in order to be occupationally successful within a society. These goals are concerned with adult society and directed toward a future world that students cannot yet perceive. Consequently, motivation for learning has a tendency to weaken. While this condition is growing more true of impoverished students who have little contact with educated adult society outside the schools, it has always been true for the highly disabled in our society. Abstract knowledge so necessary for social adaptation fails to be acquired by students who are isolated and cannot see how the volume of abstractions they must learn as children of this century is relevant to their real world.

From a critical analysis of social tasks to be learned, Abt

concludes that contemporary models for learning have become alien and new models are required. His utopian design for education was predicated on the serious use of games. Serious games, Abt says, should be used not for themselves or for the pleasure that they give, but for the ability of games to instruct, inform, and educate. Inasmuch as games are designed as simulations of abstractions of reality, they provide models of logical thinking specifically integrating thought and action. Participants in a simulated situation learn the logic of a process by actually going through the action and seeing the consequences of decisions. The game or playful mode of behavior confirms the Confucian prediction that to talk about an event is to forget, to see is to remember, but to do is to know. Or to rephrase Confucius, to hear is to forget, to see is to remember, but to do is to understand.

In comparing the Coleman utopia with the oxymoron learning strategy, both design action into education. Coleman would reorganize the total education structure including the industrial or workplace structure of American society. The Abt utopia would reorganize the internal dynamics of the student, while the Coleman proposition would require a considerable investment in large-scale institutional engineering. The Abt reorganization is by far a less costly venture. Serious gaming requires research and development on social problems so the games may simulate reality, and encourage students to play out strategies according to the rules of altering circumstances and without cost in the real world. Simulated games exercise such ways of looking at reality as sharpening and analyzing information about problems, needs and resources; broadening and deepening the assessment of program and goals; the consideration of alternative goals, priorities and programs; decision-making on goals, priorities and programs, and courses of action which will achieve the greatest impact in the shortest time consistent with available resources; and evaluating the results of program operations in order to capitalize on successes, correct deficiencies, and modify future plans on the basis of experience. The output of oxymoron strategizing was to provide a foundation for game theorizing. Student experiences in many logical and quantitative analyses of competitive processes would provide the seedbed for innovative use of the higher more theoretical abstractions of game theory.

The most serious proposal of this century about making play a serious behavior was made by John Von Neumann and Oskar

Morgenstern. Their game theory was based on the preceived similarities between certain conventionally standardized games and certain recurrent social situations. Where such similarities existed it was held more profitable to analyze the games rather than the far less sharply defined social situations. While similarities had long been recognized, the transformation of competitive social interaction into formal mathematical representation forced a sharpness into social action that had been lacking.

Game theory attempts to quantify and work through the actions of players by measuring their options continuously. Incorporated in the system are conflicting interests, incomplete information, and the interplay of free rational decision and choice. The theory was designed as a speculative approach to the structural relationships involved in the formal aspects of decision-making. Because of the focus on the conflictive situation of two or more decision makers, this mathematical theory is to games of strategy as probability theory is to games of chance.

Probability theory and game theory differ on both their origins and subject matter. In the seventeenth century, Pascal, a mathematician, proposed probability theory in answer to specific problems posed by a gambler acquaintance. Game theory, on the other hand, focuses on the strategies of two-man games from which it was derived. It was the systematic study of the decisions, or the "rules," involved in the decision-making of chess and tic-tac-toes that gave rise to game theory and enabled statements of serious propositions by which advantageous coalitions could be made or alternative strategies evaluated for their chances of success. The key concept is that the rules for choices have nothing to do with a particular game being played because they are the strategic choices forced upon the players by the way they view themselves, the world, and the other players.

Interest in the theory of games promoted a new style of thinking among scientists inasmuch as complex interest could be represented in conceptually quantifiable terms. The theory is based upon three aspects of real-life situations. It deals first with the conditions of payoff or "interests" for the different players who are rewarded or penalized in terms of what seems valuable to them or what will permit them to stay in the game. This leads to sharper definitions and clearer understandings of the concepts of utility, interests or preferences, and hence, also of certain aspects of rationality in decision-making.

Player rewards or penalties depend next on the joint outcomes of their own moves and the moves made by other players. This permits a clearer analysis of the interdependence of decisions among different actors in a situation of conflict, or of cooperation, or of a mixture of these two. Finally, in many of the more interesting games, the players must act under conditions of uncertainty and incomplete information, making the analysis of such games relevant for problem-solving, or decision-making, under conditions of uncertainty.

We can agree that game theory has the potential to identify the decision-making skills basic to complex learning. It can explain and produces the skills of: (1) how to recognize one's interest and to act in its pursuit; (2) how to take into account the probable actions of possible allies and adversaries; and (3) how to act prudently under conditions of uncertainty and partial ignorance. It is, however, what it does not do that is important. Because it is mathematically based, it is not related to an ethical system. While game theory and serious games both concern themselves with problem-solving, game theory is a more ruthless decision-making model. It is characterized by what we could call an ethical inadequacy. What is fair, just, humane, or democratic is lost in "coming to a solution" in a context of "payoffs," "realities of the situation," "bargaining advantages," etc.

The unresolved and ethical weakness of game theorizing is that the logic of its analysis and its supporting conceptual apparatus rests upon mathematical neutrality. The serious games of social problem-solving are designed to sharpen the ethical issues and they are expressed visibly in different levels of solutions. The key difference is that the logic of serious games rests on systems analysis of real social change problems. The difference between the two forms of analysis lies in the way each expresses values.

WORK-LEISURE DISCONTINUITY

Utopian Design Alternatives

Fragments of the changing pattern of work-leisure are surfacing everywhere in Western society. The language describing this phenomena in the United States is the four-day week and the three-day holiday; in Europe it is the flexible workday; and throughout the world it is a well-recognized role of the retired. Gradually, the biblical mandate of "man shall earn his bread by the sweat of his brow" is being amended. We have internalized the traditional notion that work is for economic survival but what we are comprehending slowly is that this truism is becoming less true. What has greater truth is that the manner in which man earns his bread and the institutions where he makes the bread are instruments which shape his nature. The American economist, Robert Heilbroner (1972), claims that work is the critical energizer of the socialization process, and that the shift of work away from manpower and machine-power towards automation has created a new order to work and worker. The critical change, says Heilbroner, is that man will no longer be subjected to the social fatalism of economic survival. Work will become a matter of social purpose and from the new conditions of work a resocialized man will emerge.

Throughout the globe no matter what system we live under, the long period of acquiescence before laws of economic necessities is coming to an end. The production-machinery of mankind yields such abundance that for the first time in history man is freed for other purposes. The problem is to conceptualize what these other purposes will be. When capitalism comes in many forms and can take many directions, neither its friends nor enemies have predicted the consequences that freeing man from labor has for his social adaptation.

The Heilbroner warning is that economic success does not guarantee social harmony. Had anyone in 1930 been told that in the United States the gross national product would surpass a trillion dollars by 1970, it would not have been believed. But the fact is the real per capita income has been doubling within the life span of the majority of the population now alive. Heilbroner was sure that had he known then the potential for expansion he would have felt safe in predicting for the United States an era of unprecedented social peace and goodwill. The radically challenging situation is that, despite the enormous economic change which has taken place, social harmony has not resulted. Nor have countries like Sweden, England, or the Netherlands, where real living standards have vastly improved, been spared profound social discontent. The inability of a successful capitalistic system to guarantee social harmony creates a great uncertainty factor for the future.

Evidence is mounting continuously that social harmony has not been an automatic consequence of economic affluence. The new social unrest problems are the drug culture, the cry for participatory democracy, the alienation of students, the new sexual morality, and the retreat to communal life. A common theme running through this evidence is that there is a deepseated change in work and non-work patterns being reflected in the life style of modern man. The findings of the Heilbroner analysis is that just because we cannot discern the road ahead it does not mean that we are hopelessly lost. On the contrary, whenever we are forced to stop we are in a position to do something that those in transit cannot do. We can examine the ground beneath us and perhaps derive some better idea of how to map the region in which we find ourselves. A global fact of this changed terrain is the deterioration of the old stereotypes that we have held about work. The common style of mass production has already imposed a common style of social organization. Man has already been resocialized by this new kind of work. The error in our social perception is that awareness of this new socialization process is dawning so slowly upon us.

Units of production require a unique form of internal order as well as special forms of external coordination with other huge units. Bigness brings to all industrial societies a common scaffolding of controlling mechanism which surround the central structure of production. They are visible in public utilities, planning agencies, corporate headquarters, regulatory commissions, etc. The confusion lies in our ignorance about the economic bureaucracy we have erected as a counterpart of large-scale industrial production system.

The critical point about the economic bureaucracy is that it imposes a certain kind of behavior upon all who come into contact with it. Its technology must be absorbed into daily life and modern man must learn to live within it as well as with the bureaucracy. Social theorists do not claim that the industrial production system cannot eventually be decentralized, democratized, and personalized. What they do say is that whatever efforts are made to achieve these ends, will have to be accomplished within the constraints of the imperatives of mass production.

Heilbroner reminds us that the way we got into this situation is also the way we ought to get out. The same large-scale capability that enabled us to construct the economic bureaucracy should also enable us to construct new forms of social control. The necessity for developing new forms of social controls is the bais for the Heilbroner principle that we have come to the end of acquiescence and the beginning of social purpose. To live in peace and harmony with economic affluence, Heilbroner advises us, man must develop a commensurate social technology.

New social technology, like other technology, must not only rise in response to change, it also causes change. A commonplace characteristic of technology that it delays its emergence until there is some measure of certainty that problems have solutions. A critical principle of social change teaches us that the very perspective that problems can be solved, signals the knowledge of how they are to be solved. A utopian design in this sense serves the purpose of organizing the perspective about problems.

The political scientist Michael Barkun (1972) in his study of "millenarian change" says the pursuit of massive social transformation sets up peculiar resonances in contemporary man. Where such movement and plans were once dismissed as curiosities, they have in the last fifteen or so years become the subject of a large wide-ranging scholarly literature. Millenium plans in contrast to utopian designs seek to make total change in society perfected once and for all "in a twinkling of an eye." They are led by prophet-type individuals and require a committed following who actually do the change-making.

While there is some overlap between the millenarians and the utopians, the latter are a different breed of cat. Modern utopians in most instances are scientists, usually physicists or economists, followed in some lesser number by sociologists, biologists, and educators. Any utopias proposed by scientists are the result of sophisticated technological analysis and without exception they are published and subject to review. A utopia is inferred from the analysis of evidence attending some failing social structure. It discusses the consequences of total failure to society and proposes a new order of direction which would salvage the pursuit of perfection. The proposals are widespread scholarly dialogues of an interdisciplinary and international nature. Those who take part in the dialogue are the watchdogs of human progress, or the cackling geese that warn Rome of its impending downfall. In the more commonplace language of the day, utopians are the epistemologists who give the warning bark to the error they find institutionalized into an organized body of knowledge.

If we accept the notion that utopia is a large-scale design for social change, then there are inferences to be drawn from utopian designs which focus on the most powerful discontinuity of the American society, the changing nature of the Western economic system. The major influence that shapes a society and the members within it is economics. The process energizing the capitalistic system has been the belief that this economic system is a structure largely moving toward the perfect society. A change in this belief is emerging at an ever-rapid pace. Whatever modifications of this belief come about will change both the society and the way society socializes its members.

A number of these utopians are presented so that a review of their proposals may facilitate future courses of action. Inferences may require that the expected outcomes of the new man be conceptualized at different levels of adaptation. The elite output of a utopian may provide a behavioral description of the desirable goals of adaptation.

Description of average behavior may identify the working mechanism by which the process of change is made. Marginal man may yield operational descriptions of how some remain unsocialized and suggest by analysis, kinds of interventions upon which corrective mechanisms may be built. The disalienated from the system in this sense are the disabled and the poor who may be too weakly socialized to survive.

The utopians selected for their relevance to the work-leisure problem are the economist John Kenneth Galbraith, the biologist Gunther Stent, the physicist Dennis Gabor, the psychiatrist Thomas Szasz, and the theologian Harvey Cox. Each of these utopians shift back and forth between a penetrating knowledge of some discipline and unresolved questions the larger society has about work and leisure. Using a wise perspective gained in another field, a utopian strikes out to design a whole new social structure. He envisions new forms of social existence without first asking if they are possible. As Lewis Mumford says "utopia has long been a name for the unreal and the impossible. We have set utopia over against the world. As a matter of fact, it is our utopias that make the world tolerable to us: the cities and mansions that people dream of are those in which they finally live."

Affluent Man

John K. Galbraith (1967) began the great debate this century on the coming change of economic man in his *The New Industrial State.* Some time during the forties Galbraith sensed an irreversible change in the Western economic system. His analysis implies that there will be a sharply increasing number of weakly talented, technically obsolete, disabled, and old people who simply will no longer qualify for work in a technical society. His problem statement is that the sheer volume of machine production creates a "marginal urgency for goods" and this, in turn, creates a need for reduced work hours and a reduced work force. His analysis suggests two classes of people in the coming society. One he is most concerned for is an unemployable class; the other is a class of workers who will be exempt from toil in their work. Both new classes he projects will require a redefinition of their leisure accomplished primarily through a changed education system.

The new working class in the Galbraith affluent society will work in occupations from which they would derive satisfaction and deep commitment but could control the struggle or toil. The malfunction of the affluent system lies in its inability to include the poor and the weakly capacitated. The emerging crisis says Galbraith, is one of freedom. For the two questions most asked about an economic system are (1) whether it serves man's physical needs, and (2) whether it is consistent with his liberty. The problem is not so much the freedom of the affluent beneficiaries but of the rejected unable.

An affluent society acceptable to Galbraith requires that economic achievement be coterminus with social achievements. Conditions for the new balance depend upon the freedom that the social institutions within society are permitted by the industrial system. The pivotal process in the change, Galbraith claims, will depend on the freedom the educational system manages to seize to educate toward alternatives other than service to the industrial machinery.

The Jeffersonian principle that the viability of the democratic process is vested in an educated participating citizenry emerges in a new perspective. When an affluent society does not need the work of all its people troublesome questions arise. Do the people need a political system which rests upon participation by all? Do a small number of expensively trained and paid workers who dominate the production machines require the governance of the democratic type of system? If we want to keep participation open to all in the United States including the young, the disabled, the unqualified, what are the options? The answer, Galbraith suggests, is the intellectual and artistic development of affluent man.

Faustian Man

The American biologist Gunther Stent (1969) in his *Coming of the Golden Age* was troubled by what he describes as the enduring persistence of a man whose joy it was to struggle with nature. If the affluent society is here, Stent speculated on what might happen to this struggle-oriented product of social evolution. For contemporary man is an evolutionary product of a long period of struggle in an ambiance of economic want and insecurity. A biological perspective would see the will to struggle, as having both an ontogenetic and phylogenetic origin. In the ontogenetic sense, the will to power is inherent in the structure of the human brain and the experiences acquired after birth. As far as the phylogenetic origin is concerned, it follows that the will is a peculiarly human attribute whose appearance was a crucial step in the humanization process.

According to the survival-of-the-fittest slogan, natural selection favored those who struggle successfully. Along with the evolutionary transmission of will, man passed along the psychological attributes necessary for environmental ascendency. Man-made societies favor curiosity, ambition, and imagination. Somewhere in the course of evolution, when success no longer was defined by gratification of psychological needs, the will to power shifted to environmental mastery. Oswald Spengler called this archetype, Faustian man. The boundless will to power caused man to view himself as being locked in endless strife with his world, endlessly engaged in overcoming obstacles and conflicts.

Stent treats the will to power as a biological fact which until now has been a favored characteristic. He concludes that Faustian man has been the prime mover of progress but with the disappearance of the need to struggle for economic survival, the adaptive value of the will for power should diminish. Faustian man is being signaled off the stage by the arrival of Dennis Gabor's Mozartian man. Mozartian man is an ideal type of which Mozart was believed to be the forerunner, "whose art does not live on conflict and who creates for joy, out of joy."

Stent doubts that Mozartian man is a biological improvement upon Faustian man. His predictions on the adaptive value of man powered by pleasure rather than by will is negative. The evidence for his conclusions was drawn from comparing Mozartian man with an earlier prototype of man, Polynesian man. His conclusions were that paradise has low adaptive values for man.

Whether it is a natural paradise of Polynesia or a technological paradise of the affluent society, the survival of man is not favored for long. Man is evolutionarily programmed for struggle and he and his society deteriorates without it. If economic struggle is self-limiting, then the culture which nurtures this form of behavior is also self-limiting. The Stent projection is that we are about to recreate a Polynesia on a global scale. A comfortable air-conditioned ersatz beachcombing society.

The will to power, Stent projected, will not vanish entirely, but will be redistributed among individuals whose will has been drastically altered. At one end of this distribution will be a minority of people whose work will maintain a high standard of living. In the middle of this distribution will be a larger population unemployed whose main pursuit in life will be aesthetic. At the other end of the spectrum will be the unemployable for whom the boundaries of the real and unreal will have dissolved and where physical survival is marginal. Faustian man, says Stent, better face up to the fact that the natural fruit of his frantic efforts is a Mozartian man and it does no good now to wish it otherwise. The conversion of Faustian man to Mozartian man is the result of society's response to leisure. The danger is that in the process of the conversion Mozartian man may become the self-destructive Polynesian man.

Mozartian Man

The leading utopian whose work has stimulated the most discussion and debate of this century is a British physicist, Dennis Gabor. His detailed analysis, global synthesis and radical propositions for social change are contained in two books: in 1964 he published *Inventing the Future,* and in 1972 *The Mature Society.* The conditions in society that Gabor warns about is that the growth in numbers and material consumption have led to a crisis of saturation. The hope of progress, without which man cannot live, must shift from quantity of goods growth to quality of life growth. In the course of this change there will emerge a new kind of man, Gabor calls Mozartian man, and a new kind of society he calls the mature society.

Gabor suggests that a trilemma of nuclear war, overpopulation and the age of leisure faces society. If either of the first catastrophes is realized, mankind will be equipped to deal with them. The possibility of surviving Adams and Eves is statistically possible. The possibilities of an aggressive elite surviving in the presence of overpopulation is a known historical fact. But the third catastrophe, the advent of an age of leisure in which mechanization and automation will have rendered human labor largely superfluous, will find man's psyche unprepared. For leisure made possible by an economic system is a complete novelty in human history. The restless, unsatisfied ever-conquering man whom Stent called Faustian man is no longer needed. The danger to an emergent society lies in the possibility of sublimating Faustian man and converting him to what Gabor has named Mozartian man. A mature, post-industrial society will require man to change from being driven by needs to being driven by social values. The hazard inherent in the proposed shift is any future society must recognize that man is wonderful in adversity, but weak in comfort, affluence, and security. Evolution has not designed man to appreciate what he gets without effort.

While man's traditional relationship to adversity gives us a warning as to the dangers in the shift, it also defines the constraints and the problems of moving toward a mature society. The problem will be how to make reasonable compromise between the needs and wishes of individuals and the requirements of a highly developed, technological society. Gabor proposes that there is no need to break with the Protestant ethic that "he who does not work neither shall he eat." All we have to do is not to interpret work as production. The alternative definition for work is social utility. Decent people want to work because they want to feel useful.

In the mature society of the next century, man must necessarily exist freed from the narrow occupational alternatives proposed by a dominating economic system. Work of the new society will be of a different order and supported largely by the enormous gross national product of the affluent economic system. The labor force that will man production machinery will be very small. The real workers will be the highly gifted and well-motivated minority who need obstacles to overcome and who enjoy competition in the interest of social usefulness. The production system maintained at this level will be sufficient to support a consumer society, in the sense that it will supply its citizens lavishly with material goods and will also provide them with work.

A level of employment not very different from the present needs to be maintained but a different distribution of occupations must gradually come about. Instead of paying people to be idle in stores or providing inflated service in offices, the taxpayer will pay for larger educational institutions and he will receive services formerly limited to specialized groups within his society. This shift can be made possible by the conversion of the gross national product as a financial support system for the growth of services involving health, education, transportation, new towns, slum clearances, and so on. The bulk of the workers in the new society will have freer and more open occupational choices in these service areas.

As a major descriptor of this society itself rather than its members, Gabor proposes the critical principle that the more permissive and open a society is, the less it can do without a hard apprenticeship. While a mature society must be an open free society because without these characteristics for development it will not deserve to exist, to this extent it must also be permissive. But a permissive society can exist only if coercion is replaced by inner discipline. For a mature society the internal dynamic of discipline is imparted by the right sort of education. Until the age of six, education in the family should remain loving and permissive. Between the ages of six and eighteen, education must contain an element of hardship and a preparation for responsibility. By late adolescence social responsibility must be sufficiently inculcated and a certain measure of effort must be made to become a habit so that the education years can become an introduction to a permissive society. The educational system will need to be redesigned so that the facts of an abundant reality can be converted into values, processes into purposes, and hopes and plans into consummation. The intent of education will be to replace the pressures of economic scarcity with personal responsibility.

In the coming mature society Gabor offers mankind hope, play, and diversity. Hope is an individual value for man and is expressed in his hopes for climbing a differently structured occupational ladder. Open chances for changes in occupation have always been an old utopian idea now coming into its own time. The second promise that the mature society offers is play. While play is not serious, it can be played very seriously. It is not real life though it can exercise much of the dilligence, courage, and ambition of the player. A game is an artificial universe with milder rules and can be enjoyed actively or vicariously. The third offering of the mature society is diversity, for man will be freed from the straightjacket of regular work and different life styles will not only be tolerated but will also be fostered.

Home Festivius and Fantasius

The theologian Harvey Cox in *Feast of Fools* (1969) proposed in the classical utopian tradition a renaissance for the spirit of man as a precondition for social transformation. Cox charges that as the efficiency of industrial production increases, the pathology of living becomes more visible. The social pathology of daily life is linked in the Cox perspective to the failure of man's imagination and expressed in his inability to play. The monumental achievements of Western science and industrial technology have produced a man with a shrunken psyche. Contemporary man is in as much danger from industrialization as were the luckless children who were once confined to the English factories from dawn to dusk.

Man, says Cox, is essentially festive and fanciful. To become fully human, Western industrial man, and his non-Western brothers, must learn again to play and to dream. The cost of purchasing economic affluence has been a staggering impoverishment to the vital elements of life. The weakened elements are "festivity" which, in the Cox lexicon, means play, and "fantasy," which means imagination.

Festivity and fantasy, or play and the imagination, are posed as not only worthwhile in themselves, but vital to human life. They enable man to relate himself to the past and the future in ways that are neither possible nor necessary for animals. Festival is defined as a special time when ordinary chores are set aside while man celebrates some event and affirms the sheer goodness of what is, or observes the memory of a god or a hero. It is, Cox reminds us, a distinctly human activity. It arises from the peculiar power of man to incorporate into his own life the joys of other people and the experience of a previous generation.

Imagination, from which play springs, is uniquely human. While a hungry lion may dream about a zebra dinner, only man can invent by dreaming wholly new ways of living as an individual and a species. If festivity enables man to enlarge his experience by reliving events of the past, fantasy is a form of play that extends the frontiers of the future. The social crisis, Cox warns about, is the failing imagination, the failing fantasy of man.

Cox blames not so much technology per se, as the dreary fact-ridden world that is its product. Because technology has not been subjected to playful encounter, man is growing more sober and industrious and less playful and imaginative. Work schedules squeeze festivity to a minimum. The habits formed are still so much with us that we use our technologically provided leisure either to moonlight other jobs or to plan sober consultations on the problems of leisure and to wonder why we are not enjoying our free time the way we should.

The claim that the age of science and technology has been hard on fantasy reverberates with its own truth. For while scientific method deflected attention away from the real of fantasy and toward the manageable and the feasible, the paradox continues that science without hunches or visions is a poor thing indeed.

The problem is that we live in a culture where fantasy is tolerated, not encouraged. There was a time, Cox reminds us, when visionaries were canonized and mystic admired. Now, they are studied, smiled at, perhaps even committed. But why should we care if fesitivity and fantasy play a smaller role in human life? Is there, asks Cox, any loss to the world when the society becomes sober and rational, and when man forgets to play? The Cox projection is that the loss to mankind is great not only because the disappearance of festivity and fantasy simply makes life duller, but more seriously, the very survival of man as a species is placed in jeopardy when human imaginative faculties are repressed.

The Cox position argues three theses: first, that man is both homo festivus and homo fantasia as well as homo sapiens; second, the survival of mankind as a species is placed in jeopardy when highly adaptive innovative behavior is repressed; third, the loss of the capacity to play and to imagine has profound spiritual significance. Religious man, Cox reminds us, was one who is able to grasp his own life within a larger historical and cosmic setting. As man becomes more secular he fails to see himself as part of a greater whole, a longer story in which he plays a part. Then he becomes something less than a man. Understanding neither his origin nor destiny, his life is without meaning. His spirit and his psyche shrink. Without understanding his own moral nature, man becomes a cripple within his own environment. Man is not capable of living in disparate spheres and has need of an integrating cosmic perspective. Playfulness and imagination enable man to deal with his past and apply his understanding to contemporary life while he envisions his future. When this disappears, hope disappears too and man has ceased in a spiritual sense to be man.

Homo Acedia

The puzzling questions running through the utopian themes are: if play with its underlying support to the realm of imagination is a crucial ingredient of survival, why then is man so suspicious of its presence and grieved by its absence? Why, if play carries with it so much good for man and society, does it have to be defended against resistance and hostility and its very existence protected? Why can we not accept it for what it is and exploit it for all it may be worth?

The historians of Western culture tell us that there are two conflicting explanations at work. Greeks viewed the notion of leisure which we call play, as behavior worthy of a free man. They included in leisure all those activities we would call culture. Politics, debate, philosophy, art, social rituals, and athletic contests were considered worthy of a free man because they express the desired core of a life style. The nobility believed themselves compromised and deluded when they became engaged in productive work. Productive activity was regarded as below the dignity of a free man and seen as fit only for slaves and women. Leisure was concerned with the maintenance of a style of life expressing the highest values of the culture. The pivotal difference is that in classical times there was no resistance to leisure because members of the society were bred to it. Members of a technological society are schooled to other values.

The second explanation concerns traditions inherited from the Protestant ethic and the industrial society. Calvinism is said to have sanctified work and industrialism enobled it. What followed naturally was a hostile separation of work and leisure. The emphasis was on economically productive functions as being the most significant aspect of life. Play was relegated to the status of spare time. Even for children spare time was vigorously committed to wholesome purpose, such as prayer, Bible reading, and chores.

While the reality of the Greek concept of leisure rested in slave labor, the reality of industrial society rested on the labor of free man. The post-industrial society, however, rests upon neither free nor slave labor. If, as the utopians tell us, the economic affluence of contemporary life is to rest upon automation, how then can we explain the fears that they have expressed for the new breed of man?

The American psychiatrist Thomas Szasz (1961) in *Myth of Mental Illness* proposes as an explanation the concept of homo acedia. The fear of non-work or idleness has had a history as long as the behavior of man has been recorded. All religious beliefs contain references to the danger of idleness. In the Christian religion the seven deadly sins of man numbered prominently the sin of sloth. When man was committing the sin of sloth he was "homo acedia," meaning "man acting without caring."

Acedia is a rarely used term for a syndrome characterized by listlessness, apathy, and melancholia. It is the despair from weakness which Kierkegaard described as the despairing refusal to be oneself. Metaphysically and theologically, the notion of acedia means that man does not relinquish his will so that it may interact with the outer world. The concept of acedia is related to idleness in that idleness, according to traditional teaching, is the source of a deepseated lack of calm which makes leisure impossible.

In homo acedia the linkages between imaginative play and work may be seen in a new light. In a sociological sense, homo acedia can neither be thrilled by life nor address himself to role-behavior of others, because this would call for a commitment to the act of caring. He cannot internalize his society. In a psychological sense neither could he, who was without caring, commit himself to puzzle, and least of all to doubt or tease his outer world. He cannot allow the conflict of knowing and not knowing. Play, under these conditions, cannot emerge to spark the relationship between the inner world of the imagination and the outer world of reality.

Szasz claims that the failure of psychiatry to conceptualize acedia maintains the myth of mental illness. What man needs and demands from life, Szasz reminds us, is not wealth, comfort, or esteem, but games worth playing. Critical to being alive is the presence of the challenge, the quest. When man cannot find a game worth playing, he falls prey to acedia. Religion would name acedia sloth, psychiatry calls it apathy, and society sees it as alienation, the dropping-out symptom. Call it what you will, acedia is a paralysis of the will; a failure of the appetite; a condition of generalized boredom, total disenchantment of "God, O God, how weary, stale, flat and unprofitable seem to me all the uses of this world."

Such a state of mind, Szasz tells us, is a prelude to what is loosely called mental illness, which makes multitudes of people a burden to themselves and to society. To seek, above all, for a game worth playing is the advice Szasz gives to modern man. Having found the game, play it with intensity. Play it as if your life and sanity depended upon it, because indeed they may.

The momentous change in contemporary social conditions Szasz warns as a social psychiatrist, requires that for man to adapt, his social relations, like his genetic constitution, must undergo mutations. It will be imperative that all people, rather than just a few, learn how to play. The term "learn" he used broadly, and meant by it the adaptation that man must make to his environment. More specifically, he refers to the rules that must be learned. First to be learned are the rules governing life in the family, the group and the society in which man lives. Further, there is the learning to learn the rules of the technical skills, that is, of science and technology, because there is no limit to the learning except that which man imposes upon himself. Szasz defines maladaptation as the inability to forget the old rules or the unwillingness of a person to relinquish playing old games. Man, he has observed, can go on strike against himself by refusing to play any of the games that others play.

To revolt against the challenge to live is to find no new game worth playing. The health of man requires that old games be constantly scrapped and new ones started. Man and his society both regress when one type of game playing cannot be shifted to another, or when the same game is played over and over again. If man can find no games worth playing, or if the game he is playing is not worth playing, then man is sick and his behavior is maladaptive.

SUMMARY

The work of selected utopians have been examined because these designs, more than any other conceptual form, describe social evolution. They do so by identifying critical shifting of gears in and between social systems. The reviewed utopias suggest that contemporary society is in a transitional stage from which eventually there will emerge a social structure and a socialized man new in history. Most utopian designs reveal rare agreement about areas where the world seems to be out of joint. The rapidly weakening linkages in Western society were identified as a dangerous interruption in the continuity of knowledge and action; the irrelevance of education for occupational preparation; and changing balance between life style patterns of work and leisure.

Utopian ideologies that describe social change have not emerged out of a vacuum. They were the outcomes of disciplined minds which engaged in complex analysis of reality, constructed global syntheses, and proposed responsible projections. Contemporary technology enabled utopians not only to speak from a single discipline but also to address themselves to the larger-scale social issues and problems. The tidal overwhelming conclusion that utopians leave us with is that contemporary society is softening its position that the economic survival of its members depends upon fitness for the production-market system. Fitness may now be defined by social criteria.

There are specific implications in this conclusion for the weakly abled and highly disabled within an affluent society. A new time in history is promised by these transformations. For changes within the larger societies may permit a new perspective for the socialization of marginal members. The key to the new perspective is contained in propositions regarding leisure. Utopian propositions, almost without exception, have indicated the need for a new look at leisure. Leisure, along with education, is seen as the critical vehicle for social transformation. The relevant domain requiring a reconsideration is leisure and its underlying dynamic play.

REFERENCES

ABT, C. C. (1970) Serious Games. New York: Viking Press.
BARKUN, M. (1972) "Movements of total transformation." American Behavioral Scientist 16 (2).
BOGUSLAW, R. (1965) The New Utopians. Englewood Cliffs, N.J.: Prentice-Hall.
――― (1961) "Situational analysis and the problem of action." Social Problems 8 (3).
CARTER, H. E. (1971) "Science policy and the idea of a university." Keynote address to the American Assocation of University and College Deans. (mimeo)
COLEMAN, J. S. (1972) "The children have outgrown the schools." Psychology Today.
CONANT, J. (1967) Comprehensive High School: A Second Report to Interested Citizens. New York: McGraw-Hill.
COX, H. (1969) Feast of Fools. Cambridge, Mass.: Harvard Univ. Press.
GABOR, D. (1972) The Mature Society. London, Eng.: Praeger.

——— (1964) Inventing the Future. Harmondsworth, Eng.: Penguin.

GALBRAITH, J. K. (1967) The New Industrial State. Boston, Mass.: Houghton Mifflin.

HEILBRONER, R. (1972) "Capitalism alive or dead." INtellectual Digest.

STENT, G. (1969) Coming of the Golden Age. Garden City, N.Y.: American Museum of Natural History Press.

SZASZ, T. (1967) The Myth of Mental Illness. New York: Dell.

VON NEUMANN, J. and O. MORGENSTERN (1947) Theories of Games and Economic Behavior. Princeton: Princeton Univ. Press.

WAYS, M. (1971) "How to think about the environment." Fortune.

WHYTE, L. L. (1954) Accent on Form. New York: Harper & Bros.

CHAPTER 2

DEFINING A COBWEB

Mary Reilly

We do not know when man begins to play. Play may start before birth, with the kicks and turns of the fetus; it certainly is present in the infant; and it continues throughout our lives.

When play is suppressed, both the individual and society suffer. When play is encouraged, both benefit. The reasons for this are not clear, but somehow play is essential for man and many other social animals.

Unlike most behavior, play has not been exhaustively studied. Scientists have difficulty taking it seriously. They argue about what play is. Some have narrow definitions; others would agree with Tom Sawyer that "work consists of whatever a body is 'obliged' to do. . . . Play consists of whatever a body is not obliged to do"

Editorial in *Natural History,*
Journal of American Museum of
Natural History, December 1971.

A SEMANTIC BABBLE

In the course of history civilization used leisure for varying functions, and its name changed as use shifted. It was called *schole* by the Greeks and first meant "devoted to learning." Games, music, and mathematics were intimately related in the culture and were included under the word schole because of their formal school purposes. In later Roman times the word leisure was reserved for those activities in which children and adults were freed or "permitted"; hence the Latin *licere,* to be lawful, became the root of the word leisure. The nature of the name change suggests that leisure has a functional significance to the society in which it exists. The industrial revolution confirmed the principle inasmuch as some time in the Middle Ages the word was changed to recreation and meant relaxation from and refreshment for work.

While the phenomenon may have been institutionalized around the term leisure, investigators theorized around the generic term play. But even "play" was subject to some linguistic slippage. In the United States, at least, there is a label change by age of the player. Common usage reserves the word play for children, shifts to recreation for adults, and shifts again to the word leisure for the retired. It includes solitary and group behavior. The term covers motor and mental manipulation of games, aesthetic manipulation of the arts, material manipulation of the crafts, temporal manipulation of music, and role manipulation of dramatics. Atomizing play into elements is a relatively easy task; the difficulty lies in synthesizing the elements into a coherent structure. It has been said that play is as elusive as the wind and can no more be caught by theory than the wind can be caught with a paper bag. Robert Frost would add about puzzles of this sort that "we dance around in a ring and suppose/But the secret sits in the middle and knows."

Classification

Play being a universal behavior is presumably vital to human existence. Its relationship, however, is speculative primarily because it eludes classification. Religion incorporated play in its rituals. Society dichotomized the activities of its members into work and play. This taxonomy lacks discrimination because while work may include play, when play becomes work it no longer is play. The sensory excitement in play has theoretical meaning to psychoanalysts who proposed pleasure and nonpleasure as analytical categories—pleasure, of course, being play, and nonpleasure being work. Social scientists such as the anthropologist, sociologist, economist, were inclined to use the categories of serious and nonserious. It is truer, however, to say that the relevant knowledge of the times defines play; while the dominant values held by scholars, historians, and theorists pretty much determined what play is called and how it is described.

Carrier function. The further confusion about play that adds to definitional uncertainty is that its presence is found in association with other things. The "other thing" characteristic suggests that play serves a carrier function. When it was found in association with religion, it carried worship. In scientific strategizing or military training, games become carriers of decision-making. In education, play serves as a carrier of learning. In psychiatry, the games people play become carriers of treatment.

The carrier theme was emphasized by the educational philosopher John Dewey (1928) who claimed that as regular occupations failed to engage the full scope of impulses and instincts in a lasting and balanced way, play and games could be used. They not only fill a basic human need for make-believe activity, they also provide fresh and deeper meaning to the usual activities of life. Dewey saw no antipathy between play and school work. Instead, he postulated that the playful involvement in the learning process could only enhance learning. A later educator, Coleman (1962), examined play under the concept of simulation and found that games could be designed to have a measurable impact on intellectual learning, attitudes, and strategies. Based on fairly complicated models of political, economic, historical, or social processes, simulation games were designed by educators and social scientists. They were played by students for learning payoffs that could not possibly be acquired except in the complex natural situations. In education simulations students could take the roles of national leaders, corporation presidents, pressure-group members, and make decisions based upon their assessment of a situation and simulated consequences. The close association of thought and action in this form of educational experiment appears to accomplish for learning what Dewey had hoped and Abt had predicted.

If play could be defined as the bearer of healthy behavior, it could as easily be a carrier of illness. The histories of psychiatric children are replete with descriptions of sick play. They describe children who have played little, either with other children or alone. Toys were observed to have superficial attraction for the disturbed child, and the desire to romp with other children was either absent or weakly present. From reviewing medical histories of the mentally ill, it is possible to pick up as commonplace parents reporting that a child does not play. Equally common are the admissions of the adult patient that as a child he had played neither easily nor enjoyably.

Psychiatric-ill children, when observed, or adult patients, when questioned, give evidence of being without playfulness. They were without the ability to deal playwise with either the toys, the raw materials, or the people of their world. While a kind of play impairment or deficiency in playfulness may be correlated with diagnostic symptoms, play was confined in psychiatry to the purpose of diagnosing emotional dysfunction. In this instance, play as a carrier of mental illness was used to reveal the symptoms of illness.

Eric Berne (1964) was one of the few psychiatrists who moved beyond the diagnostic function of play and used games for treatment. In his treatment system he exploited the games that people play. The rules and goals, or payoffs, of the game were used as content to be worked on in group psychotherapy.

Spinoff effects. Highly visible among the carrier effects of play are the skills that are valuable spinoffs for the functioning of society. We have long known that a plethora of skills gather incrementally around play. The intense participatory involvement of the player facilitates the acquisition of skills across the broad spectrum of arts, crafts, drama, music, sports, games, and hobbies. Play, in addition, enables the player to have access to a multiplicity of groups which promote a diversity of experience and interests. In the reality of social interactions, the required skills are nurtured. The development of powers that might otherwise be dormant goes on as a child moves through the play agenda that his age and way of life require. Hence, the filling in of a continuum of skills and interest patterns goes on in any changing social context in which the child lives.

The conditions of play, particularly the make-believe stance to reality, provide safety for risk-taking and promote in children a no-nonsense operational ethics about failure. The essential repetition and competition, controlled as they are by voluntary intent, act to reduce discouragement and to strengthen courage as a response mode. All these desirable spinoffs occur because of that one characteristic that keeps the action going. Fun, pleasure, and enjoyment are the great spinoffs, with the payoff going to the player alone. When pleasure fades play stops, because a player no longer plays when the fun is gone. It is this very element of fun that challenges while it baffles the theoretical technology of those who attempt to conceptualize play.

Finally, play offers expanding· possibilities for actions which include both the acquisition and practice of mental strategies along with their concomitant physical skills. Such a reciprocal process, Abt would reiterate, serves the critical purpose of reuniting action and thought, a necessary integration task which grows in value as we reconsider the complexity of modern civilization.

But even if all these defined "goods" were only partially true, play is a hunch, a theme, a hypothesis worth exploring. We might suspect that play could be a missing link, a critical prerequisite for occupational success and social adaptation but in reality we find it to be an obvious commonplace behavior that grows complex and elusive upon examination.

* * *

The real treasure, that which can put an end to our poverty and all of our trials, is never very far; there is no need to seek it in a distant country. It lies buried in the most intimate parts of our house; that is, of our own being. . . . And yet—there is this strange and persistent fact, that it is only after a pious journey in a distant region, in a new land, that the meaning of that inner voice guiding us on our search can make itself understood by us [Heinrich Zimmer, quoted by Mircea Eliade in *Myths, Dreams and Mysteries*].

. . . "Man" is playing a game of hunt-the-thimble, searching every corner of the room, but taking it for granted that the thimble is not in his own pocket [Colin Wilson, *Origins of the Sexual Impulse*].

EVOLUTIONARY EXPLANATIONS

Whenever the inquiring mind of man explores his world for meaning, he asks about purpose. World knowledge has grown up around the questions of what this or that means. An issue that is caught up in the pursuit of purpose the philosophers call a teleological venture. By the middle and late nineteenth century a major teleological dialogue emerged about evolution. Play was a theme in its arguments. Since the time of Darwin in 1859, scientists have studied play, but their concern was with the play of lower animals. The research of biologists and primatologists indicates that play is a behavior innate to the entire class of mammals. The lower the species is on the evolutionary scale, the less frequent and diverse are its play activities. And it follows from this that man among the many forms of life, is the supreme player. The curious tendency to compare the behavior of man with the lower scaled species of rats and cats has seriously undermined our understanding of play.

The evolutionary significance of play has been a matter of fluctuating interest among scientists of the past and present centuries. Play is, however, a significant evolutionary behavior. The theory of evolution holds that any biological trait endangering a species' survival will be eliminated by natural selection, while a trait with a value for survival tends to become established by the process of natural selection. Edward Norbeck (1971) an American anthropologist phrased the evolutionary problem of play as: if we accept the idea of natural selection, then we are faced with the problem of finding survival value in human play.

The teleological search for meaning in play began with the German poet Schiller in 1810, who blithely suggested "an animal works when the mainspring of his activity is a deficiency and it plays when this mainspring is a wealth of energy, when superfluous life itself presses for activity." This became known as the theory of surplus energy. Herbert Spencer (1855), an English philosopher, carried it further by speculating that faculties that had been quiescent for some time of necessity push for expression. He proposed that play is an artificial exercise of powers which become so ready for discharge that they relieve themselves by simulated action in place of real action. Essentially, the surplus energy notion defines play as random behavior.

The surplus energy theory was opposed by a recuperation or relaxation theory attributed to Lazarus, a German physiologist. This theory regards play as an opportunity for the restoration of exhausted powers. Actually, these two interpretations are not contradictory, because both could operate under different conditions provided the energy that arises after exhaustion could also be categorized as surplus energy. Both of these positions were weakened by the evidence of children and kittens, who play continuously without evidence of arduous activity.

Recapitulation

An American psychologist, G. S. Hall (1904), having a dual interest in evolution and education, proposed that children are a link in the evolutionary chain that passes behavior progressively through the species hierarchy. Infants pass through all the stages from protozoan to human in their lives as embryos. Some of the stages through which the human fetus goes from conception to birth are similar to the developmental sequence of structure and behavior in the specific change from fish to man. Evidence of this nature was summarized in the biological hypothesis that individual development (ontogeny) repeats that of the race (phylogeny). Hall, in his famous recapitulation theme, extended the idea to the world of childhood. His theory was that a child relives the history of the race as an embryo relives that of its more remote ancestors. The experience of ancestors is handed down and the child reenacts in play the significant occupations in the sequence in which they occurred in man and his civilization.

The literature in the early part of this century flourished with examples of children's delight in playing with water, which in turn was connected with the fishy ancestral joy of the sea. The insistence of children in climbing trees and swinging from branches showed vestiges of the life of their monkey forebears. Boys between the ages of eight and twelve validated the recapitulation theory when they evidenced delight in fishing and hunting, and went about this business in groups. The Hall theory was based on the assumption that skills learned by one generation and the resulting cultural experience could, in some way, be inherited by the next.

Culture as an inherited form of behavior was challenged by subsequent knowledge about the function of genes and heredity. Western geneticists rejected the notion that acquired characteristics can be inherited, at least in any form which would make the recapitulation theory credible. Because there is no tidy linear progress accounting for the route that primitive man took from his simple life to the more complex civilization, popularity of the recapitulation theory waned. Yet, it did have a stimulating effect upon identifying the ages and stages of the child play phenomenon. It dampened, unfortunately, subsequent speculation that evolution might have some utility for identifying play sequence and content.

A theory that play is practice was advanced by Carl Groos, a professor of philosophy at Basel, in his *Play of Animals* (1896) and *Play of Man* (1899). He proposed that animals must practice and perfect their incomplete hereditary skills before a serious need to use them arises. According to Groos, what was true for animals was true also for man. His practice theory was demolished by the observed instances of children playing at being younger. While Groos may not have been evolutionarily accurate, he identified some principles of learning that have since been obscured. He found that to learn by imitation is the preference of those young whose inherited modes of action are scanty. Groos concluded that the more adaptable and intelligent a species is, the more it needs a period of protective childhood for the practice gained in play and imitation.

Why Kittens Play

The evolutionary theory continued to chain play into locked step with animal studies far into the twentieth century. It became tradition to measure a principle of play for its truth utility in explaining why a kitten plays with a ball of yarn. We are left with a variety of choices: the kitten plays because he has surplus energy; is exhausted from hunting mice and is playing to recoup his energy; is recapitulating an alien primitive hunting style, or is practicing for a future contest where the hunting is for real.

By the mid-twentieth century the methodology for studying behavioral purposes had converged around the communication theory of feedback. Norbert Wiener (1943), an American physicist, proposed that the kitten playing with a ball of yarn was not jumping directly toward where the ball would be at any given time but, in playing, jumped toward a predicted future position of the ball. While the feedback principle was proposing play to serve a decision-making function, psychology began to assert a position. The kitten jumps, says the Freudian theorist, to reduce his psychic tension caused by sexual conflict. Not so, says the Skinnerian behaviorist; the kitten jumps for his reward, the ball of yarn which in turn disciplines the play of the kitten.

The Primate Studies

By 1971 a primatological view emerged with the findings of Suomi and Harlow, researchers at the University of Wisconsin Primate Laboratory. While observing monkeys to gain psychological information, they found that of all monkey behaviors play was probably the most informative. They noted that the manner in which a monkey plays in a social situation reveals the approximate age, sex, social position on the dominance scale, and nature of his rearing history. The play behavior also served as a fair predictor of a young monkey's future social capability and status, adequacy as a mother or father, and likelihood of developing abnormal behavior patterns. The laboratory studies of monkeys at play identified variables that not only determine how, where, and with whom a monkey will play, but promoted an understanding of the general function of play in social development.

The Suomi and Harlow studies described the process by which a helpless infant gradually becomes a competent participant of monkey society. They hypothesized two functions for play which have implications for understanding human play. First, play provides a behavioral mechanism by which activities appropriate for adult social functioning can be initiated, integrated, and perfected. Second, monkey social play acts to mitigate aggression as it emerges in the monkey's behavioral repertoire. The play repertory of monkeys under a year of age, in rudimentary forms, contain all behavior that characterizes adult social life. Patterns of social grooming, aggression, sex, and dominance were found in infant monkey play activity. When they first emerged, the patterns were not at an adult level of competency, but after months or years of practice the clumsy, unsophisticated behavior of childhood became truly adult in form.

The practice necessary for social functioning, the studies showed, came about through peer play. In early play development the infant progressed from a recognition that social objects differ from mother and the rest of the environment to a state of living with and loving fellow monkeys. Presence of peers was sought and the infant picked up such social graces as how to behave in the presence of a dominant, as opposed to a lower, status monkey. Dominant hierarchies established among peers persisted through adulthood. If the infants were raised in isolation, with no mother or peers to provide stimulation, they developed compulsive stereotyped rocking behavior reminiscent of the human autistic child. When they were finally exposed to peers they initiated aggressive attacks, but more often they were the victims of aggression. Infants raised with a mother were referred to as "together-together"—reared monkeys. In contrast to "mother-peer" groups, the together-togethers had no mother to send them out to play. Consequently their group behavior was characterized by a clinging to each other. Eventually, play behavior did emerge in the together-togethers but it was unsophisticated, retarded, and passive.

The observation of aggression and retardation in isolated or motherless monkeys suggests these behaiors are subject to the influence of play. One of the critical conclusions of the Wisconsin study was that aggression is genetically predisposed in the rhesus monkey. All monkeys showed aggression by the seventh month, and the situation in which aggressive behavior was exhibited was controlled by social and not genetic variables. Playing monkeys expressed their aggression in their activity, and because aggression was a part of play it was relatively mild in form.

The important evolutionary finding in the monkey studies was that aggression has survival value provided it is socialized. Different patterns of child-rearing showed up the relation of aggression to play. Infants reared with mothers, but isolated from peers, expressed hyperaggression in future peer interaction. Adequate maternal contact provided the courage and boldness to deal with peers, but inadequate peer contact provided poor control of aggression. When isolated monkeys reached maturity and were without either maternal or peer contact, they were virtually incompetent in every aspect of social activity. Like all other monkeys they exhibited aggression, but it was neither under effective control nor appropriately targeted. Such monkeys were observed to aggress with equal ferocity against infants, dominant males, and their own bodies. They suffered from want of practice in channeling their aggression through alternative forms of social behavior.

The spontaneous frivolous play of monkeys under the systematic observation of primate research supports the conclusion that play is an important aspect of social development. Without aggression an individual monkey has little protection from predators, but when aggression is directed randomly toward fellow group members, it destroys the society. The aggression response therefore, it was postulated, is attenuated in intragroup behavior. The adaptive value of play was seen as related to the control over both the intensity and the target of aggressive behavior. The conversion of aggression into social competency through play, the Suomi and Harlow (1971) studies concluded, serves the continuity of the monkey society.

PSYCHOLOGICAL EXPLANATIONS

By the turn of this century evolution was no longer the major point of reference for knowing man. The interest in species adaptation shifted to questions about man. The mind, unconscious processes, learning, and motivation became the objects of investigation. The differing routes that these inquiries took were called by variously named theories. The most prominent among them were theories of behaviorism, the Freudian theory, and Piaget's theory of cognition. None of these theories had a direct relationship to play except possibly the Piagetian theory which drew inferences directly from play. Most theories, in fact all theories, of this century have had difficulty explaining a behavior such as play.

Intrinsic-Extrinsic Issue

Behaviorism ignores instinct in favor of drives. For instance, hunger was proposed as a drive which raised tension that could then be relieved by food (the goal). Since a goal, or a collection of goals, was purported to shape behavior, the learning process involved was called goal-striving. The data from which the conditioning theories were built were drawn from animal experimentation. The Russian conditioning theorists used dogs; the American psychologists favored rats; while biologists preferred cats. Rats, cats, and dogs do not occupy the most optimal positions on the phylogenetic scale. Consequently, the evolutionary inferences which can be drawn for play are slight.

But there is still another reason why findings of behaviorism do not touch upon play. The absence of immediate goals in the frivolity of play has already been identified and a theory conceptualized on goal-striving has little relevancy for goalless behavior. Extrinsic motivators such as the primary drives of hunger and thirst, or even secondary drives of security and wealth, were found to be incapable of shaping the behavior of play. If play behavior is not motivated by extrinsic motivators, and subject to explanation of behaviorism the field is then open to define play as being intrinsically motivated.

Investigators have long agreed that the kinds of activities that make up play could be classed as self-activating and self-rewarding. White (1959) categorized any self-induced state of tension as intrinsic motivation. He proposed that the playful interactions with the environment that characterized this need state did not occur in the presence of strong drives, particularly in the presence of the primary drives. Play is directed, selective and persistent, but is not continued because it serves primary drives. Indeed, it cannot serve these drives until the capabilities or competencies are perfected. It is because play is intrinsically motivated that we find it serving the function it does. Freed from the subservients to other purposes, play goes about its business of preparing environmental adaptation. The self-arousal state of excitement associated with play is a concept critical to any theorizing about the nature of play.

Covert-Overt Issue

The rationality and irrationality within the mind of man caught the attention of two powerful investigators. Freud explored the irrationality of the unconscious and Piaget explored development of man's rational or cognitive processes. There is a difference in the directions that their investigations took. Freud used the data of overt abnormal behavior to build a conceptual superstructure about the unconscious or covert sphere of behavior. Piaget used the highly observable behavior of play to propose a more limited theory of intellectual activity. Although Piaget used the overt data of play for his conceptualizations, he did not develop a theory of play. It is only with considerable difficulty that the generalizations of Piaget's theory can be extended to the commonplace play of children. The generalizations of the Freudian theory can be extended to play, or any other form of overt behavior. But because the generalizations are linked to interpretations, the yield is more to the understanding of the Freudian theory than toward the understanding of play.

In moving back and forth between the thinking and feeling states of the mind and an activity that occurs in the environment, play becomes an innocent bystander that is inadvertently stripped of its identity. Freudian theory is a dramatic example of this dilemma. An examination of its relation to play points up the need to construct an overt and covert continuum along which the phenomenon may be described. Freudian theory required the overt to be subsumed under the covert because it was a theory that did what it set out to do which was to describe the unconscious.

Freud assumed a basic instinct or libido, an urge to live, as the force of all motivation. The libido was a broadly defined sexual impulse. Because it is in nature the strongest of all impulses, it was postulated as the determinant of behavior. The theory proposed that the mind was made up of three realms: the conscious, the preconscious, and the unconscious. While the functions, properties, components, operating principles, and mechanisms of each realm were admitted to be different, they were viewed as interacting so closely that it was difficult to disentangle their effects and weigh their relative contribution. The genius of Freud was that he recognized that man was generally unaware and unready to recognize the processes that influence behavior within his own consciousness.

Three systems through which reality was processed were proposed as: the id, the ego, and the superego. The theory was heavily conceptualized around the id, touched the forces of the ego lightly, and left the social forces of the superego in a fairly primitive state. The id was postulated as the original system of the mind. It consisted of everything psychologically inherited that is present at birth, including the instinct. It was conceptualized as the reservoir of psychic energy and furnished all the powers for the operation of the ego and the superego. Freud called the id the "true psychic reality" because it represents the inner world of subjective experience and had no knowledge of objective reality. The id, being the source of power, was sensitive to and intolerant of tension. Its need to discharge tension was called a striving for pleasure, or the pleasure principle. The ego was described as a structure developed on the basis of experience for regulating instinctive activity in the interest of promoting adjustment to outer reality. It conducted the appropriate transactions with the objective world of reality. The superego was proposed as the internalized moral arbiter of conduct and provided the guidelines of appropriateness for the ego functions.

Play as Primary Process

Reality was seen as an intrusion upon the unconscious, raising the state of its tension and requiring a reduction mediated through the mechanisms of conflict resolution. Tension reduction, rather than tension anticipation, was seen as the pleasure principle upon which the system operated. Students of both play and Freud indicate that it is the primary process, and its related core constructs of displacement, condensation, and symbolization, that has significance for a description of play. The primary process has its own form of logic and makes no distinction between the contents of the mind and the contents of reality. It appears to be a vehicle for both the formation and the storage of wish-fulfilling images. The primary process makes no distinction between perceptions and memory images, ideas, or hallucinations.

It is because of this very freedom from reality that the primary process has much in common with the goallessness of play. When the primary processes, driven by the pleasure principle, confront the secondary processes, driven by the reality principle, conflict is the inevitable consequence. For this reason childhood play has been considered a valuable instrument for observing unconscious conflict. It holds a second place position, however, to the analysis and interpretation of dreams. Freudian theory explains play, as it does most overt activities, simply as a striving for pleasure, escape from pain, reduction of tension, and just another way to master disturbing events.

The energy of the id is in a very fluid state, which means that it can easily be shunted from one action or image to another action or image. The displacement quality of this instinctual energy is due to inability of the id to make fine distinctions between objects. It is characteristic of the id not to distinguish between subjective imagery and objective reality. It behaves through images. The images of the mind are visual, heavily camouflaged in the language of the sexual-drive system, processed in dreams and interpreted through dream analysis and free association. In dreams, the mind is freed to regress from environmental noise and cultural noise. Wish-fulfillments come to life and function according to their own laws of distortion. The mind is protected or defended through the symbols it chooses to use, and the function of symbolism is to disguise and distort the underlying wish.

Symbolic language was conceived by Freud as the secret code of the unconscious. The majority of symbols in the Freudian theory are of a sexual nature. Sticks become the male genital. Little boxes are seen as the female genital. Sexual pleasure is disguised as dancing, climbing, or flying. Sexual castration may take the form of teeth or hair falling out. While mother or father become queen or king figures, little children become small animals, and death becomes a journey. Maturational stages of behavior are conceptualized around modes of reaction related to particular zones of the body. The oral, anal, phallic, and genital stages become the maturational levels around which behavior is organized.

Play seen through the inner processes of the mind and through the lens of Freud becomes a covert behavior stripped of its own meaning. In the interest of understanding the unconscious forces that might be expressed in the conflictual data that play revealed, play had little identity of its own. When play as a form of overt behavior was converted into covert meaning, it was fragmented into nonsense. Slobin (1964), a Harvard psychologist, identified this tendency in his description of a game, "The Fox in the Hole," played within a large circle drawn on the ground. It is played by a group of children. One child stands in the circle holding a knotted handkerchief in his hand. The fox comes out of his hole hopping on one leg, chasing the other players, waving his handkerchief, trying to touch one of the fleeing children. When touched, that child becomes the hopping fox, and all the other children chase him until he seeks refuge in his hole and is safe, until he sallies forth again; and so the "fox in the hole" goes on for hours.

In analyzing the game using the Freudian frame of reference Pfeifer, a Viennese contemporary of Freud, claimed that the playing children are manifesting infantile erotic drives, and that the main role of the pleasurable activity was to express the same forces that are present in dreams. The latent content of the game was wish-fulfillment, effected by the use of symbols. Pfeifer interpreted the symbols as the child striving to gratify his repressed sexual wishes. The circle of refuge, the hole becomes the genital symbol of parental significance, particularly the mother's lap where the child is protected from all the dangers of the external world to which he is drawn by his erotic interests and to which he always strives to return. The presence of the fox in the hole represents incest followed by the punishment of castration in that the player must hop on one leg while leaving the hole. So the sexual decoding goes on and on at the expense of any meaning the game might have.

While the Freudian theory performed a powerful service in decoding unconscious motivation, play comes off badly under the rigid constructs of the theory. The nature of play as a discrete behavior serving adaptive and necessary functions becomes chewed up in the psychoanalytical process. While Freud made some references in his work to the phenomenon of play, almost all his statements dealt with the role of play in working out individual problems and in yielding individual pleasure. Thus, his contributions were forms of interpersonal explanations of conflict. In 1905 he responded directly to the work of Groos, which had appeared six years earlier. Freud accepted Groos' general interpretation that play appears in children while they are learning how to use words and connect parts, and that play was probably the result of an impulse which urges the child to exercise his capacity. At that time his disagreement with Groos was over the interpretation of repetition which Freud believed was based on the pleasure of rediscovering and recognizing the familiar.

Eventually, Freud (1952) synthesized a new concept which he called the "repetition compulsion." While he had first placed the phenomenon of repetition within the explanatory framework of the pleasure principle, that children repeat endlessly what they have enjoyed in the past, by 1952 Freud believed that this failed to predict why children failed to tire of certain kinds of play. He synthesized the phenomena of repetition in children's play with the phenomenon of the reenactment of dramatic events and proposed the construct of repetition compulsion. When a trauma clashes through the protective barrier erected by preparing oneself for a psychic shock, the event hits full force, stirring up greater excitement than a person can handle all at once. Repetition permits the mind to develop some self-preparation for the trauma in retrospect and, by practicing, the playing child gradually gains control over it. This compulsion to repeat a dramatic insult until such time as it can be accepted through the forms of reconstruction remains an important part of the psychoanalytical interpretation of play.

There were some attempts made to rescue behavior from the Freudian rigidities imposed by the sexual impulse. Hendrick (1942) proposed an instinct to mastery which he belived would be a more realistic explanation of the activities of children and play. Kris (1952) subscribed to the validity of functional pleasure. Propositions in these directions were not acceptable to the Freudian theorists, although there is some indication that the ego psychologists may eventually recognize mastery needs as a necessary construct for the executive processes of the ego. It remained for Eric Erikson to free Freudian theory from the narrowness of the libido and to broaden the understanding of the behavioral effects of social conditioning.

In *Childhood and Society* Erikson (1963) developed concepts regarding ego identity and group identity. He proposed that play was an effective safeguard in maintaining the stability and continuity of one's meaning for other people. Personal identity, he suggested, forms the matrix for developing identity as a group member in a social or occupational role. His work provided the substance for understanding the function of the superego, in the course of which he reconceptualized the psychosexual developmental stages of the Freudian theory. In Erikson's epigenetic conception of ego development, the child passes through the sequence of developmental phases, each phase having its own specific crisis. While the child meets each crisis his behavior is predetermined, to a great extent, by the solutions that are offered or permitted by the parents and other caretakers who, in turn, are influenced by society's traditions and ideologies.

Defining play as a function of the ego, Erikson attempted to synchronize the bodily and the social processes within the self. He emphasized the ego's need to master the various areas of life and especially those in which the individual finds his self, his body, and his social role wanting and trailing. The purpose of play was retained within the psychoanalytical theory. Its function was to hallucinate ego mastery while practicing it in an immediate reality between fantasy and actuality. It turned passivity into activity, but the passivity which was a result of trauma was considered to be redesigned in play. The child, in Erikson's sense, could play at doing something that was in reality done to him. The content and structure of play were seen as having therapeutic value through the ability to convert reality and process mastery.

Children's play, Erikson proposed, was not equivalent to adult play. The playing adult steps sideward into another reality, while the playing child moves forward to new stages of mastery. He speculated that child's play is an infantile form of the human ability to deal with experience by creating model situations, and to master reality by experiment and planning. It is in certain phases of his work that the adult projects past experiences into dimensions which seem manageable. In the laboratory, on the stage, and on the drawing board the adult relives the past and thus relieves leftover effects; in reconstructing the model situation, he redeems his failures and strengthens his hope as he anticipates the future from the point of view of a corrective and shed past. Erikson maintained that no thinker could do more, and no playing child could do less, than the important task of model construction.

Piagetian Theory

The building of models, not in the interest of reexperiencing success and failure but for the purpose of building constructs for thinking, was the Piagetian theme. As a psychologist working in the Rousseau Institute of Geneva, Switzerland, Jean Piaget (1952) published a major work called *Play, Dreams and Imitation in Childhood*. He proposed a cognitive adaptation model of behavior. From observing the play of his own children, Piaget described the interaction of a child with his environment, proposed stages and sequences of physical and psychological development, and postulated that the environmental interaction was the essential ingredient for intellectual development. His major concepts were "schema," or the plural "schemata," which "assimilated" new experiences and permitted "accommodation" to environmental demands.

Piaget was biologically trained and his combined interest in philosophy, especially in the theory of knowledge, led him to study the intellectual development of children in the belief that the logical analysis of "knowing" could be determined by observing how children actually come to think logically. He found no formulated system awaiting him in the field of psychology that could be built upon or could account for the symbolization process Piaget believed went on in the inner mind of the child. Step by step he had to develop his own system of thought. His writings present formidable hazards both in style and in vocabulary. He made numerous small-print notations of what the Piaget children—Laurent, Lucielle, or Jacqueline—did on such and such a day in time. His records were filled with cumbersome equations which often make hard going for students of his work.

However complex his writing or obscure his vocabulary, Piaget manages to put across clearly the principle that action or overt behavior is the essential ingredient of knowing. His records indicate that play is where the action of thought is, and that play behavior is the natural matrix or seedbed of learning. But what we remember from Piaget's work is not how or why children play, but rather the insightful propositions about the learning process. An object is known, Piaget taught, only to the extent that it is acted upon or forms part of an action sequence. Cognitive functions not only subserve action, but are themselves forms of action. The Piaget master principle is that thinking is not "for" action, it "is" action.

At first, according to Piaget, there literally is only action without representation in the mind, but, as development progresses, the action sequences become internalized into images. Then concrete strategies appear until, finally, complex operations that are totally psychological and devoid of concrete representations are possible. The more sophisticated formal operations, such as mathematical abstractions, are all derived from and are a form of action developed in the course of this evolution. The purpose of the evolutionary course is to protect the individual in his dealings with the external world.

Assimilation and accommodation. The Piagetian theory postulates two processes believed fundamental to all information transformations. These are assimilation and accommodation, and appear to operate both separately and interdependently. The simplest explanation of assimilation is seen when it is equated with the process of eating. Food is changed in the course of being taken in and made part of the organism. Accommodation is defined as the organisms adjustment to the external world and is likened to changes in posture or changes to avoid an obstacle, or the act of contracting an eye muscle in the presence of bright light. The two processes are seen as complementary and involve each other. If the food particles to be assimilated are large, the mouth has to open wider. A number of physical and chemical processes go on in the organism, accommodating it to the type of food received, and at the same time changing what is to be digested.

As Freud widened the term "sex," so Piaget uses the terms "assimilation" and "accommodation" in a wider sense to apply them to intellectual processes. Assimilation refers to any process whereby information is changed in the process of making it part of the organism's know-how. Information is, as it were, digested. Accommodation means any adjustment the organism has to make to the external world in order to assimilate information. Intellectual development is due to, or is the product of, the continual act of interplay between assimilating and accommodating. Intellectual adaptation depends upon the two processes balancing each other or being in equilibrium. When they are not, accommodation or adjustment to the object may predominate over assimilation. In this manner, Piaget accounts for imitation. Alternatively, assimilation, that is, fitting the impression in the previous experience and adapting it to the individual's need, will predominate, and this Piaget calls play. Imitation and play are seen as an integral part of the development of intelligence, and consequently go through the same stages.

Schemata and stages. The central theme running through the Piagetian theory is the activity of the mind, that is, thinking, is not passive. The mind, says Piaget, constructs reality. His use of the word schema, or schemata, covers this notion. In contemporary scientific parlance the Piaget schema would come closest to the term "model," or the process of model building. The schemata constructed within the mind underlie all cognitive behavior, and they undergo changes throughout development. Different modes were proposed to represent different ontogenetic steps: the sensorimotor, preoperational, and operational. The sensorimotor period (extending to about eighteen months of age) is generally characterized by "action schemata" in which behavior has almost no internal image representation. Toward the end of this period internalized mental schemata replace habitual or conditioned responses.

The second period, called the preoperational phase, is characterized by representational schemata and contains images that can be manipulated internally without being acted out in reality. The external world is represented internally, but only in an erratic, subjective, or egocentric manner. During this period idiosyncratic meanings are ascribed to events as one's own experiences are projected onto objects. In the latter stages of this period the internalized schemata are gradually brought into greater objective correspondence with reality, but the basis for ordering the world is perception rather than cognition.

In the third period, the operational one, an attempt is finally made to verify statements by testing. There is a gradual disconnection between perception and thought. The child ignores the most striking perceptual elements in his surroundings and begins to think of solutions to problems that are contrary to what is naively perceived. When the schemata become "operational," the child is capable of devising strategies that involve steps in logical analysis rather than reacting immediately to a given situation. The child can go back and forth mentally through a period of sequences regardless of what has transpired in the perceptual sphere. He can recall the beginning of a series of events that have happened; his thoughts become "reversible" while reality does not. At this stage the child also begins to form lawful classes of objects that depend upon the existence of concrete objects. In the final stage of the operational period the child's schemes are composed of manipulated relationships rather than objects. By the time he reaches adolescence, a child can use strategies involving pure abstractions; that is, relational symbols that are independent of concrete objects. Similarly, the adolescent is able to formalize laws about his experience, generalize other situations, and even consider hypothetical cases. His thought is not bound to the concrete object before him.

Equilibrium. Three epochs (sensorimotor, preoperational, and operational), each with its schemata or constructions, constitute Piaget's system of development. They represent the three major levels of schemata with transitional substages between them. The transitional substages are a somewhat troublesome area in Piaget's system, as he himself and others have observed. The difficulty is in defining development as a continuous process of equilibrium while also postulating discontinuous or qualitative leaps from one level of schemata to another. The problem lies in Piaget's concept of equilibration, which is an essential ingredient of the theory. Equilibration is a product of the constant reciprocal activity of assimilation and accommodation. From a philosophical standpoint, Piaget says, life or thought is active because it constantly constructs schemata. These schemata must be able to assimilate external data as well as modify or accommodate themselves to external events. He warned that, without assimilation, there would be a pure empiricism in which the organism would be continuously modified by environmental changes. Without accommodation there would be pure solipsism, in which the organism would go beyond the reach of the external world. The struggle to maintain equilibrium is one of the theoretical points that the Piagetian theory may converge with the Freudian theory. Disequilibrium and conflict have a shared meaning.

Conservation. The three epochs of development offer maximum equilibration, while the transitional stages are unstable. Piaget illustrates this point in his classical conservation experiments. If a lump of clay is rolled into a thinner, longer shape, a child in the preoperational period will respond that the amount of clay has been altered as the result of the change in shape. At the operational period, however, he will say that the amount remains constant, despite changes in shape. Piaget explains this cognitive jump by describing a series of steps that the child moves through. As maturation proceeds, the child's attention begins to oscillate between longness and thinness, which offer contradictory perceptions of the amount of clay. Ultimately the child reaches the point where he can consider both aspects—the longness (more clay) and the thinness (less clay)—simultaneously and understand their inverse relationship. At this moment the schemata of conservation appears.

The idea of conservation explains the previously contradictory perceptions and can be generalized to other events. The stable stages of development are considered periods of maximal self-regulation. Ultimately they lead to greater horizons that require higher levels of schemata for equilibrium. Thus, the overall system describes development as a general freeing of thought or cognition from its concrete surroundings so that ultimately events or objects that defy concrete representation can be considered. The general impression is that while Piaget has constructed a complex and difficult theory about how the mind of a child works, his developmental description makes behavioral sense.

Piagetian play. Specialists who use Piaget's theoretical findings are more inclined to value the inferences he drew for cognition than the inferences which might be made for play. Psychologists, sociologists, and educators consistently emphasize the conceptualizations about cognition and as consistently ignore the significance of play. The ritual of theorizing appears to require that action data of behavior be abstracted to principles that express dynamics. Descriptions of actual playing are stripped away and transposed into forms that serve the theory at hand. In Piaget's theory the action descriptions of children playing are transposed into the descriptive-action categories of assimilation, accommodation, and equilibrium. The taxonomy operationalism of the process words, together with the construct of schemata, relieve the theory of the troublesome burden of describing the natural context of the action. Loss to the understanding of play has been enormous. The price we pay is the meager generalization that can be made to playing children in their natural settings. Whatever generalizations can be made, nevertheless, are worth struggling to make.

While Freud in his theory had to assume a special impulse for sex, there was no need for Piaget to assume an impulse for play since he regarded it as an aspect of assimilation. His explanation was that by the fourth month of life, as looking and touching become coordinated, the child learns that to push a toy hanging from its crib will make it swing and rattle, Once learned, the action is repeated again and again. This, according to Piaget, is play. Functional pleasure, and pleasure in being the cause, arise from a repetition of actions as soon as they are mastered during the successive substage of the sensorimotor period. When play is no longer a mere repetition of what was successful it becomes repetition with variations. By the time the child is between twelve and eighteen months old he is an active, systematic experimenter. As he repeats the various possibilities of what can be done with objects he becomes coordinated. In the beginning of this stage the child is engaged in systematic exploration and pursuit of whatever is new. In the final stage of sensorimotor behavior action occurs in the absence of objects and with it symbolization, pretense, and make-believe become possible.

Symbolic or make-believe play characterizes the period of about two to seven years of age. A knotted rag, at this point, can be used as if it were a doll. Actions appropriate to one object are used as a substitute. Initially, these internalized actions stand for the object as concrete symbols. Later, they act as signs indicating or signifying the object. Language is a socially ready-made set of signifiers and while words help the process, Piaget maintained they are not essential to it. Symbolic and make-believe play have the same function in the development of representational thinking as practice play has for the sensorimotor period. It is also during this time that make-believe play becomes progressively more elaborate and organized. With growing experience in the physical and social environment, there is a transition to more accurate representation of reality. This increasingly involves sensorimotor and intellectual practice so that as play becomes constructive, adapted to reality, it ceases to be play altogether. At the same time, as the child becomes more socially adapted, he consequently needs to resort less to symbolic substitutes and distortions or reality. Thus Piaget accounts for the psychological function that play serves.

Nor does Piaget ignore the socializing function of play because he is a psychologist. Social behavior is present in play, and Piaget does not bypass it with a theory intent only on psychological operations. As a psychologist he did not delimit his considerations to traditional psychological variables. He described the overt and covert inter-actions. He identified individual symbols and beliefs as they become modified through cooperation with others and described the rea-soning of the child and his use of symbols as becoming more logical and objective in the period from eight to eleven. Play was described as controlled by collective discipline and codes of honor, with games with rules replacing the individual's symbolic make-believe of the earlier stage. Although games with rules were considered to be socially adaptive and survived into adulthood, they were seen by Piaget as showing assimilation rather than accommodation charac-teristics. The rules of the games he viewed as serving a legitimizing function for the individual's satisfaction in his sensorimotor and intellectual achievements and victory over others.

A clear biological function is attributed to play because of its active repetition and experimentation which "mentally digest" novel situations and experiences. His theory affords a coherent description of the development of successive activities from pushing hanging rattles to acting out stories and playing baseball and checkers. An important play principle Piaget proposed was that when play is pure assimilation it allows the predictions that a child will play at whatever activity he has just mastered and that such play will be characterized by whatever distortion of reality suits the child's need.

Piaget distinguishes between play as repetition of an action already mastered and repetition of an activity in order to understand it. When a child is trying to understand, he is investigating or exploring and this involves accommodation to reality. Presumably, the stage between initial acquaintance and complete familiarity with any event is longer for the younger child because he is more ignorant of more aspects of new objects and effects of a new skill. Practice play occurs whenever a new skill is acquired. The need for practice diminishes as few skills tend to be totally new or when the individual grows older. Repetition, in this instance, serves to integrate the experience with the rest of the organism's know-how.

Age and play correlations were roughly postulated as proceeding in expected directions. Play, says this theory, should increase with age as the child becomes capable of more varied activities and can impose more changes on the environment. The quantity of play should decrease with age as fewer events and skills are novel. New activities are absorbed more quickly, and as specific developmental activities become mastered through play they are finally fully exploited. The quality of play, however, should increase with age as mastery needs recede.

While Freud maintained that play was almost all covert, Piaget assumed a mixed position on this issue. Freud assumed that the primary process was the single prior process leading gradually to outer expression in play. In early childhood play was regarded as fantasy woven about a real object. The play of later childhood constituted an externalization of fantasy. The work of Piaget, on the basis of his detailed observation of real activity, concludes that all imaginative thought was interiorized play. Piaget and Freud seemed to propose a theory of the Chinese boxes. The puzzle of the boxes being each box is supposed to contain the other. Action is reality, says Piaget, and play contains thinking. The conflict within the unconscious, says Freud, is reality and play contains conflict. Play expresses the covert unconscious, says Freud; play expresses the covert cognition, says Piaget.

Imagination and Play

Eric Klinger (1969), an American psychologist, proposed a single continuum upon which we might place both play and the unconscious forces underlying it. He assumed a strong interdependence between fantasy and play. Because play was highly observable and fantasy was not, Klinger speculated that a serious study of play might provide a potential source for hypothesis about fantasy. From a review of the developmental course of play and fantasy he examined the play elements for their applicability to a theory of fantasy. His hypothesis was supported inasmuch as many important aspects of the content and structure play resembled fantasy at corresponding points that could be investigated.

The Klinger findings were that the motivation of play and fantasy was autotelic, or intrinsic, because a momentum inherent in the capacity for activity and play modulated the organism's need for activation. He identified in the play process two critical subprocesses: fragmentation and preestablished bits. The sequences of any activity are fragmented, then recombined with the elements already established or preestablished in the response repertory.

The effortless of play was an element that intrigued and baffled his analysis. His major finding was that children's play contributes to the solutions of problems. The different functions of problem-solving that play served he categorized as the solution of instrumental problems, problems of emotional integration, and problems of experiential continuity. Klinger concluded that testable hypotheses could not emerge because of the substantial knowledge gaps in our understanding of play. His findings provide us, however, with a useful overall view about play and by pinpointing the relationship to fantasy suggests the possibility of understanding this phenomenon as it interfaces with imagination.

Relatively few investigators have attempted an exhaustive or fully exclusive operational definition of play. No one appears to have undertaken systematic research on the difficulties of formulating one. There appears to have been no systematic empirical attempt to dimensionalize play or to factor-analyze it. As a result an investigator like Klinger is forced to conclude that a reviewer has little assurance of any but the grossest comparability among the dependent variables of different studies. He found little agreement concerning variables in play that could be of central interest and there was, consequently, a degree of noncompatibility. This lack of agreement among investigators precludes any synthesis of knowledge or the formulation of analytical experimental designs. He found the studies on doll play, for instance, to be characterized by an interest in aggression, but also characterized by so many other issues that, in his view, they are a rather untidy array of investigations. Of all the enormous number of variables and frameworks available from which play may be examined, Klinger concluded that only a tiny portion of them had been systematically employed.

None of the studies that Klinger reviewed had obtained normative observational data concerning the structure or content of children's play in its natural habitat. Investigators appear to have kept away from children playing in the backyard, streets or playgrounds. Neither retrospective studies nor laboratory observations were found to substitute for the basic questions of how young human beings spend their free time and energies. There had been no systematic investigation, let alone analytic experiments, to verify and render precise the common clinical observation that play facilitates the mastery of emotional traumata. Indeed, the conditions under which play was most likely to reflect trauma were not very clear as far as ability to set up an experimentation for play was concerned. He found that the controversies over the motivation of play were too narrowly clustered around the primary drives.

Klinger concluded that theories other than those related to primary drives and the primary process could, in the present stage of knowledge, accommodate the data of play with less contortion and fewer epicycles. Available evidence, however, is insufficient to permit a conclusive statement as to what another theory, or other theories, might be. He suggested, as potentials for theorizing, an activation-psychotheory and a pure autotelic theory. The concepts of autotelic and activation, says Klinger, might propel play into being a researchable piece of behavior.

Imagination as play. Some valuable insights about play emerged from the Klinger study of fantasy. His global conclusion was that adult fantasy assumes the problem-solving functions of childhood's overt play. His position, therefore, tends to support the Piagetian view that imagination was internalized play. His investigation is worth critiquing.

Klinger asked three somewhat intertwined questions. First, did play and fantasy originate as a unitary process in infancy and then differentiate with increasing age? Second, do they retain sufficient structural similarity to permit some generalization from one to the other? Third, do they exhibit sufficient similarity in content to permit generalization? The conclusions were that play and fantasy appear to share a common origin and undergo parallel development until free play declines; afterwards there is some evidence for continuity between play and fantasy. They appear to be undifferentiated prior to the third year of life and thereafter until puberty develops along a parallel course with respect to such basic structural characteristics as complexity and realism. From about age three, however, play and fantasy gradually become differentiated, and play becomes increasingly socialized in the direction of games with rules and aesthetic activities. At puberty, play—as defined by Klinger—has sharply subsided and fantasy activities become more prominent.

Freud, contrary to Piaget and Klinger, asserts that unconscious behavior is to be regarded as the single prior process leading gradually to motor expression in play. Play, in this sense, is the externalization of internal conflict. Piaget, however, argues that play may be regarded as a single prior process leading through the development of symbolization in the imagination to intellectual activity. He proposed imaginative thought as internalized play. At this stage of our knowledge, there appears to be much good sense in the Klinger projection that there are more useful theories than Freudian and Pagetian to explain play.

Play motivation. A motivational explanation was another critical concern of the Klinger investigation. Piaget felt no need to propose a motivational set other than the functional pleasure of Bühler (1931). Piaget assumed that all behavior serves the ends of biological adaptation. His recognition of this principle was expressed in his concepts of assimilation and accommodation. Assimilation he proposed as a form of adapting to new material, and accommodation he proposed as a mechanism for processing new behavior into habits. The need to maintain a balance between the two was covered by his construct of equilibrium. Freud accounted for play in the mechanism of repetition-compulsion, and thereby proposed play as a means by which the child assimilates or masters an overpowering experience. Both of these explanations for motivation are incomplete. Klinger concluded that either play is autotelic, in the sense that its occurrence is not dependent on the need to attain goals extrinsic to play, or the occurrence and momentum of play are governed by the organism's "momentary needs to maintain an optimal level of activation." A theory of activation or a theory of autotelic behavior are saying the same thing. There is no empirical basis for choosing between these alternatives because both imply that play occurs spontaneously in the absence of strong internal needs for compelling external stimulation. This conclusion Klinger extended to fantasy. Fantasy becomes a kind of baseline ideation that occurred spontaneously and continuously under similar conditions. Fantasy-like play occurs in the absence of ongoing operant activity.

Fragmentation and preestablished properties. The most operational findings of the Klinger study had to do with the structure of fantasy and play. Two characteristics of structure were identified as fragmentation and preestablished properties of fragmentation. Fragmentation was found to be characteristic both of animal and child play. It took the form of interruption of the behavior sequence before it reached the normal goal by acting out of fractional sequences, repetition of fractional sequences, and reordering of sequences. Preestablished properties meant that the schemata employed by the organism were acquired prior to the occasion of play. They appeared very much like overlearned behaviors, in the sense that they contained overlearned forms, rules, and familiar classes of schematic response.

The fragmentation concept is best described by Brian Sutton-Smith (1971). There seems to be, he says, a relaxation of customary modes of feeling as a child enters play. He is on his own ground and in his own time. The special boundaries of the playing field and the temporary boundaries of recess enclose a world in which the child has autonomous power. Testing the order of this universe, the child frequently reverses the normal state of affairs. Behaviors become detached from their original goals. There is greater variation than usual, there is pretense, and there are new combinations and novelty.

For example, when a child first learns to solve a jigsaw puzzle he applies himself with earnestness, and may even cry if he is unable to complete it. After mastering the puzzle he begins to vary the process, with less concern about the final result which he takes for granted. He puts pieces in the wrong places and corrects himself with mock astonishment. Later, he takes the puzzle and playfully traces the pieces. The novelty of the new procedure is irrelevant to the original results; the means become the ends in themselves. The excitement and tension of play seem to arise from the dissonance between the old and new orders. Fragmentation in the presence of novelty, interacting with preestablished schemata, explains the observable repetition of play.

Problem solving. Play yields new solutions to old problems through the opportunities it provides to try out the combinations of old schemata. The contribution to the mastery of overwhelming emotional experiences by enabling the child to reenact them under control conditions, and to articulate them with his existing response repertory. It helps to establish opportunities to work from inter-perceptual response patterns that have already acquired meaning.

When dealing with unfinished business, however, play does so indirectly. Few would maintain that children play in order to solve problems, but the weight of observation is that, in play, certain kinds of problems are solved. A child works through the elements of a problem with the possibility of discovering new options. Theories and observations of children's play describe a heterogeneous assort-ment of problem-solving types which may be classified as instru-mental problems, problems of emotional integration, and problems of experiential continuity.

Instrumental problems are those presented by an unattained, desired or fairly specific goal, such as the acquisition of a new status, experience or manipulation, or alteration of a painful human relationship. For the attainment of fairly specific goals the child depends upon instrumental acts. Problems of emotional integration are those requiring the mastery of emotional, overwhelming past experiences, and of emotionally disturbing anticipated events. Problems of experiential continuity are those with which the child must come to grips in new situations.

Problem-solving for these different situations occurred in children's play. Fantasy or imagination provided the normal means for the solution of early childhood problems. The child attacked the problem indirectly, often symbolically and without apparent sharp awareness of his objective. The problem developed by means of successively imagined solutions, piecemeal and gradually. This described course is consistent with Piaget's assertion that play is a part of any child's problem-solving activity. Given a problem area and a substantial repertory of schemata relevant to the problem, repeated modifications and recombinations are likely to lead to new combinations that the child recognizes as leading to favorable outcomes in reality.

The role of repetitive play in mastering overwhelming images has been argued frequently, particularly by the Freudian theorists. Erikson (1940) described repeated symbolic approaches by the children toward the events that most disturbed them. Sometimes these approaches seemed gleeful but were followed by profound attacks of anxiety. At other times the approaches seemed quite joyless and even anxious. These behaviors were seen by Erikson as a product of intense conflict. Therapeutic effectiveness was explained by the extinction of anxiety through controlled symbolic repetition of anxiety-provoking events in relatively safe contacts. By repeatedly combining them with other cognitive schemata the child was likely to achieve a greater degree of cognitive integration and control. We could conclude that spontaneous fantasy may, under certain conditions, promote a similar reduction or mastery of anxiety.

Play also served to provide experiential continuity in a child's life. Childhood is marked by frequent encounters with drastically new experiences, simply because children's limited experiences with life correspondingly limit their repertory of perceptual categories and response stances. Play permits the accommodated stretching of available schemata to provide an experiential bridge between an established cognitive repertory and a strange new set of circumstances. Play thus gradually invests a new event with meaning and promotes the cultivation of new cognitive, verbal and motive skills.

Autotelic Arousal Theory

Heckhausen. An Autotelic-arousal theory as the best possible way to play and fantasy was advocated by Klinger. His perspective directs that any search for explanation include the works of Berlyne and Heckhausen. Both theorists represent post-1950 developments in motivation theory.

Heinz Heckhausen (1964), a German psychologist, starts out by noting the purposelessness as the major characteristic that play shares with certain other forms of behavior. Activities that appear to be without purpose he defined as carried out for their own sake and with an unconstrained basic feeling of "I don't have to," which distinguishes them from "necessary" activities serving the satisfaction of needs promoted by overriding demands. Purposelessness activities like play are governed by an activation cycle, which consists of alternating rises and drops in tension. Rises in tension, or activations, come from discrepancies, a term that Heckhausen uses to stand for inequalities, differences, deviations, inconsistencies, infractions, dissonance, and contradictions. They fall into four categories: (1) novelty or change—discrepancies between past, present, and earlier perceptions or experiences; (2) surprise content—discrepancies between present perception and expectation based on earlier experiences; (3) complexity—a discrepancy between parts of the present perceptual experiential field; and (4) uncertainty or conflict—a discrepancy between different expectations or between different impulses.

Heckhausen performed a basic definition task for play by describing many of its characteristics which emerged from his interest in the arousal potential. Arousal potential has properties of external stimulation that generally raises the level of arousal, dependent on interaction of the cerebral cortex and the brain-stem reticular formation. If the influx of arousal potential exceeds, or falls short of an optimal level, then states experienced as unpleasant and which are more or less severe impair sensory-cognitive and motor functions. Thus, there is a motivation to keep activation in the neighborhood of the optimum. This leads, however, to imperfect regulation with considerable time lag which, as cyberneticians have generally pointed out, causes oscillations. Upward or downward movements toward the optimum are experienced as pleasant, and even moments away from the optimum will be agreeably exciting as long as they are moderate and of short duration being quickly followed by a reversal.

The tension-relieving function is paramount in play. For example, it may contribute to the mastery of the traumatizing, as in play therapy, or of the supernatural incomprehensible, as in religious ritual. Most games, however, help to supply activation, making up, says Heckhausen, "what the everyday world has lost in unpredictability and risk, in surprise and in danger, in short, in arousal potential."

Play differs from other purposeless activities, according to Heckhausen, (1) in its moderate degree of activation, which is less than that of adventurous undertakings but greater than that of enjoyment of art; (2) in the relative high frequency of the activation cycel: tension and relief succeed one another very quickly, giving play a short time perspective.

A final characteristic which is not found in all forms is its "quasi-reality." Play is not altogether unreal, like fantasy or fiction, but it is separate from the reality of everyday life, transforming and often heightening the latter. It involves "acting on" as distinct from the more cognitive "interaction with" something or somebody that the player does not fully dominate. Players often lose this quasi-real quality as in the testing-out play of the infant and in "fascinated playing of the adult with exciting or unknown or easily manipulable material." In any case, deviations from optimal arousal potential will lose their association with fun and give rise to threatening seriousness which stifles play as soon as they get out of control.

Ludic theory. While Heckhausen studied purposeless behavior in Germany, the British psychologist Berlyne (1960) studied the same motivational problem in the United States and Canada. His concern was with the motivation of perceptual and intellectual activities when they are engaged in for their own sake. This behavior he classified as "ludic" and included under it everything usually classified as recreation, entertainment, or idle curiosity as well as art, philosophy, and pure, as distinct from applied, sciences. To gauge the strength of motivation to which these activities respond, Berlyne believed that one had only to think of the immense industries that had grown up to cater to them and to consider the economic resources devoted to them by advanced society.

Ludic behavior, in Berlyne's language, consisted of seeking particular kinds of external stimulation, imagery, and thought. His hypothesis was that most of the attempts made to express the distinction between ludic and non-ludic behavior have avoided issues. Motives associated with nonludic behavior had been referred to by terms like physiological needs or homeostatic drives. But ludic behavior must depend, just as much as any other behavior, on physiological processes.

As far as we know, says Berlyne, ludic behavior may have its contribution to make to biological implication and, in particular, to the state of bodily equilibrium and well-being that the so-called homeostatic processes serve to maintain. Berlyne made a motivational study exploring into the nature of this homeostatic behavior as it is disguised in disinterested perceptual and intellectual activities. He postulated a curiosity drive that shaped exploratory behavior. The drive acts upon an arousal system which is localized in the reticular formation of the central nervous system. As sensory information enters the ascending reticular pathway, the exploratory drive acts as a filtering device to control the ever-widening field of information.

Conflict is the critical concept in ludic behavior. It occurs when the incoming information is excessive, deficient, or discrepant. Various kinds of conflict are proposed as a stimulus selection process which forms the principle means of defense. Berlyne chose play behavior to study because his theory was not interested in the spectacular inputs that wrack adaptation. Instead, his was a study that sought to understand the most ubiquitous and recurrent patterns of information by which the mind apprehends reality.

The concept of fun, that was so characteristic of and highly observable in playful behavior is a major consideration in his study of this exploratory behavior. Incoming perceptions were, the theory hypothesized related to the subject's "category systems." A novel stimulus pattern was apt to require some cognitive "innovation" or modification of the category system so that it could be assimilated. The innovation rate depended on how rapidly stimulus changes were occurring and how much novelty they introduced, and on central factors such as fantasying and problem-solving processes. A subject at any time, according to Berlyne, has a "preferred innovation rate" (PIR), and he may use games or other forms of "fun" to keep the actual innovation rate in the neighborhood of PIR.

Four play conclusions. About ten years after the publication of his ludic theory, Berlyne (1969) described play around four conclusions. These conclusions, he maintains, discern the recurrent motifs and consonances of play behavior.

Conclusion 1 — "It is repeatedly asserted that playful activities are carried on 'for their own sake' or for the sake of 'pleasure.' They are contrasted with 'serious' activities which deal with readily identifiable body needs or external facts or otherwise achieve specifiable practical ends."

The picture of play as a class of actions that an organism indulges in because it derives pleasure from performing is encouraged by copious reference to Bühler's concept of functional pleasure. But it is clear that there is more to play than that. First, whether an organism plays, and in what form, depends on its motivational condition. Second, while an infant might very well begin by carrying out in random order a number of actions that happen to be pleasurable, selection and learning make their appearance very soon. The young child introduces variations into his playful actions and some of the variations are retained while others are abandoned. The child is evidently more concerned with the patterns, visual or auditory, that are produced through his play. The literature provides many illustrations of the constructive nature of early play, even though the products may seem primitive to the adult.

In later stages of development, when role-playing games and games with rules come to the fore, there is obviously a large amount of selective learning and temporal ordering of actions in pursuit of specific end products. Selective learning requires that we postulate some kind of feedback to reinforce some forms of behavior and extinguish others. If reinforcement does not come from some consequence effected in the external environment, it must come from inner consequence, and in particular from some effect on the central nervous system.

Therefore, when we say that play or some other activity is engaged in for its own sake, what we really mean is that it is engaged in for the sake of these inner consequences. It follows, then, that it will be engaged in only when the organism is in the kind of motivational condition that makes these inner consequences rewarding. Behavior of this kind can be called "intrinsically motivated."

Conclusion 2—"Many writers stress the unreality or the quasi-reality of play. Reality presumably refers to the forms of interaction between the organism and its environment that occupy most of its waking hours."

Play is usually distinguished from reality by being restricted to a special time and place. Special rituals are performed, special modes of speech are used, special kinds of dress, even masks, may be worn. The copious differential cues that arrive in these ways make it easy to confine playful responses to occasions when this behavior will be rewarded, and not punished. In play an animal or child, or even an adult human being, may attack each other. Aggressive responses are likely to be inhibited in the presence of another individual most of the time, but if a situation is defined as "playful," aggressive responses can be performed with impunity and are therefore disinhibited.

In "real" aggressive behavior, however, each of the antagonists tries to hurt the other as much as possible, and may even kill. In playful fighting some of the components of fighting are suppressed and most of them are under partial inhibition, reducing their vigor. Signals are given to indicate that the aggressive responses do not have the meaning that they normally have, so that the retaliative reactions of the opponent are likewise subject to inhibition.

Conclusion 3—"Several, but not all of the investigators, have noted the odd mixture of 'tension' and unpleasant excitement in play and have attached importance to it."

The German psychologists Haigis (1941) and Meinecke (1956) have gone furthest in the arousal theory in holding play to depend on courting danger. Psychoanalysis, of course, has drawn attention to the fact that many of the actions that participate in play are left over from painful or anxiety-inducing experiences. Heckhausen sees as essential the alternation between activation and relief, and credits play with providing excitement that is lacking in everyday life.

The novelty and complexity that underlie play have been classified under various forms of uncertainty which we may call conflict or discrepancy. They include the "collative" stimulus properties that have been proposed by Heckhausen and are believed to exert a dominant influence over exploratory behavior, over some forms of fear, and over aesthetic behavior, among other psychological phenomena. They all seem to depend upon the initiation of processes in the central nervous system that are somehow mutually discrepant or interfering. Although there are a number of hypotheses regarding the essential conditions that they have in common, there are arguments for supposing that they all involve conflict between incompatible response tendencies.

Therefore, a possibility that offers itself, is that conflict motivates play with or without supplementary motivation from other sources. Hence, those writers who assert that play is characteristic of a "relaxed field" are only partially right. Playing animals may be relatively free from pressures and tensions due to primary drives. There are, however, other sources of tension or drive "arousals" at work, and these may be due to collative properties. The collative properties are novelty, complexity, surprise, and ambiguity. They may be characteristics of the environment, or they may result —having been expressly sought out—from the playful activities themselves.

Conclusion 4—"The final question is, how reduction of arousal, relaxation of tension, relief from conflict, occur in the course of play."

Berlyne sees many possibilities emerging from his theory of arousal. In games of all kinds there is a degree of uncertainty about the outcome, and this is relieved as corresponding information is obtained. The infant dropping objects in the course of a practice game finds out what the object looks like as it falls, where it comes to rest, and what kind of sound it makes on hitting the floor. In a symbolic game the child finds out what it feels like to behave like a doctor or mother. In games with rules the player finds out who will win and how he himself will do. Apart from uncertainty reduction there is relief of arousal through habituation. Repeated exposure to a stimulus is known to dampen its powers to raise arousal through extinction. Fearful stimuli may cease to frighten as exposure to them without untoward accomplishment is prolonged, especially if stimuli conducive to muscular relaxation are present and, in some circumstances, especially if vigorous muscular activity takes place.

Some writers may add as a source of reinforcement the satisfaction of achievement, the sense of competence (White, 1959). This, no doubt, is important in many instances, but it may be possible, says Berlyne, to reduce competency to a freedom from uncertainty;

that is, knowing what to do whatever contingency may arise. Competency may also serve as a protection against surprise and frustration. Along with the possibility of examining competency, there is a reward value of play that appears, in large measure, to come from mastery and alleviation of conditions of uncomfortably high arousal. Finally, there is a possibility that the physical exercise component of play can itself be rewarding. There is evidence that opportunity from muscular activity can reinforce an instrumental response in animal behavior, especially after a period of restricted exercise.

In sum Berlyne, as a psychologist, argues that all the foregoing review lends little support to the position that play is a useful category for psychology. The chief element common to the infant shaking his rattle, a little girl holding a girl's tea party, the adolescent football player, and the aged rake at the roulette table is that they are all under the sway of intrinsic motivation. Yet, intrinsic motivation predominates also in exploratory behavior, hobbies of all sorts, and the enjoyment of works of art. In at least some cases these pursuits are not regarded as play. Even if we can say intrinsic motivation dependent on collative variables and conflict governs the four conclusive statements of play, the way motivation works differs widely from one statement to another. We must conclude, says Berlyne, that if psychology is to continue its investigation into purposeless behavior, we would do well to consider giving up the category of play in favor of both wider and narrower categories.

SOCIOCULTURAL EXPLANATION

Homo Ludens

Important groundwork for understanding play was provided by Johan Huizinga (1955), a Dutch historian of culture. Huizinga elaborated on the theme that culture arises in this form of play and culture is play from the very beginning of history.

As Chancellor of Leyden University, Huizinga took for the topic of an honorary lecture a subject he had been preoccupied with for some thirty years. His foundation assertion was that man playing was man experiencing culture. The idea for the lecture and the book which followed it, *Homo Ludens,* came to Huizinga while he was at work on a study of the cultural history of the Middle Ages. It is true, unfortunately, that Huizinga's style of writing, the language and metaphors he uses are obscure and frequently confusing. His writing also suffers in the translation from the original Dutch. But even so it is a treatise on play worth the difficulties involved in reading. What Huizinga did was to perceive intentively the double nature of culture. He could see the old or the former in a newer or later structure of a society.

What puzzled and intrigued the historian Huizinga was that medieval Christendom continued to maintain the cultural elements of the long forgotten past. Codes of honor, heraldry, chivalric orders and tournaments, and courtly demeanor were artificial residuals of past centuries. He speculated that these elements of medieval society the vestiges of primeval initiation rites had their origin in sacred play, and were carried on during the Middle Ages in the spirit of play.

This view of the double nature of a culture echoes an evolutionary notion that organism, an individual or a society contains as it were a double life. The theme is based on the principle that as an organization grows it passes through sequential scales of being. Older functions exist inactive but concealed conditions bound down and restrained by all that has developed subsequently. Huizinga looked at contemporary society and from that vantage point on the ladder of social evolution he was able to say that any present state society had arrived at was through the concealing mechanism of play.

Play served a serious function for society in that Huizinga suspected it processed culture. In this sense play is the basis of culture because civilization arises and unfolds in, and as, play. Homo ludens tried to integrate the concept of play with that of culture by attempting to identify the ways culture itself bears the character of play.

In Huizinga's work play is to be understood not as a biological phenomenon, but as a cultural phenomenon. He approached his examination historically, rather than scientifically. His convictions were that play could not be understood through biopsychological methodologies, because these disciplines have laid too little stress on the "supreme importance to civilization of the play factor." The objections to psychology and physiology were that they depended upon observation and description for explanation of animal and human play. Their common assumptions, Huizinga argues, are that play must have something which is "not" play, that behavior must have some kind of a biological purpose. The answers that the separate disciplines find, he concluded, overlap and confuse one another without coming nearer to a real understanding of the play concept.

If any explanation were really decisive, says Huizinga, it ought either to exclude all the others or comprehend them in higher unity. The problem is that science can only deal incidentally with the question of what play is in itself and what it means for the player. When play is attacked directly with the quantitative methods of experimental sciences, it bypasses the essential nature of play which is a qualitative factor: the profound aesthetic quality, the playful attitude, the fun, the pleasure. Instincts, reflexes, and other motivational constructs deflect the understanding from the quality of play, and direct toward theorizing the quantitative explanatory constructs. The intensity of and the absorption in play find no explanation in biological analyses, Huizinga found. Yet, analytical devices of cultural history would indicate that in this intensity, this absorption, lies the very essence, the primordial quality, of play.

The fascination that the study of play had for Huizinga was based on the strong and profound attractiveness or force that the elusive element of fun had upon behavior. He was convinced that anthropology has a potential for a cultural analysis technique that could account for or explain this phenomenon. From this reasoning he claimed that his study began where biology and psychology left off.

Nature, common sense would tell us, could just as easily have given her children all those useful functions of discharging superabundant energy, of relaxing after exertion, or training for the demands of life, of compensating for unfulfilled wishes, in the form of purely mechanical exercises and reactions. But why, asks Huizinga, did it give us play with its tension, its mirth, and its fun? In answering he employed an anthropological perspective utilizing the concepts of symbolization and competition.

Anthropology proposes that a sense of permanence and continuity necessary for truth is grounded on the identified earlier and simpler forms of social behavior. Thus, the search for and descriptions of earlier forms of events are characteristically anthropological. An appreciation of this discipline requires first that we prize the prototype or archetype models upon which later forms are patterned. The rubrics of anthropology require us next to ask whether play is an event of the mind or matter. The answer, of course, being that whatever else play might be, it certainly is not matter or materialism and it must, therefore, be a manifestation of the mind.

A next question would be about its origin. A child in play makes an internal image of some aspect of nature. His "representation" is not so much a sham or pseudo-reality as it is an imagination in the original sense of the word. Making an image is an "actualization by representation," and this process is seen as the archetype of symbolization. Huizinga maintains that this "actualization by representation" permeates the formal characteristics of play in every respect. The cultural connotation of representation is synonomous with identification, or the representation of the event as in symbol. From this principle Huizinga postulates that both play and culture can be defined around the construct of reality representation or symbolization.

Symbolization archetype. Huizinga was deeply influenced by the works of the German anthropologist, Leo Frobenius (1928), who proposed that reality imprints itself in the mind of man as the consciousness of man is developed, and play is the expression of this imprinting or programming. In the remote past man first assimilated the phenomena of vegetation and animal life and then conceived an idea of time and space, of months and seasons, and the course of the sun and the moon. He next played out this great processional order of existence through his rituals by which he actualized anew or created the events represented in cosmic order. Frobenius drew the far-reaching conclusion that man in his rituals was "playing at nature." Rituals and the play that emerged from this is the point or origin for social order and social institutions.

Questions about how mankind began "knowing" were raised by Frobenius as: What are we to think of this concrete projection of primitive nature consciousness? What can we make of a mental process which begins with an unexpressed experience of cosmic phenomena and ends in an imaginative rendering of them in play?

The facile device of hypothesizing an innate "play instinct" was discarded by Frobenius. The term "instinct," he said, is a makeshift, an admission of helplessness before the problem of reality. Equally useless and to be rejected as a vestige of obsolete thinking was the tendency to explain every advance in culture in terms of a special purpose; a "why" and a "wherefore" thrust down the throat of culture-creating community. In his own words Forbenius roughed out his view of the mental processes of the mind acting. In archaic man, says Frobenius, the first experience of life in nature takes the form of a "seizure"—being seized on, thrilled, enraptured. "The creative faculty in a people, as in the child, or every creative person, springs from this state of being seized." Man is seized by the revelation of meaning. The reality of the natural rhythm of beginnings and ends penetrates the soul of the consciousness and this invariably, and by reflex action, leads man to represent his emotion in an act. So Frobenius explains the mind "imaging" or symbolizing as it deals with the necessary mental process of transformation. The thrill of the "a ha" experience of symbol formation would be similar to the "eureka" experience of "I've got it" that accompanies the more advanced insights of thinking. "Being seized" by the phenomena of life and nature is condensed, by reflex action, into meanings which are played out in expressions that culminate in the aesthetics of ritual and art.

While repeatedly using the word "play" for these performances, Frobenius does not bother to define the term. The whole point, says Huizinga, is that Frobenius is describing play. Ritual play is essentially no different from, and indeed is merely one of, the higher forms common to child play or animal play. Archaic society played as the child or animal plays. Only in the later phase of the child's development or in civilization is play associated with the idea of something to be expressed in and by it; namely, what we would call play and games of life or nature. The organized forms of these representations evolved into rituals. Rituals are first drawn from magic, then religion, and now the sciences. Eventually they all graft themselves upon play. But the primary thing is that despite the grafted rituals, play remains play. In the long process of cultural development man's consciousness, his awareness, his thinking became embedded in the forms and functions of play.

The presence of ritual and play had been consistently observed from the days of earliest record of history. Huizinga postulated from this historical fact that play was antecedent to culture, and that play ranges from the lowest level expressed in the behavior of children to the highest level expressed in cultural rituals. Critical to the understanding of Huizinga's view of culture is his use of the word "play" or what the ancient Greeks called "agon." While Huizinga documented, from a wealth of historical material, his view of civilization as permeated with play, subsequent scholars have been critical of the way he used the term play.

Berlyne believed that his thesis might have seemed more accept-able and a little less novel to the English-speaking reader if his translator had used the word "game" throughout. In actuality, Huizinga did describe the behavior of play through the constructs of competition. In English we are more familiar with the idea of a "game" that is played in earnest, and in Homo Luden meaning is weakened because the term "play" is not subject to the rigors of definition. In several European languages, including Huizinga's native Dutch, the one word play corresponds to both games and other playful activities. Huizinga had focused in his discussion of this behavior around games with rules but he concentrated, for the most part, on what the Greeks called agon—the contest between indi-viduals or a team.

Knowledge, in the Huizinga perspective, was the result of man's competition with nature, gained particularly when man is in competition with his gods. The competitive game, Huizinga con-tends, forces the virtues required for the advancement of civilization. These he named as perseverance in striving after achievement, devotion to the social group, and self-abnegation on behalf of a cause.

Knowledge as agonistic gaming. From the "thrill" of meaning that is the root description of the symbolization process, Huizinga proposed that meaning became linked to the sacred ritual through competitive games that men played against nature. The serious occupations of life grew from the agonistic games. In the course of this growth the mind of man moved from magic to scientific thinking. As Huizinga guides us along the passage of time extending from archaic to modern civilization, he describes how play continuously served a midwifery function between knowledge and technology. Homo sapiens, the thinking man, becomes a natural product of homo ludens, the playing man. First magic, then religion and later science, were the power sources from which man seized his knowledge. As man applied his knowledge gained in the course of struggling with nature, Huizinga reasoned, his technology grew.

Knowledge and technology are the historical cultural outcomes of a power play between man and his gods. Since the time of recorded history, man has been involved in a search for whatever divine power he could seize and manipulate his world for his own purposes thereby. Primitive man began by developing rituals of dance and sacrifice in order to stave off the ill-will of nature threatening his existence. Gradually, as rituals marked the time and played out the conditions for planting and harvesting, the technology of agriculture emerged. In the days of the Pharaohs, the power to irrigate the lands adjoining the Nile River was institutionalized around a group of priestly intellectuals. The engineering profession, history tells us, grew from this source. Medicine and law likewise can be traced historically through linkages to powers of magic, religion and government, and finally the sciences.

As specialized knowledge filtered from religious into domestic practices it was subject continuously to transformations. A people, or a nation, progressing in the occupational hierarchy moves through economic dependence upon hunting, fishing, agriculture, and crafts to a dependence upon industrialism. In the course of these occupational transformations the serious work of one century becomes the play of another century and the continuity of occupational knowledge is maintained thereby. The life-supporting activities of hunting, fishing, and planting of yesterday have become the social activities of today's recreation. This historical fact supports the anthropological principle that the contemporary play of children and adults of any society contains within it vestiges of past occupations. Not only the occupations but the knowledge and skills within them are transmitted intimate linkages between sacred rituals, play, and the commonplace routines of daily life. The magic thinking of yesterday's rituals is deeply embedded in the commonplace. In ancient times a player captured forms of the magic thinking through rituals, games, and myths, thus capturing the unknown in his own reality. In contemporary life the playing child continues, even as his ancestor, to play out the knowledge and technological meanings of his own and past culture.

Meaning and myths. In the course of telling stories about other times and other villages, magic thinking becomes defined as what other people in other villages think, or "what I used to think but do not practice now." When man became less preoccupied with magic and religion, many of his seasonal rituals became institutionalized in his holidays. Life, Huizinga proposed, grows more secular each day, and outside our awareness the forms of play are changing with it. Myths he identified as another critical transformation mechanism for both knowledge and culture because they, too, are linked to the symbolization process.

Later anthropologists continued the interest aroused by Frobenius, and used play as a basic category for analyzing the logic of the imagination. Joseph Campbell (1951), in his work on mythology, built upon Frobenius' work and proposed that play and myths derived from play are the critical elements from which man built his meaning system. He argued that a vitally functioning meaning system has a fourfold purpose: (1) it creates in a man a sense of those powers or circumstances that lie outside his control; (2) it enables man to understand the natural world order; (3) it gives man a framework within which society may be seen as coherent; and (4) it gives man a way to understand the intricacies of his own psyche. These four purposes were considered not only functions for the imagination, but also for play and myths.

One particular aspect of the imagination-myths was proposed by Campbell as explaining the psychosocial functioning of the mind. Man, said Campbell, must be able to construct models that guide his enactments, and picture the world as he would like to be able to describe it. It is precisely such models, built into his myths, which man acts out in his play. He created them by the power of his imagination, and he expresses them in myths as well as in play. First man imagines the world in which he might feel at home and, on the basis of this imagination, he works to achieve the society, the world, the self for which he hopes. When man acts on his internalized model of the world, he plays.

Campbell postulated still another dimension which is overlooked in biopsychology. He proposed that play is dominated by the aesthetic, a word coming from a Greek verb, meaning "to sense" or "to know." In the Greek beliefs about reality it was the senses which were identified as giving knowledge. The "turning on" of the senses in the body in the process of image-ing. This process Campbell called the "body seeing" or the "body knowing." To illustrate seeing with the whole body, Campbell cited from Joyce Cary's novel *The Horse's Mouth* (1965), in which one of the characters is trying to show how the senses see:

> I'll show you how to look at a picture, Cokey. Don't look at it. Feel it with your eye. . . . And first you feel the shapes in the flat—the patterns, like a carpet. . . . And then you feel it in the round. . : . Not as if it were a picture of anyone. But a coloured and raised map. You feel all the rounds, the smooths, the sharp edges, the flats and the hollows, the lights and shades, the cools and warms. The colours and textures. There's hundreds

of little differences all fitting in together. . . . And then you feel the baths, the chair, the towel, the carpet, the bed, the jug, the window, the fields and the woman as themselves. But not as any old jug and woman. But the jug of jugs and the woman of women. You feel jugs are like that and you never knew it before. Jugs and chairs can be very expensive. . . . It means a jug can be a door if you open it. And a world of imagination opens it for you. . . . I'm trying to teach you a big happiness.

As-if behavior. The feeling characteristic which made man at home in his world through his imagination was seen by Huizinga as one of the essentials of play. He described this as a freedom, a stepping out of real life into a temporary sphere of activity with dispostions all its own. When a child is playing only for fun, he is perfectly aware that he is only pretending. The "only pretending" feeling of the imagination, while critical to play, is also critical to the role theory where it becomes the "as-if" phenomenon recently catching the interest of sociologists. The world of make-believe and the world of as-if have long intrigued both fiction and scientific writers. The German philosopher Hans Vaihinger (1924) wrote on *The Philosophy of As-If,* in which he argued that, in order to live meaningfully in the external world, we project fictions by which we order our lives. We do this, he argued, in politics, in science, in art, and in religion. Fictions, he postulated, have no truth in themselves, but they serve a truth function.

The as-if behavior generating a truth function for reality is, according to Huizinga, learned in play. Play as Vaihinger would rephrase it, is a fiction or a myth of the truth. Since it implies that the imagination constructs the truth, is reminiscent of Edward Albee's much quoted: "A play is fiction and fiction is fact distorted into truth." Or, to lie is to tell the truth, to tell the truth is to lie. It is precisely in the examination of this paradox that we gain insights about the relationship between play and meaning. Play processes meaning camouflaged in the paradox "as-if." The British psychologist Susanna Millar (1968) in her study of play psychology, found the paradoxical nature of play, the pretending characteristic to be crucial defense mechanism of play. The paradox, says Millar, protects all those learning subsumed under the world play.

Intermezzo behavior. Another characteristic of play, Huizinga found, was disinterestedness. Not being ordinary "life," play stands outside the immediate satisfaction of wants and appetites. As a parenthetical behavior, it interrupts the appetitive process. "It interpolates itself as a temporary activity, satisfying in itself and enduring there." Play is, says Huizinga, an intermezzo, an interlude in our daily lives.

The intermezzo nature of play anticipates the work of Robert White (1959), who postulated a need state called "effectance." He defined it as what the neuromuscular system wants to do when otherwise unoccupied or only gently stimulated by the environment. The gentleness of the environment, which both encourages and provokes play behavior, White claims, has been neglected in favor of studying sex, aggression, power or dependency. White casts the effectance drive state as the motivational force which shows itself sharply in the playful and investigatory behavior of children.

Considering, said White, the slow rate of learning and the vast amount to be learned before a child can have effective interaction with surroundings, there would not be much learned unless the child worked pretty steadily at these tasks between episodes of homeostatic crises. The association of learning tasks with play and fun, says White, is a strategy as critical as the biological strategy of associating sex pleasure with nature's need for reproduction. The moderate but persistent force of the efficacy drive favors social rather than biological adaptation.

The intermezzo nature of play provides some explanation of the curiosity drive which propels the interaction with the environment. We know that when immediate pressing needs are in ascendency, playful behavior recedes. The highly critical associative areas of man's brain might have been a suicidal piece of specialization, says White, if they had come without a steady, persistent inclination toward interacting with the environment. Thus, the exploratory and experimental attitudes of man that drive his playful behavior insure his flexible adaptation and hence his very persistence as a life form on earth.

Play space and time. Other descriptive properties that Huizinga proposed were the elements of time-place. Play is both secluded in territory and limited in time. It is "played out" within certain limits of time and place, and contains its own course as well as meaning. Play begins and then, at a certain moment, it is over. It plays itself to an end. It at once assumes fixed form as a cultural phenomenon. Once played, it endures as a new-found creation of the mind, a treasure retained by the memory. As it is transmitted, it becomes tradition, and may be repeated at any time whether it is child's play or a game of chess or a mystery play. In this faculty of repetition, Huizinga asserts, lies still another of the essential qualities of play, holding good not only for play as a whole but also for the inner structure of the imagination. Play forms contain elements of repetition and alternation which bind the play act together like the warp and woof of a fabric. The repetitious nature of play protects the interconnectedness of meaning and knowledge for both the individual and the culture.

More striking than even the constraints of time was the description of the constraint of space. All play moves and has its existence within a marked-off playground space. The arena, the card table, magic circle, temples, stage, screen, tennis court, or the court of justice, are all, in form and function, playgrounds. They represent, according to Huizinga, forbidden spots—isolated, hedged around, hallowed—within which special rules attain.

Puzzle stance. Like most other students of play, Huizinga made room in his description for the element of tension. Tension, he said, means uncertainty, chanciness, a striving to decide the issue and so end it. The player wants something to go, to succeed by his own exertions. A baby reaching for a toy, a kitten chasing a ball—all want to achieve something difficult, to succeed, to end a tension. Under the term "tense" Huizinga identified the exploratory or experimental attitude implied by "puzzle." He related it to the doubt that destroys ambiguity. To puzzle at, to doubt, to find the rule, is an element that governs all solitary games of skill and applications such as jigsaws, target-shooting, mosaic-making.

The more play bears the character of searching for the rule, the more fervent it will be. Competition in this sense is a searching for the rules that will enable man to win, and in the course of rule behavior, the player is tested. Courage, tenacity, resources, and above all the sense of fairness, are exercised. But despite an ardent desire to win, a player must still stick to the rules of the game. Thus, Huizinga continued, puzzle-based tension is reduced in the process of understanding rules, and from this understanding meaning is acquired.

Spoilsport. The pursuit of the rules in the context of competition served to set the conditions to claim sportsmanship as a cultural acquisition. The theme of sportsmanship, a product of play, accounts for much of the civilizing function of play. If sportsmanship could be accepted as serving a civilization function, the concept of spoilsport, said Huizinga, is its antithesis. The player who transgresses against the rules or ignores them, according to Huizinga, is a spoilsport. A spoilsport is not the same as the false player who cheats, for the latter pretends to be playing the game. On the face of it he still acknowledges the act within the magic "as-if" circle of time and space. It is important to note, said Huizinga, that society is lenient to the cheat, but not to the spoilsport because the spoilsport shatters the play world itself. He is alien to it. By withdrawing from the game he reveals the fragility of the play world in which he has temporarily shut himself in with others. He robs play of its illusion, a word which literally means "in play." Therefore, he has to be cast out, for he threatens the very existence of the play community.

The figure of the spoilsport is most apparent in boys' games. The miniature community of the peer group does not care whether the spoilsport is guilty of defection by virtue of either not daring to enter the game or not being allowed. Because not being allowed is not recognized, role deficit behavior is called not daring, not willing to take a chance, to go along. The spoilsport breaks the magic world, and because he is a coward he must be rejected.

In the concept of the spoilsport, Huizinga anticipated the play deficit characteristic of many mentallly ill and culturally deprived children. His description anticipates also the heretic, the innovator, prophet, conscientious objector, and, in general, the outlaw revolutionary who refuses to operate under the rules of the establishment. One who cannot or will not operate according to the rule is the incompetent, or the coward who must be rejected by society.

Rule-Bound Behavior

Erickson (1940), with reference to the Huizinga concept of the spoilsport referred to the importance of rules for role behavior and the identification process. In play, said Erikson, we learn to subordinate ourselves to rules and to internalize the meaning of roles. Whether we watch a game or take part in it, we are conscious that play is determined by rules. Childhood play, both our common sense and sociological theory tell us, provides the first contact with rules. Without experience in conduct guided by rules we cannot become either free or civilized, for it is through rules that voluntary and free selves find characteristic expression of their freedom.

A player must learn to subject himself to a rule even in those situations in which his immediate impulse would urge him toward a completely different behavior. He may play only one rule at a time, but he must play according to the rule. In the words of the Soviet psychologist Leontiev: "To master a rule, this means to master one's own behavior, to learn to regulate it, to learn to submit it to a given task."

Piaget's earlier work in moral judgment (1932) discussed the development of attitudes to rules. He proposed that a game was a microcosmic moral system and distinguished four stages. In the first stage, that of the purely motor games, ending at about the age of three, the child confronted with a novel object explores it and tries out motor patterns that he is used to applying to other objects. Out of these actions he typically forms rituals which he enjoys performing repeatedly. These represent "sensorimotor rules" as distinct from rules of handling conflicts in reality. Beginning between the ages of three and five there is an egocentric stage during which the child imitates actions of older children who play according to rules. The child, however, still plays by himself without any sense of competition or of trying to win, even if other children are playing alongside him. Genuine interaction in the desire to beat other players appears in the stages of "incipient cooperation," at about seven or eight years. There is then some observation of common rules, but the conceptions of them are rather vague. The fourth stage, that of codification of rules, begins at about eleven or twelve years. At this time there is a scrupulous observance of rules, with clear ability to formulate them and a keen interest in theoretical questions that they raise.

Efforts to investigate the development of rule-bound behavior led Piaget to develop ways and concepts describing the moral sense of children. The youngest children seem to be aware that such things as rules exist without regard to conduct in general. Some acts they see as being permitted, and others as forbidden. But their manner of playing, for instance, does not seem to be governed by any sense of obligation. Later the child believes there are absolute binding rules which are laid down by authoritative and older people, and which cannot be modified or repealed. Finally, there comes about an awareness that rules our conventions, deriving their validity from common consent that conformity to them is necessary for all to enjoy the game, and that they are always subject to modification by mutual agreement.

Competitive games exemplified for Piaget the advancement toward moral realism based upon one-sided respect for persons and authority, and beliefs in immutable moral laws comparable to the laws of nature. He proposed that the development of this moral sense was derived from the rule-bound experiences of play, and from this experience the ability to cooperate emerged. Progress toward cooperative behavior in the Piagetian sense occurs as the child internalizes the rules of motor behavior, the rules of objects, and the rules of other players.

Rules and roles. The origin of institutional order and the process of socialization are founded, according to George Herbert Mead (1934), upon the rule bound aspects of play. Mead who developed role theory was probably the most important figure in American social psychology. For many years he taught at the University of Chicago and his most important work, *Mind, Self and Society,* was published about the same time as *Homo Ludens.* Mead's notion that social roles are learned through play implies that a child must play at society and at socialization before he can take on the serious behavior of maturity. He described the social conditions under which the self arises. In addition to language, he proposed as important to self the behavior of play and games.

The play process Mead found to be most characteristic of the minds of primitive people. The key to the interpretation of rituals, Mead proposed for sociology, is located in the organization of play which can be observed in any kindergarten. The kindergarten type of behavior he described as not belonging to the everyday life of people in their dealings with the objects about them, but in their attitudes toward the forces about them, the nature upon which everyday activities depend.

The mind learns about these forces in taking the role of the "other," playing at the expression of their gods and their heroes, going through certain rites which are the representation of what these individuals are supposed to be doing. The personalities which they take, the roles they play, control the development of the child's personality. This outcome, says Mead, is just what the kindergarten works toward. Superimposed upon the organization provided by the kindergarten level is the behavior of games. The fundamental difference between play and games is that, in games, the child must have the attitude of all the others involved in the game. What he does is controlled by his being everybody else on his team. Later on in life what he does is controlled by the other, which is an organization of the attitudes of those involved in the same process.

It is in the form of the "generalized other" that the social process influences the behavior of individuals and the way the community exercises control over the conduct of its individual members. The kindergarten and the games are means by which patterns enter as a whole into the individual's experience. It is in terms of these organized group experiences, mediated by the central nervous system and play, Mead claims, that the self emerges. The game has a logic, so that an organization of the self is rendered possible. There is a definite end to be obtained; the actions of the different individuals are related to each other with references to that end so that they do not conflict.

So long as one knows the rules, one is not in conflict with himself or in conflict with the attitudes of others on the team. For example, says Mead, if one had the attitude of the person throwing the ball, he can also have the response of catching the ball. The two are related, so they further the purpose of the game itself. They are interrelated in a unitary organic fashion. There is a definite unity, then, which is introduced into the organization of other selves. When we reach such a stage it is not like the earlier situation of play, where there is a simple succession of one role after another. The early play situation is, of course, characteristic of the child's own personality at this stage. The child is one thing at one time and another at another, and what he is at one moment does not determine what he is at another. That, says Mead, is both the charm of childhood as well as its inadequacy. You cannot count on the child, you cannot assume that all the things he does are going to determine what he will do at any moment. He is not organized into a whole. The child has no definite character, no definite personality. He does not become so until he has an organized personality and he has internalized the rules, or the morals, of that society and thus becomes an essential member of it. The self becomes organized through this capacity to internalize rules derived from the experience of games.

In summing up a sociological perspective regarding the development of behavior, Mead postulated that society must be played before it can be internalized. The attitudes and movements of the other players are organized into an act under rules, and it is these rules which control the response and give to any interaction its stability and meaning. In playing a position in a game, or a part in a drama, a child learns to assume how others will play theirs. What he does is controlled by his ability to take the part of others who are playing with him. By means of rules he activates in play the attitudes of others involved in a similar process, and these become organized within the minds. Thus the learning of roles and rules converge.

Social roles are "internalized" by arousing in ourselves the response we arouse in others. As actors we practice in play all those forms of expression used by the self: the spoken word, the physical gesture, the space utilization. All these are experienced by the actor as well as the audience. Social meanings grow as these symbols are shared and meanings to the self and others are increased through practice. Symbols, in turn, depend upon the possibility of reciprocal response of actor and audience. Thus, sociology explains the convergence of rule, roles and symbols.

Experiencing authority. Sociological theory acknowledges the socializing power of rules and the influence that this learning has on social order. Children's games are valued because a game is organized through rules. The child enacting his own mind does so through his ability under rules to play the role of all the other players. He must know what others are going to do before they can play theirs. Rules become internalized through a capacity to call up in ourselves responses which are being called up in the others, and thus enable us to anticipate the responses of others. Games teach us one way, that is, the way rules order social relationships. Man learns to act with confidence because he expects others to act in certain ways. He is able to respond to these ways of acting because the social interaction game has a form, a set of rules, which determines how the other must act toward us.

The power of rules lies in consent and agreement freely given in play. The best rules, those which bind us together simply by their power as rules, are so constructed that very little is left to the decision of those who judge them. Rules are upheld by those who agree to be bound by them, not by decision of judges. Unlike the British judge who makes the law through legal decisions which are carefully codified and often become law in turn, the game umpire makes no decision about the rules but simply applies them. When a rule is broken, the umpire stops the game and penalizes those who violated the rules. The penalties, too, are determined by the rules. Thus rules are both positive and negative. When they are broken the game must stop, but the players are bound only by rules which are clear to all and which must be applied in the same way to every play and to every player. Disobedience to rules stops the game because infractions of rules destroy the equality under rules which is the essential nature of games.

Sociology, in principle, sees the funtions of rules for the individual as a form of experiencing authority and for society as a form of experiencing order. Rules appear to bind outer and inner man and enable him to construct his unique social reality. In what ways this is true we know only partially and seldom exploit that which we do know, for sociological theory merely speculates on rules and roles. In no way is it involved in the raw data of the experience. An occasional theorist may formulate propositions and these propositions agree that rules form a social bond, and that there is a behavioral utility in knowing the relationship of the laws of nature.

The laws of society, as derived from play, are frequently noted by investigators as they pass them en route to other research goals. In the actuality of daily routines a scientist's theoretical understanding of rules and roles of play is not a form of applied knowledge. The sociological body of knowledge does not seem to have an interest in rule learning. When and where rules are used, by whom, in what way, or for what purpose is a matter for theory, not for application. Sociological theory, for reasons within its own discipline, does not admit rules as a social bond equal in power to the bonds of religion, politics, economics, or the family. Probably, for the same reasons it does not admit play as an object of its research, except as speculative grist for its theoretical mill in such areas as role theory. Common practice forces us to conclude that despite the critical inferences that sociology has drawn from the play behavior, play as a coherent form of behavior remains outside its serious consideration as a concept worth study.

Serious Proposals of Play

On the record, there is little in the way of reports on play research. In a review of the literature on play Slobin (1964) commented on some work done at Harvard by Whiting (1960) and upon a study left in mimeograph form by Anderson and Moore (1960). Both of these studies raised questions regarding cultural behavior and focused on the serious purposes of play. They recognized the imitator characteristic of the behavior and were curious as to the relationship of human adaptive processes to the parent culture. The common hypothesis of both studies was that the games in which children act out social roles and events vary from culture to culture, depending on the models available for imitation. Whiting proposed the concept of status envy as relevant for such learning. He argued that a child will practice covertly those roles which seem to him to carry special privileges but which he, because of his status as a child, cannot carry out in reality. That is, a child will behave like a favored individual in an attempt to get for himself the privileges associated with the status. The sum of these envied statuses make up the child's "optative identity." Whiting concludes that a study of the role models which are most frequently imitated by children in their play should yield valuable information about social reality in various cultures. He suggests that there is a research potential to be realized in exploring the aspects of family and social structures since these are the dominant influences in the child's choice of play activities.

Anderson and Moore, while enroute to investigating other social behavior, proposed that there are sociocultural models contained in games. They developed the concept of "autotelic folk model" to deal with this critical aspect. The term "autotelic" was chosen because within play activities there were models of the culture which were being internalized. It is the internalized model, they hypothesized, which helps members of a society learn about and "play act" the workings of their society. Choosing nonserious models for learning the serious models of behavior made a kind of fascinating sense to Anderson and Moore. They based their convictions on the evidence that both probability theory and game theory grew directly out of the study of activities which people engage in "for the fun of it." The striking fact, to them, was that these mathematical theories are also successful in dealing with the "more serious matters of survival and welfare." Their thesis was that, in acting autotelically, we are "modeling" our own more serious behavior.

The conclusions of the study were that human beings in society face three broad types of problems or aspects of problem situations:

(1) noninteractional problems, in which the human being manipulates the environment without in turn being manipulated; (2) interactional problems, in which the behavior of others must be taken into account; and (3) affective problems, in which the values of the problems are important. As behavioral scientists, they were interested in examining how people learn techniques to handle problems of these three categories.

It is not enough, the Harvard studies indicated, to say that children learn from adults. Rather, it is growing more probable that as change accelerates, children may not be able to learn enough from adults to maintain their flexible adaptiveness. Some problems often entail serious consequences and require a certain degree of skill before they can be dealt with. Although every society inherits certain activities which serve as teaching devices, some societies must busy themselves with inventing more. Our present institutions, such as the family and schools, are currently revealing an all too finite capacity as teaching devices.

The question this study raises, but leaves unsolved, is: "What new devices need invention?" Anderson and Moore did, however, set down three conditions of learning which such activities must satisfy. First, they must be cut off from the more serious aspect of the society's activities. The rewards must not be too costly, nor the consequences of error too serious. Second, the rewards in the learner's activity must be intrinsic or inherent in the activity itself. The activities are to be understood as autotelic in that they contain their own motivations and goals. Third, the devices must help the child learn the relevant techniques.

Roberts, Arth, and Bush (1959), in another study, looked upon games in a similar light, proposing games as models for "other behavior." Their classification of learning possibilities was: (1) games of physical skill in which self-reliance is learned; (2) games of strategy in which social roles are learned; and (3) games of chance in which responsibility and achievements are learned. They proposed the following relationships between games and culture:

> If games are expressive models, they should be related to other aspects of culture and to variables which figure in expressive or projective mechanisms. More specifically, games of strategy which are models of social interaction should be related to the complexity of the social system; games of chance which are models of interaction with the supernatural should be linked with the expressive views of the supernatural; and there is a

possibility that games of physical skill may be related to the aspects of the natural environment.

Using the social system, religion, and natural environment as a category device, the study found that there was an identifiable relationship between the various sorts of games in a given society. For example, societies with high political integration and social stratification were found to value games of strategy, while societies low in these variables tend not to include such games. Yet, the variables were not related to the presence of games of skill in the specific institution examined. Thus it was concluded that, when looking for meaning in childhood play, we must examine the system larger than the nursery of school group. The context of play would include the social system, religion, natural environment, and, probably, the additional aspects of the larger world in which both the children and their parents live.

A child-rearing study, made by Roberts and Sutton-Smith (1962), examined the relationship between games of strategy and the special requirements for obedience present in each society. The assumption was that complex social systems require obedience. Their findings were that those involved with routine chores of an economic nature found rewards for their work in games of chance. Gambling was related to responsibility inasmuch as gambling required a transfer of property. In order to risk property, it had first to be acquired. Games of skill, however, were linked with encouragement of achievement. Further support for these conclusions regarding games of skill and games of chance were derived from the comparison between boys and girls in the United States. In line with the assumption that American boys receive more achievement and less obedience and responsibility training than American girls, questioning of school children showed more games of physical skill or of mixed physical skill and strategy to be preferred by boys. Games of chance and of strategy were found to be preferred by girls. The authors were lead by these studies to formulate a "conflict-enculturation" hypothesis, stating that participation in games resulted from conflicts induced by social learning in childhood and later.

Another study, by Roberts, Sutton-Smith, and Kendon (1963), extended the evidence for a close relationship between games of strategy and complexity of social organization. They probed the relationship between games and folk tales. It was found that societies possessing games of strategies tend to have folk tales in which the outcome is determined, or partly determined, by strategy. There is also some suggested evidence that societies with many games of physical skill tend to have folk tales emphasizing independence, and that those with games of chance tend to have tales of nurturance.

SUMMARY

Only the naive could believe from reviewing the evidence of the literature, that play is a behavior having an identifiable nature. While common sense may confidently assert that there is such a thing as play, the literature assumes a rather weak position about what this phenomenon is. Play is as concealed in theories of human behavior as it is in the actual behavior of man. The conceptualizing lenses of the mind require painstaking adjustment to detect the presence of this elusive transient behavioral form. For it does exist in both man and his society but in a concealed fashion. Beneath the sophisticated surfaces of some discipline their conceptual apparatus occasionally permits a fragmented view of play.

The bodies of knowledge sampled in this chapter were evolution, anthropology, psychology, and sociology. Evolution offered a rather clear description about the relationship between play and the phylogenetic scale. Play potential, says evolution, arises with a species position on the scale and the more complex the nervous system, the more play a species exhibits. If the society of the herd, troop, school, or family unit is sophisticated, then the play period is relatively long. As maturity is approached, play diminishes and the serious business of productive living begins. Although there appears to be little immediate utility in play, the conclusions that play is frivolous and goalless, ignores long-term benefits. For when the yield to the eventual behavior of the adult is examined, play is a good investment for both the playing juvenile and the working adult.

If play were to be judged by evolution's most critical measurement, namely survival, it would be awarded a fairly high rating. The progressive age and stage activities of development appear to have been designed by evolution to meet the demands of each maturation level. Play serves the function of adaptation by facilitating man's manipulatory and social skills, and serves society by socializing the aggression of its members.

Anthropology acknowledges the presence of play in culture. The historical evidence of anthropology suggests that play serves some partially known function in processing knowledge along a progressive continuum of magic, religion and science. Its transformational nature is proposed in the aphorism that the serious occupation of an earlier century becomes the play of a later century. Play and the traditional occupations of man are linked in some unexplained way to the productive technology of a society. A people, or a nation, progressing up the occupational hierarchy travel from economic dependence upon hunting, fishing, agriculture and crafts toward dependence on industrial production. Play is observed as the mediator of this process.

In ancient times, man captured knowledge playing out magic rituals, telling myths and competing in games that in contemporary life, man like his ancestors, will continue to need the playing out of cultural meaning. For man is destined to play with the ideas and the skills of his civilization before he can inherit them. As long as civilization incorporates playfulness within its culture, its supporting knowledges and practices will continue to develop. When a society no longer plays with its own ideology and technology, social meaning is lost and the society deteriorates. The destruction is hastened by the selfrighteousness of the social institutions and the boredom of its members.

Sociology agrees with anthropology that society must be played at before it can be internalized. Social theorists even went so far as to propose "role" as the structural mechanism for the internalization process. But play as a bond between man and his society has not been seen as sufficiently valuable to sociological theory to be studied seriously.

The absence of any serious focus upon play illustrates a characteristic common to the sciences in the United States. The main determinants of a body of knowledge about man are internal to each science and a scientist within a discipline studies only those problems considered relevant to professional interests. The sociologist, concerned with understanding man and his institutions, examines what policies internal to the profession determine to be a significant concept. Under this modus operandi each scientist, under the supposed conditions specialization, acts like a spy, reporting not what he finds, but what his superiors want to hear. When good spies report what is there, then perhaps play will be reported in a fashion that might explain its social utility. `

Psychology is troubled by the goallessness of play and finds it a form of behavior difficult for traditional psychological categories to confront. The dominant pursuit of motivation limits contemporary psychological perspectives to tension reduction, reinforcement and stimulus response. Play is a phenomenon existing far outside the interests of these themes. Whenever play is examined, psychology studied it as a form of unconscious learning and the purpose is to explain the unconscious rather than play. In this instance, however, play is valued as a highly observable expression of the unconscious.

Evidence is accumulating that play is more related to the human imagination than to the generalized unconscious of Freud. An interest in the imagination of man and therefore of play is reemerging in psychological studies. In the course of this new interest the traditional psychological methods of studying behavior are being reexamined and changed. A change is long overdue because the psychologist has been the most guilty of shaping any behavior, including play, to his own parochial theory. He asks simple biased questions and uses a linear logic giving him an unshakable conviction that by staying within his discipline he can "know" by techniques of reductionism and isolation. If play is to be understood it must, above all, have its own explanatory framework. It needs its own theoretical identity established as an outcome of serious study. It is, as the findings of this chapter show, a behavior in search of an explanation.

REFERENCES

ANDERSON, A. R. and O. K. MOORE (1960) "Autotelic folk-models." New York: American Sociological Association, Sociological Theory Section. (mimeo)

BERLYNE, D. E. (1969) "Laughter, humor and play," in Lindzey, Gardner, Bronson, Elliott (eds.) Handbook of Social Psychology. Reading, Mass.: Addison-Wesley.

——— (1960) Conflict, Arousal and Curiosity. New York: McGraw-Hill.

BERNE, E. (1964) Games People Play. New York: Grove Press.

BUHLER, C. (1931) "Kindheit und Jugend: genese des Bewusstseins." Leipzig: Hirsch.

CAMPBELL, J. (1951) "Bios and mythos," in Wilbur and Muinsterberger (eds.) Psychology and Culture. New York: International Universities Press.

CARY, J. (1965) The Horse's Mouth. New York: Harper & Row.

COLEMAN, J. S. (1962) "Analysis of social structures and simulation of social processes with electronic computers," in H. S. Guetzkow (ed.) Simulation in Social Sciences. Englewood Cliffs, N.J.: Prentice-Hall.

DEWEY, J. (1928) Democracy and Education. New York: Macmillan.

ERIKSON, E. (1963) Childhood and Society. New York: Norton.

——— (1940) Studies in Interpretation of Play. Genetic Psych. Monograph, 22.

FREUD, S. (1952) "Beyond the pleasure principle," in The Major Works of Sigmund Freud. Chicago: Encyclopedia Britannica.

FROBENIUS, L. (1928) "Paideuma, umrisse einer kultur-und seelen-lehre." Frankfurt. Cited by J. Campbell, The Masks of God, Vol. I, Primitive Mythology (1959). New York: Viking Press.

GROOS, K. (1899) Play of Man. New York: D. Appleton.

——— (1896) The Play of Animals. New York: D. Appleton.

HAIGIS, E. (1941) "Das spiel als begegnung," Psychology 150.

HALL, G. S. (1904) Adolescence: Its Psychology and Its Relation to Physiology, Anthropology, Sociology, Sex, Crime, Religion and Education. Volume I. New York: Appleton-Century-Crofts.

HECKHAUSEN, H. (1964) "Entwurf einer psychologie des spielens." Psychologische Forschung 27: 225-243.

HENDRICK, I. (1942) "Instincts and the ego during infancy." Psychoanalytical Q. 11: 33-58.

HOMANS, G. C. (1967) The Nature of Social Science. New York: Harcourt, Brace & World.

HUIZINGA, J. (1955) Homo Ludens: A Study of the Play Element in the Culture. Boston: Beacon.

KLINGER, E. (1969) "Development of imaginative behavior: implications of play for a theory of fantasy." Psychological Bull. 72 (4).

KRIS, E. (1952) Psychoanalytic Explorations in Art. New York: International Universities Press.

MEAD, G. H. (1934) Mind, Self and Society. Chicago: Univ. of Chicago Press.

MEINECKE, G. (1956) "Selbstgefährdungstendenzen im spiel eines säuglings." Psychol. Beitr. 11: 299-307.

MILLAR, S. (1968) Psychology of Play. Baltimore: Penguin.

NORBECK, E. (1971) "Man at play." Natural History J. of American Museum of Natural History 80 (December).

PIAGET, J. (1952) Play, Dreams and Imitation in Childhood. New York: Norton.

——— (1932) The Moral Judgment of the Child. London: Kegan, Paul; Paris: Alcan.

ROBERTS, J. M., M. J. ARTH, and R. R. BUSH (1959) "Games in culture." American Anthropologist 61: 597-605.

ROBERTS, J. M. and B. SUTTON-SMITH (1962) "Child training and game involvement." Ethnology 1.

——— and A. KENDON (1963) "Strategy in games and folk tales." J. of Social Psychology 61.

SLOBIN, D. (1964) "The fruits of the first season: a discussion of the role of play in childhood." J. of Humanistic Psychology 4 (1): 59-79.

SPENCER, H. (1955) Principles of Psychology. London: Longman.

SUOMI, S. J. and H. F. HARLOW (1971) "Monkeys at play." Natural History J. of American Museum of Natural History 80 (December).

SUTTON-SMITH, B. (1971) "Child's play." Psychology Today (December).

——— (1971) "Child's play, very serious business." Psychology Today (December).

VAIHINGER, H. (1924) The Philosophy of As-If. New York: Barnes & Noble.

WHITE, R. N. (1959) "Motivation reconsidered: the concept of competence." Psychological Rev. 66: 297-333.

WHITING, J. (1960) "Sexual identification and cultural patterns." Lecture, Harvard University, Department of Social Relations, October 28.

WIENER, N. (1943) "Behavior, purpose and teleology," in A. Rosenblueth and J. Bigelow, Philosophy of Science 10 (January).

WILSON, C. (1970) Origins of the Sexual Impulse. London: Panther.

CHAPTER 3

AN EXPLANATION OF PLAY

Mary Reilly

I have been surprised to find that ideas which I found difficult to grasp when I first met them on some scientific presentation spring to life of themselves when some familiar aspect of practical life is looked at with fresh eyes.

—*Sir Geoffrey Vickers*
in The Art of Judgment

SELECTING AN EXPLANATION

The Alternatives

The pursuit of the rumored goodness and usefulness that play might have for man is plagued by the difficulties inherent in the processes of explanation. One of the first problems is the very obviousness of play. It is a behavior endlessly in plain sight, and because it is a behavior there in plain sight it lacks the intrigue that the unknown has for scientists. Intellectuals go to any lengths to avoid the obvious and the mundane and theorists in particular disdain it. The real difficulty that confronts any broadened explanation of play is that it is an obvious commonplace behavior breeding contempt dampening investigatory interest.

A further trouble lies hidden in scientific methodology. We do not lack for the means of making discoveries. The deficit is in the ways

we organize discoveries theoretically. Theorizing requires us to look
at phenomena with scientific rigidity as we show how this or that
follows under a variety of given conditions from a few general
principles. The problem for play, then, is not one of discovery, but
of explanation. For play is everywhere and obvious and there is no
need to discover it.

The literature of the last two centuries leave a student of play with
a confusing array of insights which demand some kind of coherent
ordering. Since theories have the power to organize and explain, play
is a most deserving candidate for a theory. The usefulness of a good
theory is that is provides the security of naming concepts and
describing their relationships. While concepts provide categories for
observing, thinking about, and testing phenomena, an array of
concepts does not constitute necessarily a theory. Concepts, as
Robert Merton has argued, constitute the definition or prescription
of what is to be observed. They are variables between which
empirical relationships are to be sought. But only logical interrelationships between various concepts may lead to the development
of a theory.

There are, however, constraints upon traditionally constructed
theories which limit theorizing as a tool for analyzing play. Existing
theories about behavior are limited in their ability to explain
multiple dimensions and integrating mechanisms. They are at their
best when they speak to single levels of action and internal
mechanisms of operation. It would be comfortable to stay within the
familiar confines of such theorizing to explain play. But the reality
that precludes traditional theory being the preferred mode of
explanation is that it fails to look at play in the ways play needs to
be explored. For whatever explanation that is selected must, above
all, grasp the nettle of explaining complexity because the essential
nature of play is that it processes complexity. This aspect of this
behavior must be confronted and not explained away by a process of
simplification. Play, historical evidence clearly shows, is a phenomenon stretching across a knowledge spectrum which includes
biology, psychology, sociology and anthropology. Because it is
multidimensional it requires interdisciplinary explanation. This critical specification precludes a traditional theory and welcomes a
systems theory approach as the form of explanation.

The Systems Approach

The notion of systems emerged because ordinary theories were recognized as being too clumsy to deal with the intricate web of progressive complexity. The systems concept was designed to emphasize the relationship between assemblages or combinations of parts that make up a complex whole. A characteristic important for understanding is that it is composed of a hierarchy of subsystems. That is, the parts that form the major system, may themselves be systems and their parts may be systems, and so on. The hierarchical nature of this form of explanation requires that what is looked at is the effect that subsystem relationships have on the performance of the overall system.

The system viewpoint allows us to combine knowledge about the interactions of living organisms, social organizations and complex electronic systems. Consequently, a complex behavior like play may be conceptualized in the self-adaptive Darwinian sense as well as in the social organization sense of adapting to a changing competitive environment.

Problems in analyzing reality from the systems approach arise at two distinct levels: the micro-level and the macro-level. The micro-level concerns the understanding of the basic cause and effect relationships governing the performance of the lowest elementary subsystems. The macro-level concerns the understanding of the effect on systems performances of the complex chains of interrelationships between the elementary subsystems. The historical evidence about the systems approach is that micro problems are more easily isolated and studied in some detail by building models incorporating the relationships. The macro-level problems, however, have a tendency of being underanalyzed and important relationships in this area are too often ignored. Any systemic explanation of play will need to struggle for a balance of these two levels.

General Systems Theory

In the interest of promoting interdisciplinary judgment for multidisciplinary thinking, the economist Kenneth Boulding (1956) designed a progressive continuum of knowledge categories. It was called the "Boulding skeleton of knowledge" and built from inferences drawn from the many bodies of knowledge and thinking models now bombarding the behavioral science world as a result of the knowledge explosion. The skeleton conceptualized the bare bones upon which various scientific disciplines hang the flesh and blood of their bodies of knowledge. It was intended to serve both a cataloguing function and to insure some validity and reliability in the selection process of theorizing. The purpose of the skeleton, happily enough, was to reduce some of the multidisciplinary confusion which Sir Geoffrey Vickers has noted, "that in these days when the rich in knowledge eat such specialized food at such separate tables, only the dogs have a chance of a balanced diet."

The key concept underlying the universal knowledge skeleton concerned the critical relationships between the phenomena that are dealt with, and the theoretical models which explain their action. The skeleton was essentially a taxonomy of complexity defining an order of prepotency and as such is a rational device for choosing an explanatory model. It defined the two interdependent levels of a complexity as being structural and functional. The implied order of structural complexity was expressed in the skeleton, or the bare bone listing of the elements and included the progression from nucleus, atom, molecule, virus, gene, organism, animal, person, to social organization. The proposition underlying the knowledge continuum is that it is the nature of a physical biological or social discipline to identify with one or more of these elements and then attempt to build up general theoretical models relevant to the selected phenomena. Theoretical model building was defined as the technology used by scientists in their pursuit of explanations. The technology belongs to general systems theory and lies somewhere between the highly generalized construction of pure mathematics and the specific theories of the specialized disciplines.

By using systems language to catalogue the differing models of conceptualization, the skeleton clarified some of the basic conditions for a choice of a play explanation. For the ranges of complexity spread out for selection, we have: (1) the static structure system appropriate for geographers and anatomists; (2) the steady equilibrium state appropriate for the chemists; (3) the cybernetic or control systems appropriate for the physicians and the physiologists; (4) the self-maintaining systems appropriate for the physicists; and (5) the self-complexifying and self-producing systems appropriate for behavioral scientists.

The phenomenon-complexity scale and the model explanation-complexity scale enable us for the first time to make open and communicable judgments about the relative fit of a particular empirical reality to a theoretical construct.

Because technical trade talk used within any discipline was discarded as being too parochial for interdisciplinary use, the concept of "model" emerged as another form of symbolization. It was developed as a substitute for the language of mathematics which had served previously the function of being the universal language of the physical sciences. While mathematics served non-living phenomena of nature fairly well, its usefulness diminishes in the presence of such changeable complexities as organisms, persons and social organizations. Systems theory and the associated concept of model emerged out of the necessity to correct or modify the tendency of disciplines to study phenomenon abstracted to some entity rather than as a study of the conglomeration of parts. Its language and tenets preclude the study of isolated phenomena in narrowly confined contexts. Systems thinking requires phenomena to be examined in terms of their open interactions in larger and larger slices of nature. Because the context of systems thinking provides interdimensional phenomena with the best chance to be conceptualized and it offers the behavior of play an enormous potential for explanation. For if the rules of the knowledge skeleton are followed, we may conclude with some assurance that play belongs to the self-complexifying system of biology or the social organizational system of the behavioral sciences. The question is to which one or perhaps to both?

Ironically the organismic theory of biology does not confront growth or complexity in any substantial way. The study of organizing and hence the explanation of the progressive development of complexity has been achieved outside the boundaries of biology. Organization theories of those disciplines concerned with material rather than with human productivity have done a far better job of attempting to advance our knowledge of complexity. Organizational theory, driven by the needs of political science, economics and business administration, speaks to organizing and in doing so offers a highly transferable explanation of complexity. These specialties clearly analyze complexity as their concepts and propositions speak to progressive differentiation of social behavior in the context of institutional change as continuity is maintained. What relationships their theoretical framework have in common is a concern for the progressive adaptation of man in his social environment.

There is much good sense, says Anatole Rapoport (1968), a general systems theorist, in viewing social organization as behaving like human organisms. There is reason to believe, he says, that quasi-biological functions are demonstrable in organizations. They maintain themselves, they sometimes reproduce or metastasize; they respond to stress; they age and they die. Organizations have discernible anatomies and those that transform material inputs, as in industry, have physiologies. All have neural physiologies since organization without internal communication, integration and control is unthinkable. The groundwork that Rapoport set established the parallelisms between biological and social phenomena and enable us to conclude that a single explanation could serve either biological or social behavior. It sets the stage to claim that theories about organizing can explain the biosocial behavior of play.

The next question to be raised concerns the level of complexity. The danger still lurking in the selection process is the tendency to select an explanation far more complex than our present knowledge could absorb. A critical decision lies at the point of determining the "just right" level of first approximation. The goodness of the decision is judged by the capacity of the selected model to provide a coherent framework from which a play explanation could be formulated. The guidelines for level selection in systems follow a twentieth century of Occam's razor, as few concepts as you may; as many concepts as you must. For if concepts within the system and explanation of play are to be useful they should be relatively few and express relatively simple relationships that can be understood.

In summing up the process of selection, it needs to be repeated that the most critical decisions were derived from the assumption that play is a mutli-dimensional phenomenon, which can not be explained from a single discipline or by a single theory. Instead what play requires for explanation is a series of sub-theories which explain how man interacting in his environment acquires this behavior and what purposes such behavior serves. The next assumptions are that the obvious characteristics of play define it as both a biological and social behavior. It is biological because it is living behavior which belongs to man and because it grows increasingly complex over time. These characteristics place play within a biological ontogenetic framework. Since its complex structure is organized as a result of experiences acquired from interaction with the environment, it is also a social phenomenon. Play, therefore, is defined as a bio-social phenomenon.

Specifications stated in this way mandate a system approach design with the system divided into various subsystems and with each subsystem containing an appropriate theoretical explanation. The design of the system would be based upon appropriate identification of the subsystems that make up play behavior. The function of the system would be determined by the logic of the system; the rules of basic logic of the relations of the parts would then define the organizational nature of play.

Concepts of Organizing

The leading systems theorist in biology, Ludwig von Bertalanffy (1962) says that any interdisciplinary thinking about living behavior must accept as a first principle that behavior has a spontaneous nature. The concept of spontaneous activity is pivotal for bridging biological and social behavior. It means that the internal behavior of an organism will act spontaneously without dependence upon external stimulation. This proposition about the autonomous nature of a growing complexity is the link which bridges organismic theory to organizational theory. It enables both growth and organization to be viewed as different aspects of the same process. From this perspective, problems of structural growth merge almost imperceptibly into problems of structural change. What grows is not only the overall size of the structure but also the complexity or systematic intermeshing of its parts. The utility of the von Bertalanffy proposition is that the internal spontaneous activity of the organism is identified as the fundamental organizing force. What it means is learnings that are internalized do not need external stimuli to be activated. The action is automatic and their power is to regulate change. Structure and function in this sense do not have a linear relationship; they have an interactive self-transforming relationship.

The self-transforming nature of organized behavior enables us to give a new look at structure-function relationships. Physics tells us that there are laws which control the changing shapes of things. Something which grows uniformly in all directions will be a sphere; something which grows faster in one direction than in others will be long; and something which grows faster on one side than on the other will twist into some sort of a spiral. The classical analogy for evolutionary and developmental processes is the open upward spiraling shape which embraces in its sweep the behavior or organisms. The internal environment of the spiral is dominated by the experience of mankind and the external environment of the spiral is the surrounding civilization upon which it fees. The behavior of individual man interacting with the requirements of his social environment recapitulates the general spiral of mankind and civilization. The spiraling nature of the change process is conceptualized by the hierarchy model of self-transforming organization. The way the hierarchy acts to process behavior are contained in the rules that govern the work of the system.

Laws of Organizing

Organization theory defines a hierarchy as composed of stages or domains distinguished in terms of time sequences in which older, simpler forms of behavior are transformed to newer and more complex forms. The function of the hierarchy is to process change quantitatively from small to large, from simple to complex, and qualitatively from lower to higher forms of behavior. These changes are the fundamental aspects of any growth process, and they operate from the underlying assumption that what is being processed is complexity. But understanding the nature of organisms or organizations is not limited to the complexity assumption because there are other kinds of assumptions. Other assumptions concern processes which create, maintain and dissolve collectivities and constitute the work of organizing. The ways in which these processes are continuously executed are the organization. The key concept to organizing is that, while the appearance or the organization may change, the workings do not.

The organizational theorist, Carl Weick (1969), suggests that knowing the organizing process is knowing the "interlocked behaviors that are embedded in conditionally related processes." His argument is that if one could observe, describe and summarize conceptually the features of this phrase, a great deal could be understood about organizations. Weick recognizes that it is asking a great deal of any analytical device to include not only the interactions of the elements, but the analysis of the context as well. For this requires that both the macro properties of the environment be analyzed along with the micro properties of internally acquired behavior. In the case of play the micro properties would be all those properties belonging to the learning process and learned products.

The macro properties would be anything in the social surround which influences the internal behavior of the individual.

There are two laws of systems that cover the action relationship that goes on between macro and micro domains. The laws are expressed in the dyadal interaction of superior and inferior levels and in the triadal interaction of input, through-put and output. In every system where behavioral change is ongoing, there are older and newer behaviors that are being processed. Newer and more complex behaviors have the power to reorder or transform the older behavior. Older learnings are considered inferior learnings and are usually less complex but stronger. This implies that the inferior or subordinate levels have an ultimate voting influence upon the final hierarchical behavior.

In one sense, superior levels, or newer behavior are vulnerable to the control of inferior levels. The power of the inferior levels is usually underestimated for its ability to control the superior and more complex behavior. If the hierarchy is to be maintained it must be continuously re-established by the superior level, sending out acceptable orders to the inferior level below. When the orders are acceptable, the "majority rule" predominates. When the orders are unacceptable, "minority rule" or disorganization predominates.

If the behavioral hierarchy has been impaired by disease or inadequate learnings, older forms of learnings do not accept the orders of new forms of learning, and the higher, more complex behaviors become pathologically distorted. Flexibility of the hierarchy has much to do with the readiness of old learnings to make new alliances. The facts of behavioral adaptations depend upon controls made possible by the alliances or patterns of relationship and not by the traits characteristic of the individuals or elements involved in the interaction. The quality and quantity of the alliances define the power inherent in the hierarchy and power is accumulated in order to implement the business of adaptation. The laws of hierarchical ordering function to transform behavior. When older behavior is present and adequately processed, majority rule will flourish. When older behavior is inadequate to fulfill the order or expectancies of the newer behavior, minority rule or incompetency will dominate. Majority-minority rule or the interactions of subordinate and superordinate behaviors control organization as well as disorganization.

Inferences for a Play Explanation

A living organism, human behavior, or human society cannot be conceived of without taking into account what is variously and loosely called adaptiveness. In the language of systems adaptiveness is processed by the action of a ruling triumvirate dictating change and occurs in the interactive domains of input, through-put, and output. Since the increasing differentiation of complexity has these three interactive domains the explanation of this process is the system's-theory way of explaining behavioral change.

The specification of a play explanation requires that adaptiveness in some form be conceptualized. Yet the concept of adaptation is one of the most neglected and confusing areas of knowledge in the study of behavior. Adaptive behavior changes occur, we know, in three time spans. The largest period being evolution, the middle time-frame being development and the shortest span of all being learning. Biology leaves the relationship between human development and species change frozen in the aphorism that ontogeny recapitulates phylogeny. Learning theories, so far, have fragmented the understanding of behavior since they tend to focus on motivators of change. We have little coherence of systematized knowledge about learning and this fact seriously limits the development of the idea that play is a special class of learning.

There are, however, important conclusions about adaptations that can be drawn as behavioral inferences. Somewhere in the course of evolution, the behavioral energy dominating species change shifted from instinct to need. Somewhere in the course of development the behavior force for change in man shifted from need to value. The inferences for play are important if play is to be explained as serving adaptive behavior and the most plausible and possible form for explanation is to be a learning system design. Because learning is change acquired in the shortest time-frame it serves the immediate here and now problems of adaptation. The second inference that may be used for theory construction is that play is related to the energy system of value. Historical evidence is strong that play does not emerge in the presence of a need state. With equal reliability we may claim that play is not instinctual.

We may conclude then that play belongs to the class of behavior we call learning and that any explanation of play requires some prior coherent explanation of learning itself. The difficulty is that there are few learning system designs from which a special learning form like play may be inferred. Fortunately, though the selection is narrow, there is a general systems theory designed to explain complex learning. It is called an appreciative system of psycho-social learning and was constructed to support the proposition that learning is learning evaluation or appreciation. A learning system for play is designed from the appreciation system. The derived play system is constructed to explain the proposition that learning is learning meaning. Because its explanatory form is derived from a more general system, the original learning system is described in the following section.

AN APPRECIATIVE SYSTEM OF LEARNING

Sir Geoffrey Vickers (1968), a British lawyer and public administrator, believed that the critical form of learning that modern man required was a way of looking at the multi-choices presented by a complex society. What was needed for adaptation was a multi-value capacity to interpret complex reality. The Vickers' appreciative system of learning was designed for use in political science but owed some of its foundation theory to Boulding's work which was designed for economics. The system drew heavily upon general system theory, communication science and the judgment process used in law. While the appreciative system is much more elaborate than we need to explain play, it provides a general theory from which the other forms of learning may be derived.

The appreciative system starts from a series of described assumptions. The combination of knowledge on hand in the psycho-social sciences and the science of communication is here found as sufficient to provide a speculative explanation of how a multi-valued choice process is learned. Both psycho-social explanations and communication science offer somewhat incomplete explanations of the fact that behavioral changes occur in an intricate network of communication. What it fails to explain is how the learning that goes on within the network is the result of the external reality teaching and the individual learning.

The ability to develop values is the latest evolutionary adaptation of man and this adaptive capacity, which is the capacity to interpret values, is dependent upon information. In an abundant society man freed from need satisfaction may instead focus on values and social growth. Values involve a new relation with information. But so great is the super-abundance of information that the tasks of selecting, collating, storing and retrieving has outdistanced man's methods of keeping pace. The appreciative system is designed not because man lacks the means to communicate, but lacks an understanding of a way to interpret information. The critical nature of interpretation is that it gives meaning to information.

There is relevance for learning, the Vickers' system claims, to be found in the technology of communication science. Communication engineers at first concerned themselves with the problems of transmission, focusing on channel capacity and signal-noise ratio. They assumed conditions for the sender and receiver. But the problems that emerged and strained their technology were problems in the organization of sender and receiver. Information, the Vickers' system purports, is an incomplete concept when assumptions are made that the sender and the receiver are linked by a stored appreciation system or that the sender and receiver are not concerned with what is being transmitted. The appreciative system proposes that what is given and received changes the system and the change is mediated by meaning or interpretation. When the system is unable to interpret, meaning is lost and the whole system is in danger of losing the coherence and continuity upon which learning and behavior depend.

What communication theory enables learning theory to do is to look at the capacity of man to understand. This capacity until now has been inaccessible and hidden in the patterns of organization within the sender and receiver. The unique problem the appreciative system seeks to explain is how meaning is evaluated by the receiver. The capacity to learn the system defines as a state of readiness to discriminate and evaluate and these behaviors are viewed as both a product and a condition of learning. The learning readiness state was found to be subject to the analysis of the organizing process. In the course of this analysis the appreciative system claims to take a look at the fundamental processes of learning in that it looks at the capacity to learn rather than the content of learning.

The two interactive domains of the Vickers' system are (1) an external one called the realm of factual reality; and (2) an internal one called, reasonably enough, internalized reality. The rationality of the system action is dependent upon the complex operations whereby the "state of the system" is analyzed into judgments of fact, called reality judgments, and judgments of significance of these facts to the perceiver and to society. This latter process is called value judgment. The learning produced is called appreciative behavior.

The capacity of appreciative judgment is dependent upon (1) the quality of relevant mental faculties which vary in any individual in any population; (2) the material at the disposal of an individual whether stored in memory or retrievable through further mental processes; and (3) "the appreciative setting" which is the current state of readiness to see and value things in one way rather than another.

The central theorizing of the appreciative system concerns the appreciative setting which is conceptualized as "interpretative schemata." Schema is the term used in a singular sense and schemata for plural use. It is a concept synonymous with symbol and has a basis for familiarity already established by the work of Piaget, the French learning theorist. The schemata are developed in the process of classifying sensation.

The interpretation of fact and value judgments is dependent critically upon the characteristic behavior of schema action. The categories that classify sensation are viewed as not only there in the mind of man but further schemata are easily inventable and have ready disposition to combine and recombine. The facile innovation and readiness for combination are characteristics that explain the learning system's proclivity for progressive complexity. The emphasis in the appreciative system, however, is not upon the characteristic tendency of schemata to form but to link with values. The active emerging value-schema linkage system is described as having a critical action force which both seeks meaning and attaches interpretation to meaning.

The action of the appreciative system is explained in terms of: the kinds of information the system is ready to notice; the kinds of valuation ready to be made; and the kinds of action ready to be taken. The system behaves by means of its three regulatory aspects. First, it is self-regulatory in that, if not deliberately regulated, the system will regulate itself. Second, the coherence of the subsystems requires standards which act to monitor and relate the decisions going on throughout the system. The relationships are not judged by goals to be attained once and for all. Instead, regulatory action is viewed as being more like a mariner's course which must be constantly sought anew. Any attempt to reduce the action of this searching process to goal-seeking masks the essential difference between the behavior of man-thinking and rats running a maze. Third, the seeking action is to attain some standard rather than to avoid some unacceptable threshold. The regulative action, in this sense, is proposed as being guided by negative feedback.

Standards or norms of the behavioral learning are standards for success. Success standards are defined as having a double aspect of producing profit or service. Economic survival depends upon the functioning for profit while social survival depends upon service. This distinction in information meaning is not viewed as a simple dichotomy because man must survive in order to serve and must serve in order to survive. The learning system attempts to explain multi-valued choices present in a prosperous complex society and must then conceptualize the multi-standards by which performance is judged. The appreciative system is designed to assert that multi-valued choice is a central irreducible fact of modern life.

The first phase of the action of learning is to notice. The concept of interest is proposed as the elementary fact of the evaluation process at this stage. The principle is that man notices only those aspects of reality which interests him. This phase of learning is mediated by language in that there is a recognition of something, a naming of it, and then a process of "matching" it within the categorizing action subsystem of the schemata.

The second phase of learning after the matching process is a weighting process. Matching is an informational concept and involves the comparison of form. Weighting is a dynamix concept and involves the comparison of forces. Both are involved in the teaching-learning process by which values are developed. It is in this phase that the action of valuating goes on and consists of complex interactions of schemata and values.

The third phase of learning is a process derived from law and is called advocacy. It is made up of optimizing and balancing. The optimizing-balancing function involves the external as well as internal relations. New schemata emerge as a product of the interaction of standards of profit and standard of service. The combination of functional relations regulates the behavior. In the third phase learning both parts of the functional optimizing and balancing are learned but what is learned is not only how to maintain a given set of relations but what set to regard as optimal.

The standards whereby the advocacy action is monitored are already in the system but they change in the process of applying them. This transformation the Vickers' system explains by the characteristic of solubility. When new objects are presented to the senses of new ideas to thought, they must be soluble in old experience before new experience can emerge. In order to be soluble the new must be recognized, that is matched, otherwise the new event cannot be comprehended.

There are general values inherent in the total appreciative system. External reality of society is judged by whatever values the system holds for certainty and uncertainty as pledged by the rules of confirmation and disproof. The internal reality of the individual mind is ruled by whatever values held for coherence and incoherence. For instance, the schemata of everyday life are less exactly articulated than are the schemata that have been formally learned. But both value schemata are confirmed by the coherence that emerged from matching or nagged by the mismatched signals that proclaim incoherence.

The limitation of the appreciative system is defined as a state of communication crisis which occurred when the system reaches a critical limitation. The problem of the critical limit concerns the adjustment capacity of the system to preserve continuity through the variations of change over time. In the course of experience, individuals set the upper limits of their capacity to adjust and learning problems emerge when the limits are exceeded. To stay within the critical limits, the system has to learn to handle the presenting variables of change without losing that coherence which enables the system to hang together and to operate efficiently in its surround.

Inferences for a Play System of Learning

The Vickers' appreciative system can be summarized as designed to explain learning as a product of the interaction of external facts of reality with internal values. General systems theory, information theory of communication sciences, and the advocacy theory of law, explain the processes of interaction. The central theorizing of the system concerned the characteristic way that classifying categories become linked to values, then combined and recombined for the progressive learning complexity.

The assumption of the appreciative system is that the mind has a schemata formation process. The explanatory brunt of this theory is not upon the nature of the schemata formation process. Instead what it explains is that the schema-value linkage is the heart of the learning process. The process of valuation, the appreciation system says, teaches judgment.

A play system of learning cannot assume that a schemata formation process is already there and unlike the Vickers' learning system must ask how the classifying process within the mind is formed. The proposition of a derived learning system that seeks to explain play is that learning is learning to schematize or symbolize. A play system of learning is designed to explain how play teaches meaning. The difference between the two learning systems lies in the differences of their tasks. The Vickers' appreciative system is designed to learn how to evaluate reality. A play system has a lesser, but still difficult task, of explaining how reality is explored and how the exploratory process teaches meaning. The first question to be considered is how imagination per se is learned.

PLAY AND THE IMAGINATION

The problem alluded to but not addressed in the appreciative system of learning was how to expand the schemata formation process when it had reached a critical limit and there are no schema for classifying information. How is a schema or a symbol formed? The Vickers' system says an elementary decision that a "this" is a "that" is a decision to assimilate some object of attention carried out of the tissue of all that is available to fit some category, some schema, that is already learned. The process is an evaluation one and is mediated by language.

The Vickers' description of schemata action tempts the explanation of the underlying formation process to move in the direction of theories of language and theories about the origin of symbols. These areas of knowledge, however, while well examined are confusing and indecisive. The assumptions about a learning system of play must hold to the conviction that play belongs to the behavior of the imagination and that the field of imagination is sufficiently explained by its three action systems, namely, the central nervous system, a symbolization process and language. From an examination of these three areas, it is speculated, that a play system of learning can be extrapolated.

The Neurological Substratum

As neurophysiology asserts, it is the function of the nervous system to process sensation into meanings. The product of the nervous system action is the construction of a symbolical model of the external world. In this sense the brain imitates or models external processes. The function of symbolization then becomes plain. If man carries a small scale model both of external reality and of his own possible internal actions, he is able to trial-and-error the various alternatives, decide which is best, anticipate the future consequence, and thus utilize the knowledge of past events in dealing with the present and the future. The imagination, through its ability to symbolize reality enables man in every way to react in a much fuller, safer, and more competent manner to the reality which faces him.

Today the theories of the central nervous system enable us to think about the imagination as a device for processing the information and in the course of which the symbols necessary for learning are generated. The communication function of the nervous system provides a coherent stance from which the relationship between play and the imagination may be examined.

The processing action of the nervous system is complex but understandable. Roughly a hundred million nerve impulses are estimated to reach the central nervous system every second. The problem it encounters is how to discriminate the meaningful signals from the chaotic mess of background noise, because for economy's sake only certain aspects of the environment can be attended. The selection process has been described by such concepts as interests, needs and values. For instance, when we are hungry we search for food, or if we are thirsty we search for drink. The need that is predominant at any time will focus the attention on those aspects of the environment that are likely to satisfy it. But man is not an animal totally driven by needs, and therefore, there are other considerations involved in understanding the means by which the nervous system controls the sensory input. To bring the input to controllable dimensions it first has to be reduced, then arranged properly, so that information of possible importance comes in while irrelevant noise is screened out. Finally, all information that comes in has to be distributed correctly and sent to the different parts of the central nervous system for appropriate action. A selection mechanism is a necessity for the adaptation of the central nervous system of man.

Nature protects man by providing him with mechanisms that respond to the unexpected, the different, and as soon as a difference is noted the system becomes alert and seeks information. When something different happens, the central nervous system becomes alert, the receptors are adjusted to various stimuli. Both evolution and learning have prepared the receptors to become adjusted for a variety of stimuli. For instance, a certain sound will increase the sensitivity not only of the ear, but also of the eye. Alerting the brain appears to activate a central part called the reticular formation. From there, excitation is passed on to the cerebral hemispheres.

From the work of Moruzzi and Magoun (1949) we know that the reticular arousal system is a column of nerve cells extending through the lower brain. It is called reticular because it consists of a network (Latin: reticulum, little net) of short fibers and cell bodies with many synapsies, rather than a bundle of distinct tracts. It includes both ascending pathways leading up to the cortex and descending pathways with influence motor functions. There are a variety of mechanisms used by the nervous system for increasing one input and decreasing another, for making one input the important one for time and fading others into the background. Vertebrates facilitate or inhibit stimuli through their curiosity. The higher animals are notorious for inquisitiveness. Once their basic needs have been satisfied, they like to go out and explore the world. Even the timorous animals, like the antelope and deer, expose themselves to danger.

The question that occupies the sensorium is: "What is this?" The "what-is-this-state" of the nervous system drives the organism to seek information from all possible sensory channels. The central nervous system has been prepared by evolution development and experience to answer this question. For instance, receptor mechanisms operate on the environment to bring out contrast and edges so that objects stand out against backgrounds. Movement stands out from stillness, a slight noise suddenly appears as contrasted to the silence behind it. In parts of the cerebral cortex occupied with vision there are neurons that are stimulated by a contour of an edge of something. The varied receptors of vision and touch and hearing, we may conclude, have been programmed by evolution to have specialized advantages in stimulation selection.

Selection patterns energized by the question of "what is it" eventually results in sensation acquiring meanings. The meaning of sensation depends on the connections between different regions of the cortex of the cerebral hemishpere. In the higher levels of the cerebral hemisphere the brain makes a model of the world based upon inborn modes of perception and learning. This mental world parallels the real world, with some distortions. It is a symbolic representation of reality. Man, we know, has the ability to make use of symbols to a degree vastly greater than any other animal. The capacity to make and use symbols is a function of the reticular formation process and occurs in the course of information input and output.

Symbolization Substratum

Symbols serve an economic function for behavior because they provide a kind of shorthand, and like shorthand they are economical of time and space. Their effectiveness lies in the capacity of a symbol to act as an equivalent to certain things or events of the physical world. From the first set of symbols further symbols can be evolved. Finally, all symbols can be translated back into things and events of the real world. There are many different kinds of symbols and ways of using them. One of the simplest relationships is for the symbol to be a part of the whole that it represents. Instead of the total event, or the whole active behavior, a small part is shown, and the mind which understands the symbol assumes the whole for the part. Linked also to the ability to symbolize is the capacity for generalization, and this generalization ability provides man with further economy in thinking.

The capacity to form a new symbol is served by the working of many parts of the cerebral cortex of both hemispheres. Man's outstanding ability to use verbal symbols depends upon the connections in his brain between all the parasensory association areas. Man is able to see a circle, to feel the circumference of a circle with his hands or feet, to draw a circle in the air with his hand or foot. Because of the connection between the visual, tactile, and kinesthetic areas, he can abstract the common circularity from these three senses. From this common abstract one verbal symbol is made, the word "circle." Had there been no connections between the secondary sensory areas he would not have been able to recognize this one common feature. Seen circle, felt circle, and circle drawn in space would have been as different to him as anything else his senses could take in from his environment.

Indeed, it is because of these interconnections man is able to make meaningful comparisons, and from the different sensory inputs to deduce similarities and differences. The ability to perceive similarity and difference we know has a codification effect upon information. This codification ability saves time during thinking and remembering. Instead of nerve impulses having to make the complete circuit around the original path, they need only to make smaller circuits of already codified information.

When we accept the proposition that play has a crucial relationship to imagination, then we assert that symbol formation or schemata construction is a major function of play. In any subsequent conceptualization beyond the nervous sytem we are troubled by a poverty of understanding about symbols and symbolization. There is general agreement that symbols translate sensation into meaning. The definition of a symbol as a sign denoting something which is other than the symbol itself is a proposition taken from the field of linguistics. The meaning that symbols carry is what we humans bestow upon them by agreement or convention. Symbols, therefore, become the instrumentalities whereby men codify experience and create a map of the territory of experience. Their utility depends, says sociology, upon the fact that all group members are conditioned to react more or less uniformly to them. The use of symbols to store meaning, codify experience, or create a map establishes the ground plan for communication. Sociology bases much of its operational assumptions upon the premise that unless a thing can be named, it can have no conceptual reality.

Both sociological analysis and psychoanalysis are dependent upon symbolic analysis. They differ sharply in that the power of words is seen from different perspectives. It is a sociological proposition that society arises in and continues to exist through the communication of significant symbols. By significant symbols are meant those which not only signify to or stimulate others but also arouse in the self the same meaning as they do in others. Communication thus determines social relationships because language gives the capacity to indicate to ourselves what we and other persons are going to do. Man, under such conditions, is able to assume the attitude of others and to act accordingly. It is around this linguistically based ideology that sociology builds its conceptualization of symbolization.

The means whereby those in power create and control the words legitimizes their power. While it seems absurd to argue against the goodness of words, the argument here is that to name is not enough. The tendency to abstract action into words is both the intellect's strength and weakness. If we know how to look, action has shape, form, and style. Reality is too complex to be subject to the simple convenience that to name a thing is to know its meaning. Words alone provide too meager a perception of reality.

Psychoanalysis, like socioanalysis, is linked to words as a mediator of interpersonal communication processes. It differs, however, in that the realm of the imagination in the Freudian theory is named the "unconscious." While the royal road for examining the unconscious was through the dream as decoded through words, the dream itself was symbolized through visual images. Freud describes sleep as a state in which the censorship of the ego is greatly reduced and the suppressed concepts of the id manage to force themselves into disguised expression. Accordingly, much of the work of dream interpretation was to unmask the disguised content so as to create a state of freer communication between the analyst and the id. The work of the dream process, and hence of the imagination, was to express conflict for the irrational part of the mind. The conflicts within the unconscious both express and enable the decoding of reality. The symbol system of the mind is seen as being sexually constructed of visual imageries.

The dream interpretation of Freud was based on the same principle which underlies his psychological therapy. The fundamental concept was that man has strivings and feelings as well as wishes which motivate his actions, and about which he has little awareness. The unknown was stored in the unconsciousness awaiting the retrieval of dream work. The theme was that certain of the early childhood impulses became repressed, lived an underground existence in the unconscious, and appeared in the dream, paled and distorted by the adult's need not to be fully aware of them even while he was asleep. Much psychoanalytical technology was developed around the content and form of dream analysis. The content of sex was used to explain very diverse forms of the dream. Freudian theory taught that if we knew the visual images of sex before we analyzed the imagery of the dream, form could be reduced to content.

Erich Fromm (1951) studied dreams as a universal human

phenomenon of symbolism. He proposed that dreams were essentially no different from other symbolic forms, such as myths and fairy tales. To understand the language of one was to understand the language of the other. He provides the pivotal concept about both symbolization and imagination when he asserts that the symbolic language of dreams is a second language augmenting the general language function of the imagination. Language serves the function for the total imagination, functioning not only for a word symbol but for a visual imagery system as well. In symbolic language the visual images of dreams interact with the word images of myths. Fromm would have us conclude that both myths and dreams serve an information processing function. This notion is fairly old and well known to man and was expressed in the Talmud as "Dreams which are not interpreted are like letters which have not been opened." Both dreams and myths were considered to be important communication from ourselves to ourselves; but if, says Fromm, we do not understand the language in which they are written, we miss a great deal of what we know and tell ourselves in those hours when we are not busy manipulating the outside world.

The Language Substratum

The symbolic language of myths and dreams is the language of symbolism and expresses inner experiences, feelings, and thoughts "as if" they were sensory experiences, events in the outer world. The imagination processes sensory experiences into dream pictures and story plots. This language, however, has a logic which is different from the conventional one we use in the daytime, a logic in which intensity and association, and not time and space, are the ruling categories. It is the one language the human race has ever developed that is the same for all cultures and throughout history. Having its own grammar and syntax, as it were, the understanding of this language is a condition for understanding the symbol formation action of the imagination.

The linguist Noam Chomsky proposed a learning proposition about the linguistic capacity of the mind as a special feature of evolution. The Chomsky proposition is that the human brain embodies within it a universal grammar from which all other particular grammars of behavior are derived. This notion was extended by the anthropologist Fox (1970) in a position that the universal grammar is the grammar of all behavior. Because the Fox proposition has explanatory power for the symbolic language system of the imagination it deserves some elaboration. The mind of man, says Fox, is a product of an evolutionary wiring system. Man is so wired for culture that if a new Adam and Eve could survive and breed in total isolation from any cultural influence, then eventually they would produce a society which would have laws about property, rules about incest and marriage, customs of taboo and avoidance, and methods of settling disputes, beliefs about super-natural practices, and so on. In general, man would produce a society, a culture, because he is wired to do so. Fox argues that man has potentiality for action, for instinct, for learning, for the development of unconscious habits. If we were to study the behavior of man in much the same way and by much the same methods as we study other animals, we would be able, Fox contends, to identify a universal grammar of behavior that follows parallel rules in all behavioral spheres. The concept of a universal grammar of behavior casts a new light upon symbolization processes.

The logic for a universal grammar that might decode the behavior of man was built upon analysis of the constants and the variables long sought by anthropology. Culture in the anthropological parlance refers to traditional modes of behaving and thinking that are passed on from one generation to another by social learning of one kind or another. We get a little uneasy when told that animal communities also have traditions that get passed on, so Fox explains, anthro-pology retreated into symbols. Culture is couched in symbols, and it is by means of these that it is passed on. Preeminent among the symbol system is language. When all else fails we cling to language as the major characteristic of the uniqueness of man. Fox began with the theme that this human uniqueness should be interpreted in the same way as the uniqueness of any other species. How, he asked, is language wired into the behavior of man. In his answer he proposed that the learning of man was not general, that it was, instead, very specific.

Learning is not a general capacity. It is not just the capacity to learn and to learn easily, which is the cultural assumption that dominates our understanding today. Fox proposes instead that it is the capacity to learn some things rather than others, to learn some things easily rather than others, and to learn some rather specific things. It is the capacity to learn specific things that makes the learning of language possible. Man is programmed to behave in certain ways that will produce phenomena, given a certain input of information. If this input does not occur, then the behavior will not occur or will occur only in a modified or distorted form. What Fox attempted to say was that the human organism is like the computer which is set up, or wired, in a particular way. It is thus in a state of readiness at various points in the life cycle to process certain kinds of information. The information has to be of a certain type, but the actual message can vary considerably. If the information is received, then the computer stores it and uses it to go on to the next task.

If the human organism is wired to process information and the language function of man expresses most uniquely this process then we can conclude that an analysis of this uniqueness would enable us to generalize this understanding to other forms of behavior. The concept of the wiring for learning had certain constraints because man can only process information at certain times and in certain ways. The wiring is geared to the life cycle so that, at any one moment in the population of homo sapiens, there will be individuals with a certain store of behavior at one stage of the cycle giving out information to others at another stage, with the latter being wired to treat the information in a certain way. As an outcome of the interaction of these individuals at various stages, certain typical relationships will emerge. In just this way culture can be understood to teach man and man is wired for such learning. Looking at the forms and processes of the grammaticality that constitutes the universal grammar of behavior enables us to look at the imagination as it symbolizes.

THE THREE LANGUAGES OF SYMBOLIZATION

The language concept of symbolization enables us to identify at least three language systems in the imagination. A word language and dream language have already been identified. The behavior of play enables us to propose a new and third language system constructed from a class of symbols called "rules." The symbol of the rule is a product of the built-in characteristics of a nervous system that asks "what-is-this?" The concepts of conflict and curiosity explain the rule symbolization process. Exploratory action of man mediates the information processing of rule symbolization. The psychologist

Berlyne (1960) proposed a concept of perceptual curiosity to refer to states of high arousal that can be relieved by specific exploration and in which specific exploratory responses are likely to occur. The exploratory curiosity is aroused when the incoming information is excessive, deficient, or discrepant. When this difference occurs, a stimulus selection process Berlyne calls "conflict" operates. The function of conflict is to provide a defense for learning. Play is the expression of this defense mechanism as it explores reality energized by curiosity and targeted on knowing the unknown.

Play is a behavior whose central mode of operations is to puzzle, to tease, to doubt at reality. The "as-if" of the metaphor, the contradiction of the paradox, and the specificity of rule are the realities of its substance. For in play man puts himself totally and freely in a position of decoding the complexities of reality. Playing man accepts and anticipates the pleasure of encountering the unknown. Indeed, the unknown is homo ludens' adventure. Doubting the unknown is his game. And the doubting man is the man most apt to survive and become adaptive. Our contemporary civilization, it is clear, continues to require modern man, as it did ancient man, to doubt his environment and the nervous system of man continues to thrive on doubt and to seek certainty.

Doubting man, we conclude, is man living in the conjuction between the old and the new, the absurd and the serious. If he adopts the sharp-dumb approach of the oxymoronous way of thinking, man may safely interact with his environment. The incongruities and contradictions of the environment are decoded and internalized more readily by a modus operandi that thrives on uncertainty as play does.

In the confrontations between novelty and change, novelty and habit structures, the resulting conflicts build up the behavioral repertoire. The power of a particular conflict to shape behavior depends upon such conditions as: how novel the pattern is; to what extent it arouses and relieves uncertainty, and to what extent it arouses a release conflict; and how complex it is.

The natural ontogenetic arena for developing experiences with conflict is play. In the action of play reality is explored via curiosity and conflict for the rules of how things, events, ideas and people operate. As meaning is generated, the searching process produces learning. The symbolization system becomes enriched as playing man constructs the rules of space, time, and purpose. In play inquisitive man seeks out first the sensorimotor rules, then the rules of objects and of people, and finally even the rules of thinking. The capacity to know the rules enables man's intellect to know, and particularly to know-how. And this capacity of knowing is the act of symbolizing which is a prerequisite for learning competency. The self-transforming nature of the curiosity drive linked to the built-in informational processing disposition of the nervous system explains the progressive complexity of rule learning.

Koestler (1964) postulates that to extract information is as vital to man as it is essential for him to extract specific forms of energy from sunlight and food. If, says Koestler, we could assume information processing to be an inherent tendency of all living organisms, then we must also assume the existence of an inherent primary drive to explore the environment for relevant information.

The curiosity of man differs from that of animals in that man's response to the environment is to ask questions, hence the stimuli to his exploratory activities are novelty, surprise, conflict, or uncertainty. Play is the behavior in which the exploratory drive receives its purest form of expression. When the drive is directed toward specific targets, it results in latent learning and, in a more complex form, it becomes problem solving. While play is self-rewarding, in problem-solving the search as well as the solution act as incentives to move on to another problem. In this way means and ends become chained to keep the learning going as the nervous system processes information continuously.

In summary, rules process meaning in the course of exploratory action and, therefore, are a legitimate class of symbols. When the nervous system asks "what is this" to discrepant information, it is asking what is the rule of this difference. The theory of universal grammaticality proposes that man is wired not only for words and visual imageries, but he also is wired for rules. The third language says, learning is learning rules. The understanding of this language is bound up in the understanding of all the language systems acting within the imagination. Understanding play, the vehicle of the third language, is to grasp that it is a subsystem of a larger imagination system of learning.

A LANGUAGE LEARNING SYSTEM

The fundamental learning in man that distinguishes man from all other animals is that his learning is learning to symbolize. It is inherent in his capacity to be aware of his experience. Man is able through a very special characteristic of self-awareness to infer meaning. This capacity enables him to reflect upon reality by representing reality in symbolic constructs. In any population the capacity to construct symbols varies quantitatively and qualitatively. But it is the general ability to infer meanings, to symbolize or schematize which places man in a unique stance to reality. The uniqueness of man's behavior is the product of his imagination.

It is consistent with knowledge, as we understand it today, to say that within the mind is a realm called the imagination. It is a small step beyond to propose that the imagination could be conceived as a system whose output or product is meaning mediated by the process of symbolization. The mind-imagination relationship is expressed in the assertion that, while behavior may be the product of the mind, symbolization is the product of the imagination. The input to the system is the information in the cultural milieu in which the individual lives. Learning in this system is explained by the complex ways that information is processed and the resulting complex richness of the symbolic or schematic output.

The assumptions of the imagination system rests upon assumptions drawn from information theory and universal grammaticality. Information theory explains such aspects of processing as selection, collating, storing and retrieval. The forms and processes of grammaticality explain how the learning of man is specific and not general. The expressive way that symbols name, describe, and speak for reality sets the conditions to explain the imagination as a language domain and to propose that learning to construct and use images of reality is learning the language of reality. The complex interactions of the imagination system is seen as the action of converting information into meaning through a process of learning following the rubrics of language constructing.

Information within the imagination is converted into meaning through three subsystems each of which has a specific class of symbols expressing a different language form. The three subsystems are: a myth subsystem utilizing word symbols; a dream subsystem utilizing visual imagery; and a play subsystem utilizing rules of action. The word system serves the thinking behavior of man while the dream system serves his feeling behavior.

When reality is represented by what we suspected is at least three different processing forms we are able to see the specificity of learning in a new light. Words in naming captures the logic of reality, while the dreams of feeling capture the relationships of reality and the rules of action capture the technology of reality.

In the following section, the emphasis on theorizing will be upon the subsystem where the images of rules generated in play serve the action system of man. Each subsystem constitutes a specific domain of reality-representation and their multi-interactions both within and between the domains produce the symbols or schemata which express or speak for reality.

No class of symbols, the word, the visual image, or the rule acts alone. Symbolization is an interactive trilogy of words, dreams, and rules operating continuously throughout the imagination. While different people learn and use words, dreams, and rules differently, what they share in common is the capacity to represent reality in internalized images constructed from personal experience. The danger to the understanding of the system as a whole lies in the fact that the word domain tends to have a tendency to be viewed as the total system. The distortion lies in assuming one subsystem can speak for all. The general fallacy being that the word system is commonly understood as the language system, and consequently may speak for other specific behavior processed in the dream or rule domains of the system.

Of the three action systems of the imagination the word subsystem is the most studied and hence the best known while the rule subsystem is the least conceptualized. There is considerable knowledge about how a this or that acts as our enormous industrial technology testifies. The literature asserts that we probably have too much knowledge on hand about how things are formed. The necessary link in knowledge is how the action state is related to thinking and feeling states.

The first domain of the imagination to be described is the word system. Man names things because he has a passion for order and this drive for descriptive order reconstructs his internal reality and results in a final stage called cognitive behavior. The symbolic structures of this subsystem are conceptualizations that range from the simple processes involved in names and sentences to more complex hierarchies made up of myths and metaphors. The global action of this system, we speculate, is logic.

The second domain of the imagination is the dream system of visual imageries. There is much historical evidence to show that this internal dimension has two aspects of processing: one involving night dreams, and the other daydreams. The work of Freud indicates that during sleep the feeling states of anxiety process the conflicts of experience. Daydreams which anticipate the future and provide blueprints for information selection of the present have had little psychological study. The complex schemata of aspirations that energize imitation and is sustained by hope, are complex symbolic forms and processes of feelings states that we know very little about. The product of this subsystem we speculate is the organization of feelings for social interactions. The relationship-constructs of this domain explain the progressive organization of society. Daydreams linked to hope guide the social adaptation of behavior.

A third dimension of the imagination is the play system which thrives on reality problems and seeks to know the rules of how things, events, ideas, and people go together. Complex organizations of rules learned specifically from action of experience give rise to the skill configurations upon which the competency of man and the technology of his society are founded. Play in this way is viewed as processing or mastering reality.

The capacity of the total imagination system to act is dependent upon: (1) the quantity of schemata already on hand and generated from experience; (2) the freedom of the system to match and weigh combinations from all its subsystems and (3) the current state of readiness of the external reality to encourage and applaud new symbolic representations.

BEHAVIORAL TRANSFORMATIONS OF PLAY

The subsystem of the imagination most relevant to under-standing play is the dimension of rule-constructs. Play behavior we know is permeated by the exploratory drive of curiosity and this characteristic because of its critical nature needs to be further elaborated. The readiness state of curiosity, it si speculated, has three hierarchical stages, namely exploratory, competency, and achieve-ment. These progressive stages are hypothesized as expressing a higher level of excitement and requiring a corresponding need for more control. While curiosity may be the basic motivation driving the system, the three derivative areas of exploration, competency, and achievement appear to function in a relatively autonomous way.

Exploratory Behavior

Play behavior that occurs early in childhood, or play behavior that occurs when an event is very new or different, is characterized by exploration. It is a class of behavior that undoubtedly is motivated by Bühler's concept of "functional pleasure." It is engaged in for its own sake, and fulfills in all ways the requirement for intrinsic motivation. Schachtel (1954) refers to such behavior as a relatively autonomous capacity for object interest. He proposes that this interest is pursued precisely at all times when major needs are in abeyance. High pressure of need or anxiety is the enemy of exploratory play. Low need pressure is a requisite if the organism is to achieve an objective grasp of the environment. Exploratory behavior, then, is the product of an autonomous capacity to be interested in the environment and has great value for the survival of a species. Its focus is on sensory experience, and traditionally it has been associated with the free play of early childhood and the aesthetic experiences of art, music, and dance.

In the pure pleasure of doing something for its own sake, exploratory behavior teases and tests reality as the imagination searches for rules. Conditions which permit activities to be done for themselves generate in the player a feeling of hope and trust. When the environment is not safe, and therefore cannot be trusted, rule learning cannot emerge.

Competency Behavior

The second and more complex stage is dominated by the efficiency or competency drive identified by White (1959). It is characterized by a drive to deal with the environment, to influence it actively, and to be influenced by it through feedback mechanisms. This is the time when the need for excitement and novelty is experimented with, and the attitude is predominantly "wanting to do it alone and my way." The player is persistent and concentrates on the activity. Practice is the way the task is mastered and practice is absolutely essential for the learning of this period. The "wanting to do it alone" attitude, in the course of practice, transforms the feeling of hope and trust in the environment to self-confidence or self-reliance.

The action of this phase has some very special characteristics called fragmentation and preestablished properties. Fragmentation in learning has been observed by Griffiths (1935) and Sutton-Smith (1971) in the play of children. It takes the form of the interruption of an activity sequence before reaching the normal goal behavior, the enacting of fractional sequences, the repetition of fractional sequences, and the reordering of sequences. The term fragmentation implies that goal striving models or behavior represent a standard of normal behavior. The fragmentation, or repetition of play, enables the child to build skills his way with reference to normal standards.

By preestablished properties is meant that the schemata or symbols being used are acquired prior to the occasion of a specific play activity. They appear very much like overlearned behavior. They are overlearned in the sense that they appear to have acquired the characteristic properties of habits. The concept of fragmentation enables us to understand how a child absorbs a novel behavior because it contains in it the sense of Piaget's assimilation. While the preestablished concept operating in play enables a child player to accommodate, in Piagetian sense. The interaction of the fragmentation and preestablished properties, together with the attitudes of trust in the environment and confidence in self, are the major ingredients of the competency phase of behavior.

Achievement Behavior

The third phase inherits the acquired learnings of the previous two stages. Achievement is linked to expectancies, particularly to the standards of winning or losing. Because of the visible goal expectancies of this phase, there is some evidence to suggest that play has been transformed from intrinsic to extrinsic behavior. Achievement behavior has been defined, by McClelland (1953), as competition with a standard of excellence. It is a special category of person-environment relationship which involves an achievement theme. It focuses on performance. Outcome, or the capacity to produce it, is viewed, experienced, or judged within a frame of reference consisting of a more or less gradual slope of better or worse.

A standard of excellence, unlike the competence stage, is not linked to the player's individual private sense of excellence. The behavior is more real and serious because it is linked to a standard of excellence with more public classification of alernatives: pass, fail, good, bad, win, lose. It is characterized by competition either with self or others, and is linked, research indicates, to levels of aspirations. Hoppe (1930) found, for instance, that success and failures occur only within an area of medium difficulty; achieving something that is too easy is not experienced as success, and failing at something too difficult is not experienced as failure. It is progressively easier to reach a goal, then the achievement-related incentive dwindles until it finally disappears even though the external and environmental relationship remains unchanged. The same thing happens if something turns out to be unattainable. Hoppe postulated that hope of success and fear of failure are evaluative dispositions that shape achievement.

Achievement motivation lends itself to be defined as the striving to increase, or keep as high as possible, one's own capability in all activities in which: first, a standard of excellence is thought to apply, and second, where the execution of such activities can, therefore, either succeed or fail. Because achievement has a position higher on the hierarchy than either competency or exploratory behavior, it requires a correspondingly higher level of excitation. Danger, or risk-taking, is specifically a characteristic of this behavior. The hope and self-confidence generated by the other two stages must, of necessity, be transformed to a state of courage.

As persistence is a critical characteristic in the practice stage of competency, so courage is critical to achievement. Courage is realistic and adaptive when the skill of fragmentation functions in good order, and when the preestablished segments are present and appropriate to the risk-taking in hand. It is at this developmental point in time that the skills already present in the behavior repertory are subject to being reorganized in the interest of winning. Under these conditions the potential of the mind to strategize moves into realization, and man is thus enabled to move into a new position of power in his environment. He is no longer struggling with surviving. He is man controlling his environment, adapting through his capacity to strategize. He is man who has played his way gradually and safely towards the skillful mastery of his world.

REFERENCES

BERLYNE, D. E. (1960) Conflict, Arousal and Curiosity. New York: McGraw-Hill.

BOULDING, K. (1956) "General systems theory—the skeleton of science." Management Science 2.

FOX, R. (1970) "The cultural animal." Encounter 25 (July).

FROMM, E. (1951) The Forgotten Language. New York: Grove.

GRIFFITHS, R. (1935) Imagination in Early Childhood. London: Kegan Paul.

HOPPE, F. (1930) "Erfolg und miserfolg." Psychologische Forschung 14.

KOESTLER, A. (1964) The Act of Creation. New York: Dell.

MacCLELLAND, D. C., J. W. ATKINSON and E. L. LOWELL (1953) The Achievement Motive. New York: Appleton-Century-Crofts.

MORUZZI, G. and H. W. MAGOUN (1949) "Brain stem reticular formation and the activation of the EEG." EEG Clinical Neurophysiology 1.

RAPOPORT, A. (1968) "Foreword," in Walter Buckley (ed.) Modern Systems Research for the Behavioral Scientist. Chicago: Aldine.

SCHACHTEL, E. G. (1954) Metamorphosis. New York: Basic Books.

SUTTON-SMITH, B. (1971) "Child's play, very serious business." Psychology Today (December).

VICKERS, G. (1968) Value Systems and Social Process. Harmondsworth, Eng.: Penguin.

VON BERTALANFFY, L. (1962) "General systems theory—a critical review." General Systems 7.

WEICK, C. (1969) The Social Psychology of Organizing. Reading, Mass.: Addison-Wesley.

WHITE, R. N. (1959) "Motivation reconsidered: the concept of competence," Psychological Rev. 66: 297-333.

PART TWO

INTRODUCTION

Despite the high visibility of playful behavior in daily life, it is a neglected area for systematic study. The ambiguity of its concepts and the contradictory state of its themes have made this activity, as far as behavioral scientists are concerned, an undesirable category for study. Yet, if the nature of play as an exploratory form of learning is to be understood, then it is important to design an examination of this behavior. Blumer (1969) suggests an initial strategy, that of "inspection," which is used whenever the empirical date is uncategorized and lacking in propositions.

The task of inspection involves first making a focused observation of the empirical content directly, identifying elements that could be used for analysis. Missing substantive concepts and their relationships emerge as questions, or categorical statements, act to set the angle of observation, and design the scrutiny.

Explanation can occur at varying levels of focus, ranging from the full-blown theories used by all disciplines to the more limited questions tested by the psychologists or the propositions explored by the sociologists. Propositions, for instance, may be either selected from the literature or created from empirical reality. In the case of play, both sources are readily available. The unique power of propositions has not been used as a form of explanation for playful behavior, possibly because their level of abstraction is too theoretical for the state of the knowledge. It is the nature of propositions to abstract or to generalize observable relationships which are testable. In one way, they serve the function of a theory and in another, they function as hypothesis.

While the character of broad generalization casts propositions in the garments of dogma, their dogma is a strength in that propositions are long on explanation and short on rhetoric. In this sense, propositions may be viewed as guides for discussion and not as reports of "discovered" truths. They guide the process of questioning more than the process of analysis. Their failure to illuminate play may lie in the emphasis that propositions place on relationships when what might be needed is an explanation of another more elementary level.

Herbert Simon and Allen Newell (1971) suggest another level of explanation which they call the heuristic strategy. The heuristic approach consists of inspecting the most relevant observable litera-ture or behavior and asking short range questions that generate raw data through trial and error, producing the heuristics (rules of thumb) that describe the phenomena. The derived rules of thumb form the perspective and the language of inspection.

The power in the heuristic approach lies in its capability to examine small promising regions of infinite space with the intent of abstracting rules of thumb that act as a structure for inspection. The heuristic strategy has much merit as a starting device that eventually may develop understanding sufficiently to support higher forms of explanation. The higher forms of explanation are the theories that tell us how the skills of competency are generated in the process of play, what these processes are and what mechanisms perform these processes.

THE HEURISTICS OF PLAY

1. There are many culturally well-worn activities that a child does in play and he does them because he is a child and he does them with more or less skill.

2. Play is an external expression of the developmental process, and the highly observable skills of play constitute a description of the developmental, learning or adaptation processes.

3. Play acts to relate tasks to capacity and the interactive product is skill. The cultural time-worn activities of play converge with the human need to practice an emerging ability. This exercising or practice function of play is indistinguishable from its testing function. The fortuitous interaction of novelty and practice process skills. There are specific

periods during childhood when certain types of activity are essential for development. If the needed opportunity for activity is lacking at a critical period, a given skill may not appear, may be slower making its appearance, or may be only partially adequate. It follows then that play will not process all skills equally or sufficiently. But what is a fairly clear rule of thumb is that the product of playful behavior is skill.

4. Playful behavior is a mastery process. At each stage of development there are fairly specific tasks appropriate to a maturation level and which society expects an individual to master within a set time-frame. The play activities of childhood, functioning at the unconscious level of cultural learnings, parallel the maturation level of development which functions at a genetic level. Both levels converge in society's expectation. If the activities are not mastered at the appropriate developmental stage, a child will be at a serious disadvantage in moving competently through a subsequent stage. The demands for mastery could act as a harsh taskmaster of childhood if play were not present to soften this task with the benevolence of fun. The ambience of playfulness, however, cannot camouflage the reality that the demands of a given developmental period may be relatively easy or difficult depending upon how well the tasks at prior developmental levels have been mastered.

5. The major characteristic of the process is fun. The close linkage with fun puts play in a unique class of behavior. The consensus in the literature is that the pleasure of play or "functional pleasure" is the pleasure of mastery. Fun, of course, is intrinsic and the yield is confined to the player. Any observational device that intervenes between the player and the play interrupts the fun and distorts the performance. The validity of the performance lies in the total commitment to the demands or rules of the activity, while the reliability of the observation lies in its direct relation to the raw data of play. A pencil-and-paper or verbal response by the player is known to yield different results from those obtained by direct observation of play. What a player reports has been found to be different from what a trained investigator observes. Direct observation of the raw data of play controls the reliability of play testing.

6. A major mechanism of playful behavior is imitation. Play activities vary not only with the stage of development, but also with group membership. A child whose play skills have not emerged according to the expectancies of the peer group tends to regress to membership in a group where the standards of competition may be lowered but where the imitation potential has dropped. It is one of the truths about learning that those whom a child tends to imitate occupy large chunks

of life space. The peer group comprises a major life space chunk and is the favored institution for disciplining competition and cooperation. Both of these skills are learned within the peer group and depend in some partially known way upon imitation. The imitation potential of the peer group acts to shape the general developmental skills which focus on achieving a realistic frame of reference about self and world, developing the competencies needed in the culture, and learning about and preparing for problems likely to be encountered in living. The quantity and quality of the skills learned are dependent largely upon the membership within a specific group.

The perspectives and inspection devices constructed in the chapters of Part Two fall loosely within the heuristic mode. Each author uses an observational device to limit the space. In Chapter 4, Michelman designed a play agenda both as an observation and intervention device. Her intent was to describe and order the behavioral chaos of deficit children. Given the incoherent activity expressed by neurological and psychiatrically disturbed children, the problem she posed was how to specify the elements of a play environment that might evoke and provoke the integrating effect of play skills. The play agenda purports to construct a specific environment composed of tasks demands. The agenda was concerned with presenting a challenge to the interactive systems of sensation, perception and intellect. It focuses on the aesthetic experience of art, the symbolization experience of play, and the risk-taking, problem-solving experience of games. The intent of the agenda is to optimize the environment by specifying the task demands.

Takata, in Chapter 5, proposes that a play history, properly conceived and employed, could be a powerful observational and diagnostic tool. History asks questions about what has happened and what evidence supports past patterns of behavior and the collected data serves the function of explanation via chronology. The past play skills of a child were sampled by epochs whose parameters were defined. The elements within each epoch, when researched according to the rules of evidence and content, built a comprehensive mosaic from the past. As an observational device, the play history enables one to sample past behavior in order to piece together the present. The analysis of the data, Takata suggests, should produce a play deficit diagnosis which could act as a prescription guide for intervention.

In Chapter 6, Knox selected four elemental dimensions of play and constructed a scale to observe play skills in discrete contexts. Knox proposes that the observations of the four dimensions could be translated into a play quotient statement. The play scale reflects the state of balance or skill ratio present among the four categories. In the cases of deficit behavior that were used to illustrate the scale, she hypothesized the imbalance of play behavior in the observed units that lowered the play quotient.

Hurff let the popular indoor outdoor games and exercises speak for themselves in Chapter 7. She specified twenty play situations as units from which to observe sensory, motor, perceptual and intellectual behavior. The play inventory was designed as a gross monitoring device of the critical skills that accumulate over the first decade of life. The scores suggest the readiness for the adolescent struggle with occupational choice.

In the last study of Part Two, Shannon addresses himself to the process of occupational choice that extends over the long period of adolescence. The population he explored was hospitalized military patients whose medical diagnoses indicated an adolescent failure to manage the adult role thrust upon them by military service. To observe the sum of choices made over time, Shannon selected from play behavior tasks which made a hierarchial demand upon decision-making capacity. By observing measurable decision-making activities in play some potentials for intervention in life role decision-making were suggested.

REFERENCES

BLUMER, H. (1969) Symbolic Interactionism: Perspective and Method. Englewood Cliffs, N.J.: Prentice-Hall.
SIMON, H. and A. NEWELL (1971) "Human problem solving: the state of the theory in 1970." Amer. Psychologist 16 (2).

CHAPTER 4

PLAY AND THE DEFICIT CHILD

Shirley S. Michelman

Tom, Tom, the piper's son,
He learned to play when he was young . . .

—Nursery Rhyme

It is not possible to spend any prolonged period visiting settings where children are treated for disability without being appalled by the grim, intellectually sterile, aesthetically barren environments that surround many institutions. Unnatural standards of silence and enforced immobility accompany preoccupation with order, oppressive rules and slavish adherence to a time-table that has little bearing on a child's developmental needs.

There is general lack of proper play facilities and equipment. Half-hour blocks of play time are haphazardly sandwiched in between classical therapies. Yet play is a crucial part of the deficit child's treatment with vital influence on his behavior, thinking and performance. No other activity that we know of enables handicapped children to acquire a similar sense of control over their world. If play is to serve the growth needs of the deficit child, it requires continuous structuring and skillful enrichment of the environment. Without this help, the child remains like an undeveloped country outside the perimeter of technological progress and destined to struggle at a marginal level of daily living. Spontaneous collaboration of growth with health, which results in improved behavior, is not the output of the developmental process for many of these children.

For any numbers of reasons a deficit child is often overlooked as a candidate for play experiences of the type easily absorbed by healthy children. Since he, himself, may be unable to function in play unassisted, he fails to acquire skills even at the lowest level of his ability. Handicapped children have the right to develop their potentials to the fullest possible extent. To provide that opportunity is society's responsibility. In 1959 the United Nations General Assembly unanimously adopted "A Declaration of the Rights of A Child." This declaration stated that mankind owes every child the best that it has to give. It also stipulates that, "the child who is physically, mentally or socially handicapped shall be given the special treatment, education and care required by his particular condition." Play, it is herein proposed, is a neglected, overlooked key that helps unlock the door to learning. Yet it does not seem to fit or to have any place on the agenda of skilled help that society offers. It is much as Florey (1971) says:

> When a child cannot play, we should be as troubled as when he refuses to eat or sleep. The significance of the everyday play of the child requires that professionals who work with children regard it as a respectable area of concern. When children are having difficulty in play, this is not the time to call in the volunteer or to dip into the bag of scrap materials. This is the time for the immediate attention of a professional and it calls for his careful and studied examination of what might be going wrong.

If the construction and application of a play agenda for the deficit child is to have a changed priority and its visibility heightened in services to children, how do we begin? Play, as Berlyne (1960) reminds us, has a payoff to all three areas of the major behavioral systems: sensation, perception and intellect. Sensation provides the critical input for perception. The organization of sensation in the form of symbols then casts perception as the input mechanism for all those decision-making, problem-solving skills of the intellect.

This chapter will examine the role that play exerts upon the sensory, perceptual and intellectual pathways. Its concern is with childhood art experiences and the influences that art imposes on the sensory-perceptual pathway. The games of childhood will be examined for their influence upon the perceptual-intellectual pathway. A play agenda for the deficit child will be proposed from this examination.

THE DEFICIT CHILD

Who is the deficit child and how does he perform the critical developmental tasks which are the responsibility of his childhood? What kind of a worker is he actually? For a child with a disability is not only a child with special problems, he is also a child with tasks that belong to him as a pre-schooler, elementary or high school student. Although some units of his behavior, like a jig-saw puzzle, may be out of place, we do him a disservice if we fail to set expectations around his potential and then help him meet them. For the handicapped child, there are many areas of growth, many potentials for achievement that need help as critically as impaired physical or psychological areas require medical treatment. All too frequently the medical focus masks the needs the child has in the daily living areas of his life.

There are more than seven million children in the United States who are emotionally disturbed, mentally retarded, physically disabled or who are suffering from special learning disabilities. Other millions of forgotten children endure the dehumanizing conditions of environmental and cultural deprivation in our urban ghettos, barrios and impoverished Appalachias. Beyond these are the even greater numbers of children that every society consigns to the human scrapheap. These are labeled the irretrievably handicapped, the incurably ill, the incorrigibly delinquent and the hopelessly uneducable.

A deficit child lives in a restricted world circumscribed by disability. Because of a narrowly circumscribed existence, he shares with other disabled children many behavioral and learning problems whether his individual diagnosis is mental retardation, cerebral palsy, brain damage or emotional disturbance. Often, as a child, he does not know what to expect of the world nor what the world expects of him. Because of some sensory motor impairment, emotional or social maladjustment, he may learn early to manipulate his world through temper tantrums and disruptive behavior; or, fearful of change and any new experience, he may withdraw. His is an inward-directed emotional existence with impaired capacity to confront reality. Only his own needs and desires have meaning for him. He may be unable to concentrate for more than a few moments. Susceptible to overstimulation, perhaps he cannot tune out irrelevant stimuli. Usually he lacks motivation and harbors abnormal fears of failure.

And more often than not he has poor coordination, inadequate use of language and inability to deal with abstract ideas. His accumulated inadequacies summate into feelings of worthlessness and insecurity.

A cerebral palsied child, braced, splinted, in a wheel chair, is unable to interact with his environment spontaneously and cannot tolerate frustration. Unable to fend for himself, overprotected and understimulated he withdraws into passive dependency. There may be little motivation to vocalize needs or begin to postpone immediate gratification when every wish is anticipated. Purposeless, irregular movements beyond the child's control, disturbances in balance and clumsy coordination all prevent his taking in experience through action. The ensuing monotony, boredom and environmental deprivation induce either lethargy or violent acting out. Because of the inability to perform, to learn physical skills, a brain-injured child may well develop restrictions around doing and participating. His incapacity or fear does not encourage him to reach out spontaneously with his senses and mobility to investigate his surroundings. This leads to fragmentary and distorted concepts of a hostile world over which the child feels no control.

An autistic child presents a startling dramatic picture of sensory deprivation. He has massive personality deficits, disturbances of perception and motor behaviors as well as language that may be absent or pathological. His emotional reactions are shallow and inadequate. Because he is unable to distinguish between himself and the outside world, normal personality development is impaired and his capacity for interpersonal relationships is severly defective. Instead he may substitute tenuous relationships to inanimate gadgets. Bizarre, self-stimulatory, repetitive behavior might include hand-flapping or twirling. His schizophrenic world is often populated by delusional creatures. It is a timeless world where a fusion of past and present experiences approximates the dream state. He may remain in the shower for an hour or more if not encouraged to come out. As time goes on, it becomes difficult to determine whether the child does not know how to play or lacks the opportunity to do so—or perhaps some of both.

When a child sits for hours rocking his body back and forth, his sensory, perceptual and intellectual pathways are pathologically preoccupied and his development is blocked. Unlike a healthy child he cannot be stimulated by sight, sound and smell and thus discover pleasure in his own body movements. The preconditions for sensory motor play or practice games are blocked. The pleasurable exercise of such rudimentary skills as banging, shaking, learning to roll over or creep do not generalize through the sheer enjoyment of the activity itself. Repetition does not lead to learning and random action does not result in understanding cause and effect. The action of play that spontaneously leads to learning and competency simply does not emerge in the deficit child. The distortion at each level seems to accumulate as the child works at his business of internalizing reality. The skills which are the final product of his job are bizarre and the behavioral patterns that form appear chaotic. Common sense wisdom tells us that the first distortions begin in the sensory pathway. Yet, the bulk of the investigations the literature indicates are focused at the perceptual level. Society, however, deserves the power to judge the child's right to participate in life from the observations made primarily on his intellectual level and secondarily on his behavioral skills. The unevenness of our knowledge about sensation, perception and intellect and the multiple feedbacks that each has upon the others, is the problem that lies at the heart of intervention. This much, however, we do know: play is a natural integrator of these crucial levels of behavior and therefore worth investigating.

THE SENSORY, PERCEPTUAL AND INTELLECTUAL PATHWAYS

Today we accept the idea that the unborn child experiences touch, movement and sound in its prenatal environment. Salk, in 1962, after a series of experiments at the New York Elmhurst City Hospital, concluded that sensory impressions from the maternal heartbeat are imprinted on the child during prenatal life and affect subsequent behavior during the first year of life. The neonates in a maternity nursery where the "lub dub" of the mother's heartbeat was approximated were calmer, less anxious, gained weight and cried less frequently than infants in a silent nursery. Many hospital nurseries nowadays keep radios playing music which seems to soothe the infants. Studies have also noted that unconsciously most women carry children on their left hip where they are close to the rhythm of the heartbeat.

Professor Jerome Bruner at the Harvard Center for Cognitive Studies is engaged in current research from which is emerging information about levels of awareness and intelligence in infants.

Bruner has demonstrated that four-, five-, and six-week-old infants learn to suck at different speeds to produce changes in their environment. He has long been fascinated with what and how children know, how they gather, categorize, store, use and communicate information in order to organize and interpret their world. His tendency is to focus upon the symbolization problems, that is, on the perceptual pathway to the intellect. Because of this approach, much of his work is closely akin to the work begun by Piaget. Both of these psychologists share a common interest in the play of children, since their behavioral illustrations are drawn from the play realm.

The work of Bruner provides us with multiple and rich insights about the play-route to learning. We know now that infants notice many more details of their environment than adults ever suspected. Not only are they aware of their surroundings, but they seem to enter the world with a basic ability to pick up logical rules from mere fragments of evidence. They then use these rules in a variety of combinations. Bruner has come to the conclusion that there are programs of action in the minds of healthy infants right after birth for the intelligent use of hands, eyes, tools and language. He believes that infants actively invent rules or theories to explain what they perceive. Thus even at three weeks of age an infant will have fairly complex hypotheses about the world he has just been born into—and if he is proven wrong, he may burst into tears. The Center experiments seem to point to a powerful information-processing ability in the brains of infants that responds to environmental stimuli. Bruner feels that the infant's own intentions and self-activation are of utmost importance. On their fate depends what the baby will learn from his environment. Good toys placed just beyond reach will tempt self-initiated activity. Responsive parents quickly establish a code of mutual expectancy between themselves and their child which serves as a precursor to symbol formation and language. Parents or those engaged in the care of children who fail to encourage play and dialogue and who react to their babies primarily by punishing them for errors breed a sense of powerlessness which inhibits growth and learning.

Sensory and Environmental Inputs

The Bruner work reveals that the infant brain is already programmed for actions and skills that are elicited by sensory stimuli and environmental interaction. Handicapped children suffer multiple deprivations which prohibit them from the action that should result from the natural environment and programming. Environments within hospitals, homes, schools and playgrounds provide massive enrichment which is acted upon by the curiosity or exploratory impulse. The conditions for learning are accessible toys, raw materials and physical objects that engage the senses as well as behavioral models that are imitative plus adults who will applaud and encourage. Carefully considered environments which supply negative and positive feedback for the child and which will neither over-stimulate nor underestimate his potentials are probably the broad specifications for engineering the environment. Consistency and recurrent regularity help to pattern habit structures and time-sequences that are paced in accordance with reality. Only as deficit children are able to build inward models of the world that are related validly to outer reality can their adaptation proceed. Spontaneously moving into this process is not possible; therefore the structuring of learning, related to the structuring of play, may well be a critical service to learning or acquiring the competences of adaptation.

Pickard, in *The Activity of Children* (1965), writes about the nature of the child's mind which is active in both the waking and sleeping states. She suggests the mind works by means of attention and interest and that it first grasps whole situations, whether of people or things. Then in the course of ceaseless activity, it analyses, reorganizing fresh information with previous information into a more experienced whole picture of the world. When a solution to a problem is found, the mind remembers the solution rather than how the solution was reached. When no solution is found, the mind goes on worrying about the problem and does not relax until an answer is found. If a child is not provided with a blend of environment that stimulates the right experience for solving problems, or if his experiments and solutions are not encouraged or appreciated, he is unable to construct reliable life-guiding inward models.

A child who must lie inert for hours with nothing to do too often escapes into a fantasy world unless his attention and interest are aroused by active play experiences. The world of a cerebral palsied two-year-old who neither creeps nor crawls is extended, for example, when we initiate sensory experiences. Moving his hands and feet to feel the prickly texture of fresh-cut grass, the roughness of tree trunks, the smoothness of sea-worn stones and the multitude of textures that our physical world provides helps him construct a more realistic understanding of his surroundings. A child whose environment does not provide the necessary conditions for integrating physical, emotional, mental and social development may reflect the lack in unruly, antisocial or withdrawn behavior. An unruly child is easily noticed because his behavior sets him off from the group and his confusion is dramatized by the disruptive things he does. A withdrawn child is equally troubled because he has given up trying to understand the realistic world of people and things. Both unruly and withdrawn children fail to achieve an integration between experiences inside themselves and experiences coming from their environment. They are subject to what Smith (1969) in his study of socialization and competency calls the causation factor of the benign and vicious cycles.

Benign and Vicious Cycles

Smith proposes a view as old as the Bible that those who have, gain, and those who have not, lose. Behavior, that is, one level's output, is the next level's input and thus we account for the interlocking levels of Berlyne's sensation, perception and intellect. But, continues Smith, there are conditions under which the building-blocks of experience cannot function. When the ends of a system cannot function as a means, as in the case of a deficit child, learning is of a different order and requires different propositions. The causation cycle of learning competency is, developmentally speaking, a matter of trajectory.

Launched on the right trajectory, the child is likely to accumulate successes that strengthen the effectiveness of his orientation to the world while at the same time he acquires the knowledge and skills that make his further success more probable. His environmental involvements generally lead to gratification and to increased competence and favorable development. Off to a bad start, on the other hand, he soon encounters failures that make him hesitant to try. What to others are challenges appear to him as threats; he becomes preoccupied with defense of his small claims on life at the expense of energies to invest in constructive coping. And he falls increasingly behind his fellows in acquiring the knowledge and skills that are needed for success on those occasions when he does try.

The relevancy of Smith's causation cycle of competency lies in his description of the vicious cycle of incompetency. How might the undesirable trajectory be interrupted so that a desired trajectory can be constructed? Smith proposes that there might be a potential interest in following deviant or collateral pathways more patiently and requiring practice of a different order. When the sensory system fails to function as an input for the perceptual system, this experience block should be viewed as a prime focus for treatment.

THE SENSORY-INPUT PATH THROUGH ART EXPERIENCES

The created visual image that a child makes with his hands and eyes together links the inner vision with the outer vision that shapes his felt experience into symbols.

—G. Kepes

The yield of sensory input to perception is symbolization. Yet the symbolic process which links sensation to perception encounters many difficulties with the deficit child. The ubiquitous nature of environmental stimulation along with the deficient nature of his sensory experiences create many stumbling blocks. Symbolization may first be examined as the output phase of sensation as we search for clues that identify these constraints.

It is part of our common wisdom to understand that the essence of being human lies in our use of symbols in art, music, dance and language. Bruner (1968), in his *Toward A Theory of Instruction,* states "as soon as the symbol stood for something else than the act itself, man was born; as soon as it caught on with another man, culture was born; and as soon as there were two symbols, a system was born. A dance, a song, a painting and a narrative can all symbolize the same thing." The capacity to think and feel is related to the capacity to conceive, project and use symbols. Symbols enable a child to communicate his feelings, thoughts and desires through the symbolic process. There are three parallel systems for both processing and representing reality: first, action or manipulation; second, imagery; and third, symbol organization for use.

A child who is curious and interested in exploring his environment attempts to understand his world through play, drawing, painting and other forms of nonverbal grasping and symbolization. Information absorbed through the senses is assimilated and recast into new symbolic forms. Given a crayon or piece of chalk, a child will make marks on any available surfaces. Through these initial experiments with symbol formations he develops the mental set for learning symbolic language.

The word symbol is of Greek origin, "symbalon," and signifies the adjustment of various parts to form a whole. Its three variant meanings are to unite, to connect and to bring separate parts together. Any device whereby we make an abstraction is a symbolic element and all abstraction involves symbolization.

The most primitive function of symbols is to formulate experience and articulate ideas. Although the concept of symbol varies with the perspective from which it is viewed, two essential characteristics are first, their function of reference or direction of the user's interest to something apart from the symbol itself and second, the conventional nature of connection between the symbol and object, thought or feeling to which it refers. Words are our most powerful symbols; their use is universal and constant. Language is a cultural tool which helps the child interpret his environment by asking questions about it. This leads to understanding and synthesis of experience which enables him to begin to use the environment to serve his needs. However, symbolic language does not only apply to speech. There is a wide range and variety of other nonverbal signals and language systems. Art, pantomine, dance, drama, myth, ritual, action and gestural languages are also symbolic forms of communication.

The Symbolic Process

The conceptual process is a symbolic process which pervades all mental activity—perception, apperception, selfhood and emotion as well as thought and dream. Children learn to use different types of symbols as they build concepts of their world. A concept is an idea which stands for a large number of particular sense perceptions or it may also stand for less abstract ideas. Concepts are tools to think with which are then projected through verbal or nonverbal symbol formations. For example, before a deficit child can function in his environment, he has the tasks of building concepts of space and time. These concepts must grow out of his concrete experience to make them trustworthy, just as symbols must evolve from sensory experiences to make them meaningful.

Piaget, who has done the foundation work on the conceptualization process of the child, claims that the formation of the symbol is not due to its content but rather to the very structure of the child's thought. In his words, wherever there is symbolism in dreams or in play it is because thought, in its elementary stages, proceeds by egocentric assimilation and not by logical concepts. Symbolism is a positive aspect of a child's thought and expression and may be considered as a universal form of nonverbal-imaged communication. Symbol formation is the foundation from which all subsequent learning develops and is part of the developmental process. Universal or personal symbols used by a child to express his ideas, experiences, subjective feelings and objective observations are translated into visual or plastic form through his art expression. This form of expression is a natural exploratory activity which influences sensory input to perception.

The symbols of art are visual images with innate sensory qualities. Their meaning inheres in the total form. Unlike the discursive symbols of language, mathematics and science they have no fixed signs or elements which must be combined according to rules. In their total range they express the whole subjective side of existence: moods, emotions, desires, the sense of movement, growth, felt-tension and resolutions. They articulate and abstract the logical forms of subjective experience by using congruent forms. The art symbol negotiates insight rather than reference since it does not rest upon conventions but rather motivates them. Therefore art symbols are more easily handled by the deficit child who often has difficulty establishing conventional or abstract relationships in his mind.

Discursive symbols, on the other hand, have conventional connotations and describe the neutral aspects of observation or thought. Discursive symbols convey meaningful units or dictionary meanings according to the rules of grammar and syntax. Each element or sign has a relatively fixed meaning and the total import is built up stepwise by using them successively. The significance may therefore be paraphrased by synonyms and logically equivalent meanings. The great flexibility of the presentational symbols of art are that they are metaphorical. Because they may mean many things they have strong generalization power.

The genesis of symbol formation is rooted in the sensory-motor phase of infant development. The neonate has automatic responses but no envisioning. Sensory and tactile stimulation must precede perceptual and cognitive development. When sensory-motor activity is blocked in any way, as it is in handicapped children, symbolic functions do not develop normally. A deprived child imprisoned within his own autistic shell often displays identical perceptual, symbolic and cognitive distortions as those described by adults after experimental sensory deprivation. These distortions include deterioration in the ability to think and reason; gross disturbances in feeling states, and vivid imagery, often in the form of bizarre delusions or hallucinations (Solomon, 1961). Behavioral aberrations and developmental retardation are consequences of the damaging effect of sensory and environmental deprivation (Thomas, 1968).

The importance for the deficit child, therefore, of rich and varied sensory inputs, is both obvious and critical since sensory and kinesthetic experiences are the necessary basis for cognitive learning. Such experiences provide enriching cues about reality and discriminate one thing from another and self from the world. Objects are seized by our sensory organs before perception changes and acts upon what is seen. A child tunneling in the sand is learning about rough and smooth, wet and dry, warm and cool. Flying high on a swing or balancing on a seesaw, he is experiencing up and down while orienting his body in space. A child learns many things enactively through his muscles.

Stimulation to visual tactile receptors is a basic nutrient for symbol formation as well as being necessary for human health. Such stimulation must precede symbolic, perceptual and cognitive development. Experiments with humans and animals reveal an innate preparation for cognition of such elementary visual information as colors, lines and simple forms. From this rudimentary basis all future perceptual learning emerges.

It is a truism that all knowledge begins with our senses. We learn about our environment by what we see, hear, touch, taste and smell. Sensory clues help us focus experience, code our sensations, crystallize feelings and shape our goals. The image of the external world is created from this confluence of sensory impressions which are gradually integrated into perceptual patterns. The knowledge a deficit child gains through his senses helps him to process and interpret information from the surrounding world which he internalizes through play. In the process of internalization he begins to utilize symbol formations and problem-solving skills to organize the bewildering phenomena of his environment. This prepares him for purposeful action and provides feedback as he starts to use his surroundings to meet his needs.

A healthy child attracted by a shiny red ball, for example, reaches for it. He grasps it, shakes it, bites it, rolls it. Mother tells him "ball." Next time he recognizes it, giving evidence of memory and growing mental powers. Using his senses to investigate the physical properties of the object, through much repetition and language, he eventually forms the abstract concept "ball." There is immediate relationship between new sensory experiences and the use of symbols to describe these experiences. The ability to bridge this relationship is greatly diminished in deficit children. Art experiences cultivate the senses. They promote direct involvement with shapes, colors and textures and thus their importance cannot be overemphasized. Art is a multisensory investigation of the physical world. As such it provides a deficit child with the foundations for visual and cognitive learning.

Childhood Art Experience

The assumption about childhood art experience that is being made is that it is direct sensuous experience and provides basic nutrients for symbol formation. Deficit children who freely explore and experiment with shapes and textures produce aesthetic forms. Through these experiences, they develop the mental set for learning symbolic language. By mental or learning set is meant a generalized habit that comes from repeated experience in coping with problems of a given kind. For example, the child's repeated scribblings and drawing prepare fine muscle and visual skills required for reading and writing. Childhood art expression may activate a hierarchy of learning sets involved in the deficit child's intellectual development. Intellectual competence is based upon many subordinate abilities, each of which must be incorporated into successively higher levels of ability. Thus, repeated scribbling is preparation for writing while visual apprehension is the precondition for reading.

A close relationship has long been observed to exist between the child's art expression and reading readiness. Studies demonstrate that children who show good spatial coordination and visual literacy, attained through art experience, are better readers. Drawings have been excellent predictors of reading and writing readiness.

The basis for the development of formal learning rests upon twenty-six letters and ten numerals. These thirty-six abstract figures are constantly reshuffled and manipulated as they take on different and increasingly complicated meanings. However it is not the abstract function of these figures nor their rearrangement that makes for the deficit child's mental growth. It is what these figures stand for. Being able to assemble letters in proper sequence to spell "dog" does not constitute an understanding of a dog. To really know a dog the child must touch him, feel his furry body, feed him and learn his habits. It is the interaction between the symbols, self and the environment that provides the materials for abstract intellectual processes. Therefore mental growth depends upon the relationship between a deficit child and his environment. Such relationship is a basic ingredient of all art experience including the two-year-old's scribbles which depend upon his tactile and visual experiences.

As a child becomes absorbed in scribbling, his attention is spontaneously engaged in the very act of doing. Such spontaneous attention is fundamental to all learning. We cannot force the deficit child to attend, for attention is a selective activity of the mind. One thing is attended to while others are for the moment ignored. Many handicapped children have difficulty attending, for they cannot tune out irrelevant stimuli. Yet selective activity appears in the first few weeks after birth when the baby's eyes follow a moving object swung before his face. As the deficit child becomes involved in his scribbles he is learning and attending in the process. Although his drawing may seem haphazard to an observing adult, he is practicing placement patterns, a primitive sense of figure-ground relationship, and the beginning of visual-motor activity. Scribbles therefore are proposed as the building blocks of children's art expression and the dawn of symbol formation.

Symbol formation begins as the child starts to document himself. The rhythmical movements of a two-year-old's first uncontrolled scribblings initiate kinesthetic pleasure. As the child discovers connections between his muscular movements and marks upon the paper, the basis for visual retention develops. The child is learning to change from kinesthetic thinking in terms of motions to imaginative thinking in terms of mental images and symbols. This is an important step in the child's cognitive development.

Every discovery of a mode of symbolization that a child makes follows the same graphic evolution from scribbling to picture-making. Children everywhere produce identical universal forms such as the circle, upright and diagonal cross, the rectangle and so forth, and with these symbols they express what they wish to say. Modifications of these basic forms provide a symbolic language as extensive as the experience of the child permits. For example: If the arms of the cross within the circle are extended beyond the circle's circumference, the basic form becomes a symbol for the sun; if the diameter is extended laterally and two lines are added to the base of the circle, it becomes a man; other modifications stand for a house, a vehicle or a tree.

At first, this symbolic language is monochromatic and geometric. Gradually colors are added. These have psychological significance and associations for the child at simple or deeper levels of unconscious symbolization. Color correspondences may be perceptually determined by colors prevailing in the environment. They may also convey deeper implications. For example, red may be associated with fire, anger or the setting sun; blue may signify water, sky or anything mysterious and deep; yellow may be associated with flowers, joy or the noonday sun; green may represent grass or growth. It is only when the child's emotional development has been subjected to overwhelming stress or deprivation that colors assume unusual or irrational significance.

Development of artistic activity in children, when uninhibited, parallels the development of perception and intellect. The drawings are symbolic of a specific mental unity that represents an interrelationship between concepts and symbol formation. The truth of this assertion is found in the common practice of using the findings of the Draw-A-Man Test as a maturational index. The evidence is abundant that the process of symbolic presentation is the birth of the child's mentality. Symbol formation, as part of this process, should be enriched if it is to generalize to areas of problem solving and task accomplishment.

Thought or the intellect arises where ideas have taken shape and possible conditions are imagined. What is imagined is symbolically formed since the most primitive function of symbols is to formulate experience and articulate ideas. Imagination is a specifically human form of conscious activity. It is not yet present in the consciousness of one-year-olds and is totally absent in animals. Consciousness is the ability to retain, compare and combine the myriad sensations that enter our brains as spontaneous images. These images are organized into perceptual patterns which then as meaningful structures give direction to our thoughts. Where there is mental apprehension and consciousness, visual order ensues. Thus the art experience is speculation from sensation to perception, culminating in the intellect.

As a child progresses from undirected scribbling to symbolic intent, he experiments with shapes, colors and placement patterns. Feelings awaken for design and space-relationships. Initially he presents the most essential, permanent and representative features as symbols of the object, because conceptual realism precedes objective representation or optical naturalism. A child is first concerned with expressing his own ideas and feelings. His drawings reveal the emotional relationship between his inner world and the world that surrounds him. He describes not only what he knows but what he feels and includes in his pictures that which has significance for him. Thus feeling helps to integrate perceiving and thinking. The mind appears to act like a screen retaining only concentrated data, simplified geometric symbols or the most distinctive characteristics of the figure or the object. For example in drawing the human figure, the child progresses through a tadpole or cephalopod stage where the limbs issue from the head. A man, for a deficit child of six or seven years, means mainly the self which needs a head for thinking and eating and two legs for locomotion. This head-feet picturization represents a primary projection of self and persists until the child becomes consciously aware of a man's actions, movements and body parts and represents him accordingly. As the child begins to feel himself part of the larger environment he begins to represent man with conscious consideration of size and proportion in relation to his surroundings. In healthy children this does not generally occur until approximately ten or twelve years of age.

Size relationships are also symbolically determined by the deficit child. Initially, hierarchy of size is intimately related to his concept of importance, strength and power. Visual experience becomes subject to multiple simultaneous stimulations such as superimpositions of profile and full-face, plan and elevation or inside-outside presentations. As children begin to draw, they are not constricted by the artificiality of fixed renaissance perspective. Rather, unbounded space is described by an amplified perspective with multiple viewpoints.

The depiction of space evolves from a subjective ego-bound

orientation with self as center of the universe. An important concept, the baseline, is a universal space schema that generally appears in the art expression of children between the ages of seven to nine years. As a space device it indicates a conscious relationship between self and environment. The baseline may symbolize the ground on which things stand or characterize the surface of a landscape. Objects in a plane are drawn perpendicularly to the baseline or folded over even though these objects may then appear to be drawn upside down. The pictorial intention of the child determines the direction of folding-over. The grouping of objects according to the intensity of experience is characteristic of the subjective sense of space. The space to which the child has access expands as he grows and the way he perceives space changes. As he begins to understand the existence of objects as separate from himself, he represents them in some logical relationship to each other and portrays objective space relationships. The baseline becomes a unified plane, relinquishing its symbolic nature only when objective visual orientation supervenes. Depth is then described by overlapping planes when the child is approximately twelve years of age. When this occurs, there is a structural correspondence between space, symbolic intent and plastic emphasis and the simultaneous grasp of seeing, thinking and feeling in relationship. The child presents and practices this for space-time relationship in his art expression.

The handicapped child's relationship to his environment as he searches for his own concepts may be expressed in his art attempts. As he develops these concepts through constant repetition, they become his schemata. For him they become modifiable expressive symbols for man and his surroundings. It is fortunate that the schemata are not rigid. They may be altered for value emphasis, expressive reasons or new intentions. The schema is no more than a formula image of the human figure or object that has been crystallized through repetition. Its individuality reflects the personality and psychological constitution of the child who creates it. The self-initiated repetitions which lead a child to schematize reflect his need for finding order and meaning in his environment. This structuring of his world through repetition of schemata provides the basis for future abstract thinking. The quantity and quality of repetition, it is suspected, are what distinguish the normal from the deficit child.

Spontaneous repetition helps the deficit child integrate his personal vision of the world and his place within it. Such repetition evokes insight for further action and stimulates disciplined imagination. It differs vastly from the stereotyped rigid and pathological repetition of the child who perseverates to evade change and reality. Meaningless repetition must be disrupted by extending the child's frame of reference, switching the medium he is working in and helping him overcome his anxiety about change. On the other hand, meaningful repetition promotes learning as the child assimilates concepts and experience through his own artistic activities.

The use of stereotyped processes such as prefabricated stencils, molds, copying or coloring books is discouraged except for purposes of assessing organic brain damage or perceptual dysfunction. These tend to deaden the imaginative spirit and dampen self-expression. They prevent the handicapped child from taking in experience and integrating it at his own level. Enforced controls discourage curiosity and inhibit spontaneous exploration of colors, shapes and new materials. They block symbolic and conceptual development. Such imitative methods induce rigidity, dependent thinking and inflexible approaches according to alien standards.

Necessary limits may be structured for the deficit child by imposing certain specifications. For example, limiting the number of colors and materials available to the child; specifying dimensions for the working surface; or setting up time limits for a project. The limits are imposed with the understanding that a deficit child needs the self-confidence, independence and satisfaction that come from his own efforts. Art experiences that allow a child to express personal concepts cultivate his senses. They promote critical tactile and visual stimulation that provokes the involvement necessary for symbol formation. They encourage emotional outlet and purposeful achievement. As the child manipulates with meaning and purpose to convey or fulfill his intent, he is engaged in active confrontation with reality. His art expression implies planning, experiencing and activity. A handicapped child who experiments with a variety of media in an encouraging play milieu tends to develop satisfactory coping mechanisms. He becomes open to experience and more disposed to try unorthodox solutions to problems. He is less constricted by rules and less inhibited by authority figures. He displays some of the essential characteristics of the competency cycle, namely, playfulness, curiosity and resourcefulness. In other words, he exhibits the type of flexible behavior that stimulates learning. His work becomes a safe and friendly place for him to experiment and learn. These art experiences initiate multisensory investigation of the physical world, and as information is assimilated by the child and projected into new symbolic forms this is reflected in his total growth pattern. Art experiences, it can validly be concluded, encourage imaginative exploration and offer endless opportunity for varied approaches, change and modification. They have an ongoing influence upon the sensory level of behavior and thus provide the handicapped with necessary inputs that compensate for their pathologically induced deprivations.

Drawings by a child with emotional and behavior problems, cerebral dysfunction, communication and personality disorders have long been used as diagnostic aids. Interpretation deals with the projection of his inner fears, fantasies, hostilities, body image and family relations. Yet little attention has been paid to the art process as a sensory-input path and the fact that it promotes effective symbol formation and conceptual growth. Self-expressive art experiences engage a handicapped child's interest and readiness to learn. Because it is a reality regulating activity which the child discovers through his own experimentation, and because it captures and exercises his senses, its potential use is worth further study and exploitation.

Levels of Symbolization

There is no need, however, to begin from scratch to study art as a form of sensory education. There have been some eminent experts on this issue, sometimes directly and sometimes tangentially. One who focused directly on the art experiences of children was Victor Lowenfeld, an art educator whose work spanned the forties and fifties. His conceptualization of the levels and sequences of this learning is closely akin to Piaget's steps towards cognition. Both offer confirmation of the developmental sequence of learning. The Bruner studies of the developmental phases of cognition were, of course, founded upon Piaget's work and therefore tend to advance our understanding of the multiple complexities that exist as behavior flows along the pathways of sensation, perception and intellect. Because compatibility exists between the work of Lowenfeld, Piaget and Bruner, some of their most relevant descriptions of the learning sequence are presented herewith as a guiding frame of reference for enriching of sensory experiences.

Lowenfeld dealt directly with the art experience of a child and focused on the sensory motor and kinesthetic nature of the activity. He drew inferences regarding visual imagery and cognition and was convinced that art could provide a child with rich and satisfying cues about reality. His definition of the sequential stages of symbol formation and aesthetic development were divided into six stages. The six stages were proposed as descriptions of the way the environment is ordered and suggest formulas for guiding behavior:

1. *Scribbling stage (two-four years): Dawn of symbol formation and self-expression. Corresponds to Piaget's sensory-motor and pre-operational stage.*

2. *Pre-schematic stage (four-seven years): Corresponds to first representative attempts. Conceptual realism is projected through universal symbols. Piaget's intuitive stage.*

3. *Schematic stage (seven-nine years): Corresponds to achievement of a form concept that is realized through self-devised schemas. These schemas are modifiable expressive symbols for man and his environment. Piaget's pre-conceptual stage.*

4. *Gang stage (nine-eleven years): Dawning realism is projected through representational symbols. Corresponds to Piaget's concrete operational stage.*

5. *Pseudo-naturalistic stage (eleven-thirteen years): Optical naturalism and realistic symbols replace conceptual realism. Corresponds to continuation of concrete operations.*

6. *Adolescence (thirteen to eighteen years): Period of crisis and decision includes either representational or personal art symbols. Corresponds to Piaget's stage of formal operations and deductive thought.*

Aesthetic Growth

The unique contribution of the Lowenfeld approach is its rich dependence upon the field of aesthetics. He adds a new dimension by including this realm of knowledge which is one usually disregarded by the psychologists and sociologists who study the developmental or socialization process. "Aesthetics" derives from the Greek word "aisthetikos" which means perceptive by feeling. It is that component of growth responsible for the change from chaos on the lower end of the continuum to harmonious organization and adjustment of the senses to the world on the upper end. This striving for higher forms of organization refers to greater integration of thinking, feeling and perceiving. It may start at any level, conscious or subconscious, and gains impetus in both the play and art experience of a child. As a vital aspect of knowledge it is crucially dependent on the child's curiosity and exploratory impulse as they act on the aesthetic field. The exploratory drive in its unique relationship to the aesthetic field thus serves both social and cultural forces of man and society.

Sir Herbert Read (1943) calls aesthetic education "the education of those senses upon which consciousness and ultimately intelligence and judgement of the human individual are based. It is only insofar as these senses are brought into harmonious and habitual relationship with the external world that an integrated personality is built up." While Lowenfeld attempted to identify aesthetic and symbolic schema, Piaget worked on relating conceptual and social schema in children's play. Both were attempting to explain how a child orders his environment and constructs his rules for proper behavior.

Levels of Cognition

Piaget found that there are clearly marked stages in the way children think as they seek to understand the world around them. These cognitive stages, he asserted, provide clues to the deficit child's behavior and performance.

During the first 18 months children learn primarily through practice play and sensory-motor experience. Impressions about the world are received through their senses and movement. Mobility may be thought of as a sixth sense often absent or inhibited in handicapped children. From the moment healthy children, on the other hand, attend to sensory impressions, they become active agents in their own learning.

From 18 months to four or five years, children go through a phase of intuitive thinking. Intuition is immediate perception or judgment without any conscious preparatory mental steps. During this time children come to fresh decisions about their world through exploratory trial-and-error problem solving. New discoveries alter many previously held ideas. Their inward model of concepts is constantly adjusting in accord with their experiences. This second stage is a period of intense feeling which naturally colors the preschool child's thinking and art expression. At this time the child projects conceptual realism in his drawings, reflecting the intensity of his experience.

From about the ages of four or five to seven or eight children reconstruct their conceptual framework through environmental interaction. Notable changes occur in their methods of sorting out ideas. Initially the child has no settled concepts about space, time, movement, speed or number. He cannot yet understand logical relations such as whole and part serial order.

During the pre-operational period children learn to master symbols in art, language, fantasy and play. Their symbolic world initially makes no distinction between internal motives and feelings, on the one hand, and external reality on the other. This has been noted in the child's symbol formations for man and space. At the pre-operational stage magical thinking still precedes concrete conceptualization. Children may believe that the sun, like themselves, must go to bed. Perception remains a stimulus to activity and objects dictate to the child what he must do. For example, a door demands to be opened or closed, a bell must be rung, steps must be climbed. Objects supply a motivating force to the very young child's actions and determine his behavior. Crude trial and error are the preschool child's means of problem solving, for he is not yet capable of complex mental acts.

By about seven or eight years most children have established reliable connections between inner conceptual models of their world and external reality. Sense and meaning supplement color and shape in the child's perception of his environment. This is the period of conservation when children have achieved some basically constant concepts about length and number and are able to interrelate systems and reason rationally.

The period of concrete operations extends from eight to fourteen years of age. A concrete operation is an action that may be carried out in one of two ways, either directly by manipulating objects as the preschool child does, or internally by manipulating symbols that represent things and relations. In concrete operations, data about the real world are transformed and organized internally in the child's mind to be used selectively in the solution of problems. Children at the stage of concrete operations are able to carry out trial and error internally in their heads. They are learning the mastery of classes, relations and numbers and how to reason about them as they develop internalized symbolic systems for structuring the immediately present reality of things they encounter.

The period of formal operations extends from twelve to fifteen years when the adolescent's concern is with mastery of thought. This period leads directly to adult reasoning. The adolescent is now able to think not only about the reality he sees but also about the potential. He can look at a situation, ponder alternative possibilities and select one that fits the case at hand. He is prepared for the logical operations of abstract thinking and is able to tolerate hypothetical propositions and engage in mental problem solving. Many deficit children, especially the mentally retarded and under-privileged, are unable to progress beyond the stage of concrete operations. This explains the importance of direct sensory experience as the basis for the handicapped child's problem solving and learning. Stable environmental concepts come only as the child's perceptions, actions and the information he gains from them begin to conform with outer reality and the way others perceive and act.

Art and Learning

Bruner stresses the fact that learning takes place most readily in an atmosphere of playfulness. A playful attitude toward reality leads directly to experimentation and testing alternate solutions to problems. Art is an ideal laboratory for growth and learning. As an adaptive goal-seeking process it promotes flexible attitudes and freedom from fixed patterns of conceptualization. Art expression involves the handicapped child in perceiving the world he lives in, reacting to what he sees and feels and interpreting his emotions, feelings and insights through a variety of sensory media. Art is thus a reinstatement of the senses and emotions to the actuality of experience.

The created visual image that a handicapped child makes with his hands and eyes together links the outer vision with the inner vision that shapes his felt experience into symbols. Art involves elements of curiosity and the opportunity for relaxed exploration and collection of data. Implicitly it has a constructive direction and is childhood play brought to purposeful results. A child's mind is constantly striving to make sense of the world in which he finds himself. Periods of activity alternate with periods of apparent quiescence as new experiences and ideas are assimilated. If ideas are accepted without being properly digested, there is lack of integration in thinking. This explains why rote learning means so little to the deficit child. Without integration of thought, learning does not generalize nor can the child transfer his means of problem solving from one area to another.

Bruner, Piaget and Lowenfeld stress the importance of a personal experience or sensation being the foundation for perception and thinking. This principle is especially true for handicapped children who need concrete experiences to understand how problems are solved. Their own actions are thereby transformed into integrated thinking as an inward process of concept-building relates to external reality. Providing handicapped children with activities that stimulate learning through their own efforts is a play concept in developing competency. Although learning is different at various stages of the child's development, it is always dependent on the evolution of competences which in turn must be grounded in the concrete of sensory experience.

CARL AND VICTOR

The value of art as a safe arena for the deficit child to practice risk-taking, problem solving and decision-making is demonstrated in the description of two Mexican-American brothers hospitalized for six months at a psychiatric institute. The children, Carl and Victor, were admitted because of emotional and learning problems associated with increasingly withdrawn behavior. One purpose of hospitalization was to determine the degree of mental retardation and its relationship to sensory and environmental deprivation. Carl was five and Victor eight years and four months old on admission. Although both children functioned fairly close to average norms in motor development and self-care skills, initially it was difficult to assess their other capabilities. Neither child would perform, answer questions or take chances by guessing. Nothing seemed to reassure them that error would be tolerated. Each child was studied separately but both exhibited identical behaviors. Carl and Victor were untestable by classical means since they were unable to attend verbal instructions. Their characteristic response was "I don't know" followed by subdued, fearful silence. They sat with lowered heads, would forget and suddenly burst out crying and run from the room. In play sessions each tended to isolate himself from group activities, particularly if supervised by an adult.

It was felt that a nonverbal approach such as art might decrease their inordinate fear of failure and increase their ability to take risks, experiment and solve problems. The goal was to increase their flexibility of response and sense of security which might then generalize to other areas of endeavor and thus encourage a receptiveness to learning. They needed opportunities for successful achievement which would thus increase their self-esteem and self-confidence.

Carl and Victor were included in a small art group with five other boys and girls who ranged in age up to thirteen years. A nine-year-old schizophrenic boy with minimal cerebral dysfunction was also in the group. His behavior was characterized by negativism, irrelevant talk, referring to himself as "he," and extreme anxiety at any extraneous noise such as a vacuum clearner or aeroplane flying overhead. Other group members were a six-year-old cerebral palsied girl retarded in speech, movement and general maturity and eleven- and thirteen-year-old girls who, as wards of the state, were declared "incorrigible." These girls exhibited acting out destructive behavior. There was also a hyperactive or hyperkinetic seven-year-old boy who constantly clung to adults but was belligerent to his peers.

The group met three times weekly for one-hour sessions. Emphasis was placed on sensory exploration with all types of art media, paints, clay, pastels, crayons, charcoal and inks, as well as every kind of natural, raw and manufactured material for collage and construction. The idea was conveyed to the children that in art there is no right or wrong, only different ways of seeing and experiencing the world of people and things. Independent choice and decision-making about materials, subject matter and colors were encouraged. Each session centered around some motivating idea to stimulate the children. Some of these ideas were: painting the kind of landscape or house the child would like to be in; painting a picture of traffic sounds; an experience or feeling the child had enjoyed; a circus or fair; what the child felt when looking out the window at winter or spring; painting a picture of happy or sad feelings and making a collage of rough and smooth, hard and soft. Other sessions involved painting large cardboard cartons with big brushes. These cartons the younger children later used in their imaginative play as cars, boats, a market and doll carriage. Many periods began with reading a story to activate the children's thinking. Some of these fairy tales, myths and fables became favorites that were asked for over and over again. Three periods centered on a joint project of creating a city from discarded milk cartons, clay, sponges and wood scraps. The children became scavengers collecting all kinds of materials in the hospital and on walks out of doors. These they transformed into buildings and bridges, freeways and train tracks. One session was spent painting to different types of music, another to creating imaginary animals and still another to building space designs.

As the sessions and their experiences progressed, Carl and Victor became less inhibited. They began to sing, dance and joke and appeared visibly relaxed. Carl was able to work cooperatively with others in a group project and no longer acted threatened by his peers. When left to himself he persisted in an activity he would ordinarily have been afraid to try because of fear of failing. Victor too became more flexible and seemed at ease. He began to take risks as he experimented with new media and symbol organizations. When encountering an unfamiliar art medium he would first manipulate it until his tactile impulses were satisfied. Then he would play with it and experiment to see what he could make it do. Finally as form consciousness developed he would use the material to fulfill his intended idea. As he dared to give form to his feelings and concepts in a nonthreatening play milieu, he began to take chances, solve problems and make independent decisions. After a while Victor was able to participate cooperatively with peers in playground games and a cooking group. He could tolerate fairly close adult supervision.

Both children showed improvement in their daily behavior. It was concluded that Carl and Victor needed freedom from the pressure of mastering formal learning tasks. They needed more time for their learning of those activities that other children learned in a faster and more spontaneous way. They needed opportunities to practice problem solving and decision-making in carefully engineered settings. The structured stimulation of their art and other play experiences helped them to achieve the success for which they had the potential. Although Victor was chronologically at Piaget's preconceptual stage, his drawings showed that he was still thinking intuitively and needed much practice play with concrete sensory inputs. The degree of mental retardation was minimal. Both children were suffering primarily from deprivation at sensory level and this in turn added to their perceptual and intellectual deficits. Because the sensory input that art provides can be the basis for symbol formation and hence perceptual and cognitive development, it is also a safe area for the deficit child to practice risk-taking, problem solving and decision-making so that he can arrive at better understanding of himself and his environment.

GAMES AS INTELLECTUAL INPUT

*And so young and old come forth to play on a
sunshine holiday*

—John Milton

In 1560, Peter Bruegel painted a famous genre picture of Flemish boys and girls boisterously engaged in "Children's Games." Bruegel depicts 75 different games in his pictorial catalogue of children's play. Most of the games in which the rustic toddlers-to-teenagers were delightedly absorbed are still played by contemporary youngsters. There is evidence that these very games were also played by the children of ancient Athens. Many identical childhood pastimes are also illustrated and described in a seventeenth-century French book, *Les Plaisirs des Enfants* (1657) by Jacques and Claudine Stella. These art treasures cause us to inquire what there is about children's games that transcends the centuries. What is it about this universal form of behavior that can be so vitally important to our deficit children? What should we know about play that might enable the deficit child to partake of this behavioral nourishment?

Healthy children, we know as part of our common wisdom, are irresistibly drawn to play as if by some powerful magnet. Through play they move forward dynamically to new spheres of activity. A two-year-old can be engaged busily for long periods of time at a kitchen sink or in a wading pool as he watches a leaf scoot round and round while he is deeply preoccupied in filling and emptying bottles. A four-year-old hobbles in Mother's high-heeled shoes, laughing and chattering to herself as she sets out cups pretending to have a tea party. Two nine-year-olds are engrossed for days building a tree house where food and comics are stored for secret meetings. Some ten-year-olds chase each other down the block tossing a ball as they attract others to their game.

Why are certain play experiences so absorbing to healthy children at different periods of growth? How does play behavior change as a child matures? Piaget describes three distinct stages in the evolution of children's games. These stages overlap each other and much of one is retained as the next emerges. We have noted how children at different periods of maturation have characteristic ways of viewing the world and explaining it to themselves. So too in their play development do children practice different skills which help them exercise their capacities as they learn about the world.

It is important to understand the indirect, sometimes nonlinear progression of the normal play stages if we are to ensure beneficial environments and experiences for handicapped children. Because a deficit child does not reach out through play to interact with others, the deliberately designed game experiences must be brought to him. Evoking new play behaviors at the moment of a child's readiness arouses interests that enhance learning. The game experience is provocative learning.

Game Stages

The earliest childhood games are the practice games of the prelinguistic child. These are the pleasurable exercise of developing skills as the baby shifts from enjoying bodily sensations and movement to manipulating objects. Physical activity is the noticeable characteristic of this period which extends from what Piaget calls sensory-motor experience and recognition of objects to intuitive thinking and judgment. During this time the playing child is learning to orient himself to the outer world as his environment expands from mother, to objects, to other people. Through play his interests become increasingly active as he probes to discover what his surroundings are like.

Symbolic games of the preschool child are those that he invents for himself. They are the work of the two-year-old and the seven-year-old child. They are generally played alone and involve much imitation and make-believe. As the child seeks to master emotional problems and symbols in fantasy and play, he is learning to establish relationships between his actions and experiences. Piaget views the imaginative stage of play development as assimilation of reality by means of symbolic make-believe. Action in the imaginative sphere and children's creation of imaginary situations in their play exemplify a fusion of affect, perception and activity.

During this imaginative play phase, children are frequently not certain about what of their experiences comes from inside themselves and what from outside. When their thinking is strongly colored by emotion they often imagine that their feelings are also shared by people and things around them. They believe that others are also part of themselves. This has been noted in the child's early symbol formations for man and space when his symbolic world makes little distinction between internal motives and feelings on the one hand, and external reality on the other. The young child's double process of projection and introjection is eventually rectified by additional experience. However, many emotionally disturbed children are unable to rectify this diffusion or separate their internal feelings from external reality. Influencing their actions through play experiences begins to change their patterns of behavior and thought.

In imaginative play and symbolic games the child's behavior begins to be guided by meaning rather than immediate perception. Objects lose their motivating power as the child acts independently of what he sees. Because certain brain-damaged children lack this ability to act independently of what they see, persistent repetition of experience in structured game situations helps them acquire rudiments of action severed from perception.

Imaginative play is an important stage in the child's process of mastery as he assimilates reality at his own level through imitation and symbolic make-believe. The objects used as symbols in deficit children's play supply clues to the concepts they are calling to mind. The more vague the symbols, the more easily are they adapted to the child's imaginative requirements. Raw materials, therefore, such as water, sand, paints and clay, as well as indestructible toys, blocks and household objects are far better than the miniature replicas of the adult world designed by commercial manufacturers.

In symbolic games children actively repeat what formerly they experienced passively in real life. Through active repetition they assimilate and gain mastery over the event. A child playing going-to-the-doctor weeps as they play patient, reliving and relieving his distress. Each repetition of the situation seems to strengthen his understanding of the former real-life experience. Manipulating the people and objects in a fantasy world created according to the deficit child's own needs is a prelude to coping with a reality that cannot be so easily controlled.

Symbolic play allows the child to experiment with life-tasks and social roles and teaches him rules of behavior. When a child plays mother and imagines her doll to be her child she is reflecting rules of maternal behavior in her actions even though this is not a game with rules formulated in advance. What the child is internalizing in real life becomes a rule of behavior in her play. Vygotsky, the Russian psychologist, suggests that every imaginary situation contains potential rules of behavior in some concealed form. The literature from the psychoanalytical field regards symbolic play as a defense against anxiety, a resource for control of mood and impulse and a vehicle for mastering conflicts. It is also considered by other applied fields as a valuable cognitive skill with personally and socially adaptive functions. Imaginative play, in any guise, is an important stage in the child's mental development as he integrates reality at his own level of understanding. There is considerable evidence to prove that children who show relatively little imaginative capacity also lack adequate planning and problem-solving abilities.

During this second period of play development, children's inward models of the world around them change from unsettled notions to reasonably constant ideas. Through imitation and ceaseless repetition in symbolic games children absorb the quality of things and people as they act out their feelings and experiences. From chugging like a train, creeping like a kitten or flapping arms and flying like an airplane, the child advances to making believe he is father going to work or mother taking care of baby. In his symbolic games he experiments with adult roles and rules of behavior that help him understand the social realities of life.

The third level of play involves games with rules played by the school age child with his peers from seven to twelve years of age. This period is often thought of as the gang stage because as healthy children achieve increased independence from adults, they increasingly enjoy playing with their peers. During this stage children begin to appreciate the need for rules and regulations as they come to realize that rules are based on mutual consent and can therefore be altered.

In their desire to be like each other, children at this time often make up their own secret rules and chants which are insisted upon with utmost rigor. There are gang chants to patch up quarrels, chants of ostracism and inclusion, and chants that scorn those who show indifference to conforming. Iona and Peter Opie have collected scores of chants and children's games over some 25 years of studying the complex folklore and culture of childhood. The Opies have compiled many of the special rites, codes and beliefs that children have evolved for themselves, out of sight of grownups, in two valuable resource books, *The Lore and Language of School Children* (1959) and *Children's Games in Street and Playground* (1969). Their work is rich in the description of how the gang stage functions as an innate movement of child development towards community loyalties. The impulse to work with others, so clearly defined in gang play, should be fostered at this time by providing the child with increased responsibility in his home, school and community.

Games with rules are social games that involve regulations imposed by the group for violation of rules. They deal with interactional problems in which the behavior of others must be taken into account. In kickball or monopoly, for example, the playing child must know the roles of the other players as well as his own role. He must develop the ability to take the role of the other in order to anticipate what will happen next and adjust his behavior accordingly. Thus the child begins to assess his own abilities against those of others and in so doing he develops his self-image and feelings of identity. Games are self-motivating and form an end in themselves. The reward or payoff for the child is the pleasurable experience of the activity itself.

Piaget distinguishes what he calls two moralities in the child, or two distinct sources for rules of behavior. The first morality is externally imposed upon the child by adults. Mother, for example, teaches him not to touch other people's things. The second morality arises from mutual collaboration between child and adult or between children themselves. These latter are rules which the child himself participates in establishing. When the child tells himself "I must behave as the 'It' person in 'Follow the Leader' or 'Red Light' " he is imposing his own rules of self-restraint and self-determination as he exercises control over other players. In other words, he is disciplining himself, for these are internal rules which prevent him from acting out on immediate impulse. Through self-discipline the child learns to master his behavior and regulate his conduct in such a way that he is able to follow first the rules of the game and eventually some rule of life. In play, then, the child learns to renounce his impulses as he coordinates his acts of behavior to the rules of the game. As he masters his behavior he leans to submit it to a given task. This learning is not only useful, it is essential for the deficit child. Through games with rules, handicapped children are helped to achieve social-interaction, self-determination, a sense of responsibility and cooperation.

During this third level of games with rules, children are busy testing in concrete situations their now increasingly reliable inner concepts of the world as they add fresh information constantly. But even at this time healthy children are not yet able to engage in prolonged abstract reasoning. They must still solve problems concretely through their play experiences.

If the game stages are understood as play opportunities for the handicapped child, intervention can be planned that will be appropriate to the child's capacities and maturity level. The use of games under the conditions of understanding developmental sequence serves to reduce the deficit child's pressure of impulses and activates incentives for learning. As we interject play experiences that neither overstimulate nor underestimate the child's potentials, his understanding of the physical and social realities of life develops. Through games, the handicapped child learns in a safe way that the outcomes of various activities are not so extreme as he had either hoped or feared. Limits are thus placed on the anticipated consequences of an activity. As the child absorbs the game attitude, which is a sense of playfulness constrained by a set of rules, he senses that the consequences are limited because of rules that govern the procedure, be it "Looby Loo," baseball or twenty questions. In the safe arena of play, he begins to risk decisions and experiment as he interacts with others.

Play and Decision-Making

While games may be a superb vehicle to entice a child to interact with his environment, they are also practical experiences in trial and error risk-taking and decision-making.

The healthy child engages in trial-and-error learning, early in his development. He wants to find out whether he can do something, fit boxes together, for example, so he tries this way and that until he finds a way that works. Trial-and-error learning is the basis for later ingenious persevering work in consciously finding the solutions to problems. As children investigate, information is gained and decisions are being made.

The one-year-old is making decisions constantly about what pleases or displeases those around him. If he screams, he is generally not given what he wants. When he smiles he usually gets it. When children are surrounded with consistent behavior they learn more rapidly. They do not waste time in wrong decisions which must later be unlearned.

There is a deep inner drive to repetition that leads children to perform certain actions and experiments over and over again as they gain in understanding. This repetition not only leads to success in their learning by trial and error, it also transfers knowledge from the immediate setting to other environments. In setting up sequences of play activities for the handicapped child, operationally speaking, every task requires giving impetus to these things: getting started; maintenance of novelty and new interests to keep it going; alternatives to be tried out and tested; and clear terminus built into it to keep it from being random.

To be just right, a task should be neither so familiar nor so uncertain that it arouses confusion and anxiety. As a handicapped child plays at the carefully constructed but just right task, his interests are spontaneously engaged in the very act of playing. This type of spontaneous attention is fundamental to all learning. When a child's actions are influenced through problem-solving experiences, his patterns of thought and behavior are also affected.

When a child is able to assume a playful attitude, he learns that outcomes of various activities are in reality not so extreme as he anticipated. In games like "Run Fox Run" or checkers, he learns that the consequences are limited by the rules of the game. As play increases, impulse control and fear recede and intrinsic learning begins. This is learning where the self-reward inheres in the process of doing things for pleasure. Intrinsic learning provides its own reward. It represents the beginnings of a conflict-free sphere of the ego which is characterized by curiosity and competence-seeking. Learning that is dominated solely by extrinsic rewards, such as praise and prizes or punishment, becomes specific to the requirements of one particular task. On the other hand, intrinsic learning generalizes to many areas of task accomplishment.

A deficit child's interest and readiness to learn increase through the discoveries he makes through his own experimental activity. Problem-solving behavior involves curiosity, flexibility and the courage to risk. Such behavior fortifies a child's capacity to cope and adapt and hence live comfortably with changing self and changing world. Deficit children need the opportunity to make the right decisions in their play. The problems they must solve become increasingly complex—from fitting boxes together to learning to sort shapes and classify objects. With increasing numbers of successes, handicapped children stole valuable information for future problem solving. Active learning accumulates for future references as the child discovers solutions by a process of successive decisions in concrete play experiences.

When adults do things for the child or give him answers before he has had the chance to find out for himself, the child learns passively. On the other hand, as a child tests out solutions and discovers answers for himself, he learns actively. In play, the handicapped child becomes an active agent in solving his own problems. Problem solving requires the exploration of alternatives. Like any other child, a deficit child, in trying to push a wagon through an opening that is too narrow, quickly discovers that he must either widen the opening or find another way around it.

Problem-Solving and Coping

Bruner describes three conditions that induce problem-solving and coping behavior. The child needs a task that will gain and hold his interests. He needs models of exploratory older children or adults. Finally, he needs time for quiet reflection and the opportunity to pace himself. These are good criteria to follow in structuring deficit children's play experiences.

The human tendency toward mastery of skill is present in the young child's play and fascination with games and puzzles. Evidence of mastery is seen in his need to solve problems. The 16-month-old child who never tires of taking a ball-point pen from daddy's pocket, removing the top and fitting it back together again, is problem-solving. The little girl pretending tea party is mastering simple problems of arithmetic as she counts out cups and saucers, plates and spoons. She is also mastering the task of becoming a woman as she practices mother's way of walking, talking and working. She becomes mother by imitation before identification takes place.

Unless certain basic skills are mastered by deficit children, more elaborate skills become increasingly out of reach. The gap may be reinforced to irreversibility by the handicapped child's sense of defeat unless an outside source intercedes and provides necessary inputs and tutoring. A mentally retarded child begins to feel effects on his environment in such a simple game as switching the lamp on and off time and again. As the child senses his effect on the environment, he feels that he makes a difference. The best games with young children flow easily and naturally from the situation of the moment. The spirit behind such games, like that of all play, should be joy, fun and exuberance. Basic skill practice begins as a child counts "One, two, button my shoe . . ." or disciplines himself to keep in step and clap in time with a rhythmic song. The feeling of belonging and the element of sharing is evoked in circle games and singing songs together. Repetition and imitation keep the learning going.

Games help a deficit child understand cause and effect and encourage trial and error. The try-out, correction and revision process is most apparent in games of imitation. Brain-damaged children will imitate, compare and correct at a concrete physical level while engaged in games like "Did you ever see a Lassie go this way and that . . ." or "Simon Says." The child's ability to think, speak and act is coordinated as words supplement actions. Children want to get things right and will continue trying until they do. Action songs and games help retarded children to carry out imitative acts at a physical level that they cannot carry out mentally in imagination.

Handicapped children, like all children, enjoy playing at household chores like washing, sweeping and tidying up. These experiences bring them greater understanding of what adults do. When dishes are being washed the child wants to help. When mother is cooking he wants to cook. If a child wants to set the table, the wise adult will allow him to try, even though it may take more time and cause damage. Early obstruction of the child's efforts at his moment of readiness leads to frustration and feelings of ineffectiveness. The deficit child needs special encouragement in independence at every juncture. Washing dishes is a form of water play, tidying is a form of pattern-making. Given a chance to spring into action at the moment of readiness, deficit children move forward to new stages of competence and responsibility. Learning happens as behavior is modified by experience. Adaptation is generalized as mastered skills are applied to new situations. But the absorbing business of practicing new skills must persist for a long time before it is thoroughly ingrained in the deficit child.

Games and Skill-Building

As children fit, fill and pull, the fun is more and more in the doing. It becomes self-evident that play, with its emphasis on action, trial and error and repetition is learning. Gradually children begin to enjoy what they have achieved. Not only the filling but the full pail, not only the stacking of blocks but the towering skyscraper give pleasure. As the child's delight lies more and more in the completed task, his actions are governed by the instinct to master. This instinct affords the deficit child a growing feeling of competence.

The instinct to master may also be thought of as an instinct for workmanship. This is noticeable as we watch the loving care with which a child smooths off a sand-cake or pats and shapes a mud pie. Children strive to make things successfully to satisfy themselves.

In play activities deficit children of any age become grounded in mathematics, physics and language as they fill and empty pails or pitch and toss a ball. Unconsciously they calculate, estimate, and test gravity, weight, capacity and volume. Playful investigation of the environment entails concrete problem-solving. Through solving problems in play, deficit children begin to think from soundly constructed inward models based on reliable concepts of the real world. After such concrete experiments in play, future reasoning is not so likely to collapse in the face of external reality.

The will to learn is an intrinsic motive, finding both its source and reward in its own exercise. Deficit children must have the will to learn aroused through play and games. Only then will they build serviceable models of what the world is and what it can be.

In *Thinking Is Child's Play*, Evelyn Sharp, a teacher of mathematics, illustrates many brain-sharpening games to be played with preschool children. Her games can also be used to the advantage of deficit children who need mental as well as physical and social stimulation. She describes the actions whereby concepts of permanent objects, of representation, enduring characteristics of quantity, of number and conservation, emerge slowly. Her suggestions for games are based on the belief that concepts are constructed layer upon layer and are based upon related perceptual experiences which are reorganized and assimilated with more familiar ones.

The expansion of concepts involves: (1) choice and making discriminations between belonging or not belonging to a particular class, set or category; (2) decisions to select appropriate instances and reject inappropriate ones; and (3) assimilation or internalizing and integrating the new with previous related learnings. These abilities result in a generalization or abstraction which forms the child's current conceptual level.

Manipulating concrete materials for computing and measuring in a game situation leads the child to use his previous background of experience as he makes more precise discriminations and forms more adequate generalizations. Children can be taught to count by rote but an understanding of number develops only from personal experience with manipulative materials. As a child develops number concepts through play, his encounters with size, shape and weight form the basis for more advanced mathematical understanding and problem-solving.

The 40 games that Sharp introduces focus on the logical operations of classification and seriation which underlie the concept of number and all types of analytical thinking and problem solving. Experience in classification requires the ability to recognize likenesses and difference between objects and to group them accordingly. Seriation is based on comparison and entails arranging objects in a series according to some specified order or characteristic such as size. These games could very well provide a handicapped child with different levels of visual and tactile experience in many areas and provide concrete exercise for the principles proposed by both Piaget and Bruner.

Sharp assumes that the mind functions to build into its symbol formation process elements that implement both the ability to qualify and quantify. We would also augment her work with the Lowenfeld perspective drawn from the field of aesthetics. Art qualifies and enriches meaning and description as it helps the child build concepts about self, time, space and distance. The integrated behavior of play quantifies and measures as the child investigates number, size and quantity in his games and his environment. The blend of all these elements provides an important source of understanding how to influence the learning capacity of handicapped children.

A PLAY AGENDA

The circumscribed existence of deficit children can be expanded beyond their deprivations and disabilities by application of art and game experiences. A play agenda is constructed to apply this proposition. The agenda is constructed to encompass three levels of learning and experience: the first level evokes interaction with the environment; the second level promotes mastery of symbols in art experiences and play; the third level develops risk-taking, problem-solving and decision-making abilities.

Multihandicapped children in manipulating their physical and social surroundings actively develop basic skills and symbolic modes of representing and assimilating reality. Effective patterns of habit-structures and task-accomplishment lead to improved coping that influence the deficit child's behavior, thinking and performance. The play agenda is proposed as a guide to ensure that the sensory, perceptual and intellectual development of behavior is exercised in a balanced manner.

Art and games are suggested for the attainment of each learning level and are proposed as catalysts for evoking certain behaviors in a deficit child. The hypotheses of the agenda are that the environments, the play events and experiences of the child that optimize learning will influence positively the thinking, feeling and doing of a deficit child; and that achievements learned in play may later be applied "for real" in school and work.

Specifications for Environment

1. Environments that carefully consider a child's capabilities will neither overstimulate nor underestimate his potential capacities. Indoor and outdoor environments that are adjusted to the child's physical and mental powers will assure a good match between his abilities, interests and environmental expectations. This means that not only chairs, tables and play equipment are to be adjusted to children's size and developmental level, but the complexity of the task should evoke both action and pleasure. Play equipment should adjust to more than one purpose, more than one child and more than one developmental level. It should encourage action that can be completed in a relatively short time for distractible children

with limited attention span as well as challenge the ingenuity and perseverance of those with increased ability to concentrate. Play materials such as blocks or paints and a series of related toys like Kiddie Kar, tricycle and bicycle, encourage graduated use for developing minds and bodies.

2. Environments within hospitals, homes, schools and playgrounds that provide substantial sensory-cultural enrichment arouse curiosity and stimulate investigation as children gain competence for living in the world. Such environments will incorporate visual stimuli, accessible toys that lend themselves to being used in many different ways, raw materials like sand, water, paints and clay, physical objects and playground equipment that engage a child's senses and activate his interests.

3. Environments that include play materials and activities that meet the requirements of children at different cognitive, kinesthetic and play stages foster growth and learning. Such play materials and activities would include:

A. At the Sensory-Motor Stage of Practice Play:
   Toys that attract the eye, ear, senses and muscles as they challenge growing powers.

   (1) Toys that appeal to the senses and muscles:
       soft toys for feeling, squeezing and throwing
       large rubber or plastic blocks that rattle or tinkle
       washable unbreakable dolls
       squeaky cuddly toy animals
       wrist bells
       sandpile with bucket, scoop, and other sand toys
       wading pool with containers, tumblers and other
         objects to fill, empty and float
       rocking chair, rocking horse
       swings, see saw, slide

   (2) Toys that challenge growing powers:
       nests of hollow blocks or boxes to pull apart and put
         together, to pile up, convey and drag
       empty containers with removable lids to take off and
         put on
       cartons or boxes to climb upon or into, hollow barrel
         to crawl through

large soft ball to push, lie on or roll over

toys with openings of different shapes and sizes to
  receive equivalent blocks of varied shapes

hammer boards, peg boards

large "ride-'em" toys, tractor, locomotive, etc. for
  straddling

wagon or truck to ride in

picture books, nursery rhymes, jingles to look at and
  listen to

large crayons for scribbling

B. At Symbolic, Imaginative Play Stage:
Toys and games for strengthening large muscles, for
stretching the mind and activating problem-solving, for
make-believe, pretending and practicing grownup role
behavior, for creating and expressing feelings and ideas and
practicing symbol formations.

(1) Toys that strengthen large muscles:
    steps for climbing
    kiddie kar
    push-and-pull toys
    large balls   -
    bean bags
    simple rolling and throwing games
    large hollow blocks
    ten pins
    mallet with peg set

(2) Toys for stretching the mind and activating problem-
solving:
    put-together trains, trucks, boats, etc.
    wooden inlay puzzles
    nests of blocks, colored cone
    colored wooden beads of different sizes for stringing
    lock with key
    magnet, magnifying glass, mirror
    water-play toys, bubble set
    abacus, toy cash register
    aquarium, terrarium
    view master with slides, filmstrips
    globe of the world

books with simple stories, poems, fairy tales, fables, etc.

(3) Toys for make-believe, pretending and practicing grownup roles:

washable unbreakable dolls that can be dressed and undressed

housekeeping equipment of all sorts including cooking, laundering, gardening, cleaning

toy tea set

costume box for dressing up with hats, shoes, purses, tie, scarves, gloves, etc.

doll house and furniture

space hat

toy luggage

small family figures

farm, zoo and animal sets

transportation toys: boats, trucks, planes, cars, trains, etc.

steering wheel

ride-a-stick horse

sheet or blanket for play tent

large cartons for making stores, houses, schools, stations, theatres and for climbing into

puppets

(4) Toys for creating, expressing feelings and ideas and practicing symbol formation:

crayons, colored chalks, pastels

thick poster, tempera and finger paints

large bristle and sable brushes with short handles

large sheets of varied textured papers

clay, play-dough

materials for collage and constructions

blunt scissors and paste

hammer, nails, soft wood

record player and all types of music to sing, dance, clap, march, and listen to

percussion instruments to play, tom tom, bells, drum, triangle, cymbals, gourd tone block

C. For Children Who Are Learning To Play Games With Rules: Activities, materials and games that elicit risk-taking, decision-making, skill-building and social interaction as well as all those activities previously listed.

(1) Toys, games and apparatus for developing skills, teamwork, and group participation:
bicycle, skates
baseball, bat, gloves
basketball, shuffleboard, table tennis, dodgeball equipment
camping equipment, etc.

(2) Materials for creating, for practicing risk-taking and decision-making and for building confidence and self-esteem:
clay, paints, pastels, colored inks
materials for collage, constructions, space mobiles, paper sculptures, etc.
craft sets
jewelry-making and bead work equipment
sewing, embroidering, knitting and crocheting equipment
materials for making doll clothes
tools, lumber and wheels for making vehicles boys can drive
models for making rockets, planes, trucks, ships
camera
musical instruments
harmonica
record player

(3) Materials for stretching the mind:
magnet, magnifying glass, binoculars
kite
meter stick, tape-measure (steel and cloth), protractor, compass
three-minute egg glass
scales
models of geometric figures
hobby sets
jigsaw puzzles

> typewriter
> chess, dominoes, checkers, parchesi
> anagrams, lotto, word games
> games of chance
> slides, films, filmstrips
> books, some to read, some for listening to
> share and tell sessions
> games that present the basis for concepts of number, measurement and mathematical understanding (see Sharp, *Thinking is Child's Play*)
> games that develop language and communication skills (see Hurwitz and Goddard, *Games to Improve your Child's English*)
> art games that encourage flexibility, risk-taking and decision-making (see D'Amico, *Art for the Family*)

(4) Environments that offer opportunities for success evoke confidence and self-esteem. Permitting and rewarding exploratory problem-solving behavior will stimulate further experimental activity. Appreciating a child's efforts will help him build reliable inward models of the world that are related to outer reality. Pacing of rewards should gradually shift from extrinsic rewards of praise and prizes for successful efforts to the intrinsic rewards of solving a problem for oneself. Immediate rewards for performance must eventually transfer to deferred satisfaction attained through task-accomplishment. ·

(5) Environments that include models of exploratory adults and older children to imitate and learn from encourage adoption of desired behaviors by handicapped children. Meaningful contacts with accepting responsive adults will stimulate action, interaction and initiative. Well-informed adults are sensitive to children's changing needs, incentives and moments of readiness. They will neither expect things too soon, which will confuse and distress a child, nor will they miss the moment of a child's readiness which may forfeit opportunity for all time and make learning difficult at a later stage. Supplying the material,

experiences and appreciation adapts the environment so that a child can come to terms with his own strong fears and feelings.

(6) Environments that are structured by consistency and pervaded by a spirit of playfulness encourage adaptation as children begin to understand what is expected from them and what to expect from the environment. This enables them to make decisions that do not have to be unlearned.

(7) Environments that structure time and space help children understand these concepts as they build habit structures for dealing with such realities. The recurrent regularity of days that are patterned with a balanced routine of chores, play, work, rest and relaxation assist handicapped children to gain the internal capacity to make use of time and comprehend its sequences. With this capacity they are better able to accept and adjust to change. Time provisions should be made for active group games as well as for periods of quiet reflective assimilation. Space provisions should be made for indoor and outdoor activities.

Specifications for Experiences

1. Play experiences that correspond as closely as possible to the normal play stages of healthy children are most beneficial to deficit children. However, consideration must be given to the child's current needs and abilities.

2. Sequences of play activities that alternate group experience with periods set aside for solitary play with materials and ideas allow the child to proceed at his own tempo as he practices basic skills and gains understanding of his environment. Group experiences, on the other hand, will evoke necessary imitation, social interaction, cooperation and competition. A child's sense of self and personal awareness often develops in relation to his awareness of others. Discouragement may be avoided when frustrating experiences are rapidly adjusted and when "losers" in a game, for example, are given a chance to redeem themselves quickly. Letting other children help the loser

increases their feeling of security and personal worth. Shared experiences will solidify feelings of companionship and pleasurable learning. What is agreeably learned is long remembered.

3. Art experiences with sensory media and imaginative play activities enhance a child's capacity for adaptive emotional behavior. Such experiences encourage practice in symbol formations and integration of inner and outer reality. The child's pictorial and perceptual development may be stifled when adults ask a child "What is it?" A child will spontaneously tell you what his drawings mean when he is ready to. Avoid showing a young child how to draw a person or object. Instead allow him to make the exciting discovery that his scribbles look like a man or animal for himself.

4. Play experiences that provide opportunities for repetition, imitation and problem-solving promote learning and help the deficit child find order and meaning in his environment. Repetition enables a child to master basic skills as he symbolically gains understanding of past experiences. Thus he digests learning which then transfers to other areas. Play actions performed over and over again lead to success through trial and error learning and provide the groundwork for future perseverance in problem-solving.

Imitation in group action songs helps children learn body parts, discipline and group awareness. Imitating mother bathing the baby for example, in imaginative play, allows the child to rehearse adult social roles and rule-bound behavior.

Problem-solving involved in such simple games as taking things apart and fitting them together again or mixing colors will help children understand the qualitative and quantitative aspects of experience as they confront reality based obstacles which must be overcome. Problem-solving will elicit flexibility and the courage to risk as children test alternative methods of solution.

5. Games with rules of graduated difficulty encourage children to practice the discipline of self-restraint and control of immediate impulse as they submit their behavior to a given task. Opportunity to try out different roles within the game, the "it" person or the follower, for example, allows practice in leadership and group membership.

6. Experiences that evoke the instinct for workmanship and a sense of pleasure in mastering things for their own sake, as in activities like making sand-castles, mud pies, painting, sculpting, constructing and model building enable handicapped children to savor intrinsic satisfaction and reward. Cooperation and attention span increase in proportion to the pleasure and sense of achievement derived from the experience.

7. Motivation stimuli keyed to the child's interests and developmental level as well as models of enthusiastic adults are devices that get a play experience started. Novelty introduced at crucial junctures maintains interest and further incentive for continued participation. A clearly defined terminus will avoid boredom and end a play experience before the satiation point is reached.

8. Variables to be aware of in play experiences are:

   A. The degree and range of required rules and the form and source of personal or impersonal controls exercised over the child participant. Leapfrog, for example, involves simple rules as opposed to chess which is governed by a complex set of procedures. The "it" person exercises low control in "Hide and Seek" and high control in "Follow the Leader," "Red Light" or "Simon Says."

   B. The provisions for learning, thinking, repetition and imitation involve the competence or minimum level of ability required to participate in a game. For example, group singing and dodge-ball require low-level beginning competence, whereas chess or the pitcher's role in baseball require fairly well-developed skill.

   C. The provisions for verbal or nonverbal interactiveness. For example, a child absorbed in his own painting or model-building interacts minimally whereas participation in a group mural project, square dance or team sport requires increased communication and group interaction.

   D. The provisions for reward structure: intrinsic rewards inhere in creative activities like painting or sculpting whereas group games or team sports involve extrinsic rewards in the form of praise or prizes for excelling or improving skills.

9. Individual and group variables to be cognizant of are:

A. The child's readiness, capability and motivation at the current moment: children with low motivation and capability may be lured into activities whose rewards are immediate and abundant, for example, making a necklace of beads, which will be noticed and admired by others. The more complex the activity the higher the child's motivation must be to ensure its successful conclusion.

B. The degree of self-control available to the child at a given time influences play activities—for example, the hyperactive child may need a structured solitary play experience to control his behavior whereas the withdrawn lethargic child may need incentives to draw him into a game with an adult or peer.

C. The degree of group cohesion, composition and mood, influence the course of play experience—that is, for a group of deficit children with little solidarity, parallel activities may be preferable to those that require much interaction or interdependence.

D. Timing and sequences of play experiences are important variables to control. For example, large group activities are often not successful first thing in the morning when individual egos are too fragmented and shaky to be exposed to interactional games. Body contact sports before bedtime may induce undesirable aggressive play that overstimulates children and prevents relaxation.

Specifications for Activities that Promote
Risk-Taking and Decision-Making Abilities

1. Art activities that encourage experimentation with numerous solutions to a problem involve children in risk-taking and decision-making. Because there are no "right" answers and any number of possible solutions or outcomes are correct in painting, drawing and sculpting, art is a safe arena for the deficit child to practice decision-making behavior. Through such behavior the child will learn to adjust to new situations. When for example, the paint runs or spills onto unintended

areas of their work, children can be helped to take advantage of the unexpected by shifting ideas and coming up with new solutions and decisions. The very process of painting requires constant revisions and changing viewpoints as the work progresses. Using a box of scrap materials to make a picture of "Daddy" today and using the same materials tomorrow to make a feeling and seeing collage of toys the child enjoys, develops flexible and imaginative thinking as well as constant decision-making about shapes, sizes, colors, textures and placement patterns.

2. Table games in which errors and wrong decisions are not irreversible will promote risk-taking and decision-making. As the child comes to realize that scorepoints can be made-up on the next move or won again in a return match, he becomes less fearful and anxious about choice. A deficit child's anxiety about failure and uncertainty may be dissipated by the game attitude which is constrained by a sense of rules and demands no real-life consequences.

3. Activities that allow alternative solutions to problems and adults who refrain from making a child's choices encourage decision-making and active learning. Such learning remains with the child for future reference On the other hand, when a child's decisions are made for him he becomes dependent and learns passively as his insecurity increases. Encouraging handicapped children in independent decision-making, unless unsafe or detrimental to their treatment, will fortify their self-esteem and competence. Allowing them to choose stories, music, art and play materials, games, etc., and abiding by their choices whenever possible will encourage children to become active agents in their own learning.

4. Activities like imaginative play, painting, drama, dance and creative writing allow children to revise and alter many previously held wrong decisions about themselves and the world which they inevitably make in the course of conceptual development. As they rectify decisions they begin to understand that decisions are not irreversible and may be changed with new experiences and learning.

5. Activities that are dependent upon group choice, such as the subject matter for a mural painting, a story to be read aloud or

the destination for a group excursion, help handicapped children learn the dynamics of group decision-making and the manner in which cooperation and consensus can be reached.

6. Any play activity or game that provides experience in success promotes feelings of confidence and competence in handi-capped children, and builds a framework of security from which the child draws courage and flexibility for his daily living.

SUMMARY

This chapter has explored the vital role that play exerts, through childhood art experiences and games, on the deficit child's behavior, thinking and performance. As play promotes inputs to the major behavioral systems of the sensory, perceptual and intellectual pathways, handicapped children begin to acquire rudimentary skills that expand their marginal level of daily living.

Sensation is the critical input to perception. As sensation is organized in the form of symbols it casts perception as the input mechanism for all the problem-solving, decision-making skills of the intellect.

When a breakdown or deprivations are suffered at one level of input experience, the sensory, for example, deficits accrue that are compounded at all subsequent interlocking output levels of per-ception and cognition. This stumbling-block of experience then interrupts the self transforming trajectory cycle of learning com-petence and should be the prime focus for intervention and treatment.

A play agenda is proposed as a guide to skillful intervention. Such intervention will ensure that the sensory, perceptual and intellectual development of behavior is exercised in a balanced manner. It is based on the hypothesis that environments, play experiences and activities that optimize learning will influence positively the thinking, feeling and doing of a deficit child. Those achievements learned in play may later be applied "for real" in school and work. Specifica-tions are set up for environments, experiences and activities that: promote interaction with the environment; foster mastery of symbols in art experiences and play; and develop risk-taking, problem-solving and decision-making abilities.

Relevant descriptions of the learning sequence of symbolization, cognition and game stages as presented by Lowenfeld, Piaget and Bruner are presented as a guiding frame of reference for enriching sensory experiences and provocative learning.

Intervention considers not only a deficit child's growth needs but also his capacities and current level of maturity. It requires continuous engineering of experiences and environments to integrate the sensory, perceptual and intellectual pathways.

Providing handicapped children with activities that stimulate learning is a play concept in developing competences. Although learning is different at various stages of development it is always contingent upon the evolution of competences which must in turn be grounded in the concrete of sensory experiences.

Handicapped children have the right to develop their potentials to the fullest possible extent. It is society's responsibility to provide that opportunity.

Because deficit children may be unable to function in play unassisted they are often overlooked as candidates for activities that healthy children engage in spontaneously. Yet art and games assist the handicapped in acquiring skills that foster security and competence for daily living. Structured play experiences are therefore advocated for crucial intervention in the treatment of deficit children.

REFERENCES

BERLYNE, D. E. (1960) Conflict Arousal and Curiosity. New York: McGraw-Hill.

BRUNER, J. S. (1967) On Knowing. New York: Atheneum.

––– (1964) Toward a Theory of Instruction. Cambridge: Harvard Univ. Press.

––– (1963) The Process of Education. New York: Vintage.

D'AMICO, V., F. WILSON and M. MASER (1954) Art for the Family. New York: Museum of Modern Art.

FLOREY, L. (1971) "An approach to play and play development." American J. of Occupational Therapy 25 (6): 275-280.

HURWITZ, A. and A. GODDARD (1969) Games to Improve Your Child's English. New York: Simon & Schuster.

KEPES, C. [ed.] (1960) The Visual Arts Today. Middletown: Wesleyan Univ. Press.

LOWENFELD, V. and L. BRITTAIN (1964) Creative and Mental Growth. New York: Macmillan.

OPIE, P. and I. OPIE (1969) Children's Games in Street and Playground. Oxford: Clarendon Press.

––– (1959) The Lore and Language of School Children. Oxford: Clarendon Press.

PIAGET, J. (1962) Play, Dreams and Imitation in Childhood. New York: Norton.

——— (1959) Judgement and Reasoning in the Child. Paterson: Littlefield, Adams.

PICKARD, P. (1965) The Activity of Children. London: Longmans, Green.

READ, Sir H. (1966) "Art as a unifying principle in education, ' in H. Lewis (ed.) Child Art: The Beginning of Self Affirmation. Berkeley: Diablo Press.

SHARP, E. (1970) Thinking is Child's Play. New York: Avon Books.

SMITH, M. B. (1968) "Competence and socialization," in J. Clausen (ed.) Socialization and Society. Boston: Little, Brown.

SOLOMON, P. [ed.] (1961) Sensory Deprivation, A Symposium. Cambridge, Mass.: Harvard University.

STELLA, J. and C. STELLA (1969) Games and Pastimes of Childhood. Reprint of the 1657 "Les Jeux et Plaisirs de L'Enfance." New York: Dover.

THOMAS, A. (1968) "Variations in temperament as a factor generating psychological deprivation." Perspectives on Human Deprivation, Biological, Psychological, and Sociological. Washington: Department of Health, Education, and Welfare.

CHAPTER 5

PLAY AS A PRESCRIPTION

Nancy Takata

DEVELOPMENT AND HISTORY

In many obvious yet subtle ways development is history. A selective combination of data and historical techniques could emphasize a number of mutual ideas: timeness, continuity and sequence as well as context and environment.

The term development refers to the emerging and expanding capacities of the individual for greater facility in overall functioning. The phenomenon of development involves interaction between maturational qualities and resultant changes that occur in behavior from experience with the environment. Development is, for the most part, a continuous process which proceeds sequentially. The continuity is not necessarily a smooth one. It is subject to peaks and plateaus. The order unfolds in step-by-step fashion and moves from the simple to the complex or from a state of undifferentiatedness to differentiatedness. Each succeeding step needs every preceding one. Ultimately, they merge and coordinate. The result: a developmental milestone. The child then moves to a higher level of performance.

TIMENESS, CONTINUITY AND SEQUENCE

History comprises a special form of thought which starts with the perceptible fact or facts observed by the historian (Barzun and Graff,

1957; Collingwood, 1970). Matters concerning the historian deal with the concrete rather than the abstract, with the individual rather than the universal. A mark of history is that it is time- and space-bound. It must be defined by time and more precisely, recorded by time. There must be a where and when, yet these dimensions cannot also be the here and the now. Collingwood (1970) indicates that the origins of history lie in man's awareness of continuity and the sense of time.

It is intriguing that a requisite for understanding nature of man lies in understanding just this developmental quality of self-awareness. The additional advantage of the historical approach is the fact that man develops in such an orderly manner, there is predictability from one step to the next. In this sense history and development are one in the same: both are bound by time and continuity. But there is yet another requirement to which historical evidence is subject. The evidence is not judged by what is known about similar events as much as it is measured by its relation to what is known about other things happening concurrently. For a necessary condition for historical observation is that an event of history must be returned to its milieu and to time.

Developmental phenomenon shares common properties with history but quite frequently we fail to allow the principles of one to illuminate the principles of the other. By definition development refers to a dynamic interaction between growing and maturing internal human structures and the external environment. A human individual functions in a particular setting not in a vacuum. Events, things and people within the milieu evoke responses. Just as the events of history require the plasma of time and of context, so development occurs as human potentialities are evoked and satisfied by an environment that is sufficiently challenging and rewarding.

The techniques of the historian deal with the principles for organizing the facts as well as their conclusion and the explanations. His efforts are supported by the rules which bind the data to time, continuity and context. Evidence in this sense is the critical ingredient for reconstructing the past. It is a kind of perceived fact which must exist here and now and may take the form of a written page, a spoken word, a picture, an article of clothing, and so on.

The investigation of any problem is furthered by asking answerable questions. In asking a question, the historian has in mind some preliminary idea of the evidence that he will be able to utilize. In historical method, the question and the evidence are correlative. If the right question is directed toward a perceptible thing, it becomes usable as a piece of evidence. Therefore, in principle, the variety of evidence that may be sought is infinite; the entire perceptible world furnishes potential evidence.

HISTORY-TAKING

History because it belongs to the behavioral sciences, begins by asking relevant questions so that the data may be organized and interpreted. First, the method used for data gathering, the content of questions or the type of information to be sought need to be discussed. One of the systems selected to guide the fact gathering is called the "personal history." It is concerned with either the course of an individual's life experiences or with broad underlying feelings and motivations. The interviewer knows beforehand those aspects of experiences he wants the respondent to verbalize. This method requires that the historian be free to probe, to rephrase questions and to reprobe. This is necessary to maximize understanding and involvement, hence, to maximize the reliability of the verbal report. Since heavy reliance is placed on reported evidence rather than on observed facts, the information to be collected must be what the respondent (eyewitness) is willing and able to report. The face-to-face encounter involving the historian and respondent serves particular value for appraising the validity of the evidence. The history taker can observe not only what is said but how it is said. Affective and value-laden responses can be determined. In addition, he can immediately follow up any contradictory statements. Although an interview that is less structured demands more skill it is at the same time more flexible.

THE TAXONOMY

Identifying critical patterns of play requires the construction of a nomenclature or taxonomy. Such a classification is a primary tool for any historical analysis of child's play. It serves to provide appropriate terminology and consistent language of the play phenomenon and to map the common threads underlying play behavior throughout childhood. The milestones of play can then be illuminated throughout from the points of view of cognitive and psychosocial development and be subject to classification systems proposed by Piaget and Erikson. In addition, Florey (1968) has classified play according to stage appropriate patterns spanning the period from birth through eleven years. The characteristics within the categories may then be more easily described and explained.

The designation of phases is somewhat artificial since life itself is a continuous process. Child's play follows that same principle—actions ebb and flow; new ones are built upon old ones which the child continues to have at his disposal. While there are no clear-cut lines of demarcation between phases, the emerging categories and new directions of behavior occur within certain time periods and follow an order.

Although different investigators have identified classification of age periods in play, the periods for the most part are developed from differing points of view. There is lack of agreement regarding the numbers of play periods existing in child development, the length of each period and the name of each period. An aged based classification of play is proposed here arbitrarily and its purpose is to serve the function of analysis. Because the developmental process and play parallel each other, it is assumed that the following epochs will describe play behavior.

The Epochs

Sensorimotor	0-2 years
Symbolic and Simple Constructive	2-4 years
Dramatic and Complex Constructive and Pre-Game	4-7 years
Games	7-12 years
Recreational	12-16 years

Sensorimotor Epoch

During the first eighteen months of life, play is qualified in Piaget's terms as sensorimotor. It begins as the infant experiments and enjoys such sensations as touching and hearing. During the first quarter of his life play is entirely autotelic. The child gazes at his hands intently, follows moving objects visually, listens to and makes sounds, and moves his hands to his mouth. He produces an effect only upon himself. For Piaget this characterizes the second substage of the sensorimotor period called primary circular reactions.

Following this time, the infant begins to produce effects on objects in his environment wherein each repeated effect is the same. For instance, he shakes a rattle repeatedly or hits swinging objects to make them swing. This comprises the idea of "shaking for the sake of shaking" or "mouthing for the sake of mouthing." It is characteristic of the third substage according to Piaget, the substage of secondary circular reactions.

By the eighth or ninth month the infant acquires more complex ways of dealing with the environment and engages in such feats as picking up objects and dropping them from heights. Of significance is the emergence of objectification—the child pushes an obstacle away in order to find a hidden object. At this time hiding and finding games such as "peek-a-boo" delight the child no end. He begins to explore objects in a number of ways. He can fill other objects, touch them, turn them, move them and so on. This characterizes the substage designated the coordination of secondary circular reactions.

Beyond this time and roughly to eighteen months of age, the child engages in active trial-and-error processes. He accomplishes actions characterized by a varied response to an object or he can try out new responses to achieve a similar goal. The essence of problem-solving behavior comes to the fore at this period. The child becomes engaged in actions such as making an object roll, slide, fall from different heights, or splash in water. It is more than haphazard for his actions are produced to observe a result and set feedback into motion. He is engaging in discovery of object spatial relations; he puts small objects into larger ones, places toys under the table, or aligns them in some fashion. His behavior illustrates the substage of tertiary circular reactions.

The child's increasing abilities to exercise actions using trial and error expands his repertoire of skills in dealing with novel situations and things. Thus he continues into the sixth substage of the sensorimotor period, intentional invention of new means. The striking feature of this behavior involves the emergence of a form of representation, a kind of imagery necessary for solving problems. Mental trial and error replaces active, overt trial-and-error responses. This is demonstrated by the child who can reproduce a task or action at another time as actions can now be represented mentally. Mental representation is made possible by the ability to represent objects and their spatial relations. Or, put in another way, the child who can imagine displacement in space and who can internalize a cause-effect relationship demonstrates the faculty of mental trial and error.

According to Florey, play interaction with human objects includes the infant himself and involves the practice of newly acquired motor skills such as pulling himself up and letting himself down in a repetitive pleasureful way. Involvement with parents takes the form of pat-a-cake, of chasing-hiding games, of imitating actions such as reading or dusting when demonstrated. Playing with a peer group is virtually nonexistent in a true interactional sense. Rather, the child under two years engages in play alone or assumes an onlooker role (watches others). If in close contact, the child may treat others as objects which he pushes or hits.

During the first two years of life, play begins with actions and sensations directed by the child himself. These actions are translated to produce effects upon objects and materials and are highlighted in the child's beginning ability to find a hidden object. As manipulative and physical powers mature and emerge he possesses an increasing capacity to deal with materials more actively and can meaningfully do this until he reaches a stage of first active trial and error and then covert trial and error in solving problems. The mode of social participation in play remains self-centered and individualistic. Play companionship of others does not yet involve a true sharing and interchange.

Symbolic and Simple Constructive Epoch

The significant changes in play during this period are influenced by (1) increasing growth and mobility, (2) advancing use of language and (3) increasing manual dexterity. The continued practice and maturation of general physical coordination and verbal capacity of the child reaches a critical point in his ability to interact with the social milieu. Thus, play actions change from practice play to symbolic play in the Piagetian sense and from solitary play to parallel play as described by Gesell. The toddler engages in such actions as climbing and running; he carries objects, builds, digs and tears things apart. Make-believe and pretend play begins to develop and are applied to the representation of objects and situations that the child encounters. Blocks, lines and so on begin to stand for other objects.

As the child begins to distinguish himself apart from other objects he can regard them as different and as occupying space different than his own. The toddler is armed with schemata for action and schemata for representation. This latter aspect distinguishes the current stage of symbolic play and is significant for two reasons. First, it repeats and organizes thinking; that is, what is in the mind exists in terms of images and symbols already mastered. Second, it serves to assimilate and to consolidate the child's emotional experiences. What happens to the child can now be reproduced in his play.

In Piagetian terms this constitutes the stage of preconceptual thinking. Explained in another way, for Erikson (1963) play is no longer centered on the body (autocosmic); it extends to the small world of manageable toys (microsphere).

Dramatic, Complex Constructive and Pre-Game Epoch

During this time play undergoes further expansion. A milestone is the widening of social participation in play. The child seeks companions and begins to play with them in an associative manner. For Erikson, the extension is into the world shared with other persons (macrosphere). Materials can now be shared in the company of others. Common occurrences are seen in shifting groups of two or three children. There is increasing interest particularly in novelty. Increasing control of hand dexterity makes possible actions that demand small muscle activity. Hammering, sorting using small objects, putting things together are at a high premium. Constructing simple projects that can be completed rapidly are important. The quantity of a collection surpasses the importance of the quality of items collected.

Imaginative play becomes increasingly reality-oriented, especially in the form of role-taking play. In this sense, the situations being played may relate to living conditions to which the child is exposed—animals, family relationship, school, and so on.

Symbolic play provides a helpful avenue for the mastery of external reality. It links pure practice or sensorimotor play to that highly organized form of play, games with rules. Thus far the origin and history of play has stressed its relationship to the development of the individual. Mead (1934) adds another dimension and postulates emergent stages of play according to its service for establishing social order. The child begins his mastery of symbol making ability by moving from playing "play" to playing roles. This period of early childhood reflects the first stage suggested by Mead, the "play period."

The child imagines himself in different social roles and in

make-believe imitations, such as mother, father, fireman and so on. This is essential for knowing the differences of oneself from other selves (or "roles") and enables movement to the next stage. A more precise term for Mead's play period is drama. It occupies a fundamental function for the child's developing awareness of himself as apart from, yet also related to others. Drama serves as a prime vehicle affording the child enhancement of a variety of roles to practice and learn. Fantasy drama keeps viable the past of the society through myths, legends, villains and heroes. Symbolic significance of play for a society is a much overlooked aspect in the study of man's social behavior. Since the myths and legends of a society are maintained through play, much of the continuity of society may be due to this form of behavior.

The early childhood years is a daredevil period in which strength and skill outdoors are practiced considerably. Locomotion is the vehicle of development of this period. There is need for increasing physical space and freedom.

The four- to seven-year-old enjoys action. He talks about his performances and his constructions. This is the time when his products need to be saved, displayed and named. His efforts are bent on realistic representation of things. Growth in language skills greatly influence the child's play during this time. Exploring verbal humor, chanting rhymes, creating rhythms are the new and exciting forms of learning.

Game Epoch

Entry into school provides expanded opportunities for learning about a world beyond the boundaries of family. The child is earnestly concerned with the real world and with its practical aspects. This is reflected in his play. The late childhood years are spent in play as a copyist, rather than as a designer. Real places replace picture books. The urge to find out how things operate reflects keen enjoyment in a sense of industry to use Erikson's term. The child wants not only to make things, but to make them well and to make friends and to get along with them. This latter task is illustrated in the school aged child's friendships and growing strengthening of these relationships. The agents for enculturation continue to extend far beyond the family. School experiences and the changing complexity of play enhance the process.

A significant change in social participation in play is seen in the movement from symbolic games to games with rules. Mead described this stage as game-playing. The child is fascinated by the rules of the game. He masters them and even makes up his own rules or his gang does. Rule-making helps him to escape difficult situations that could not be handled or would be difficult to handle otherwise. Additionally making rules and mastering them assist in building a self-identity. When the child risks his own identity in the presence of others he can advance to the next stage, the game stage. He learns first to play with others before he can play against them. Social participation is transformed to cooperative or organized play behavior as the child approaches the tenth and the eleventh years. He moves from difficulty in abiding by rules and needing to win to a phase of fascination with rules. He participates in inventing new ones and strongly adheres to them. Concerns about his peers and his status in their eyes increase in importance.

Imaginative play that straddles the end of the previous phase and the beginning of this phase requires heroes be imitated and costumes be worn. Some of this behavior is applied and becomes incorporated by experiences encountered in daily living. Milestones of this period according to Hartley and Goldenson (1957) now include: (1) curiosity about nature; that is, pets, gardens, insects, scientific facts; (2) attributing a value to everything; and (3) maintaining secrecy of the gang. In sports activities wind, speed and coordination predominate. Participation in formal organization such as scouting, recreation groups emerge and assume importance.

Recreation Epoch

This period continues the mastery of a variety of skills previously learned. Team work and cooperation demonstrate the need for very strict rule-bound actions and a respect for them. A variety of games appeals to the pre-adolescent because they are avenues for using and developing strengths, skills and mental abilities to the fullest degree possible. Continued emphasis of contemporary peers reigns. There is also high interest in constructive projects and manual skills aimed at increasing competencies. Activities are primarily group-oriented, such as group singing, team sports and in sports there is strong competitiveness. The Mead's concept of the generalized other, during the game stage is in ascending. It increases the more serious activities of adolescence. The serious activities, while recreational in nature, verge on the service aspect. The development of social role behavior continues in the context of such activities, as club work, altruistic organizations, dancing, singing, and so on. The necessary ingredient at this stage is involvement in heterosexual groups.

Oftentimes play is assumed to occur naturally. It is not regarded as a behavioral domain that might need to be monitored stimulated or simulated similarly to reading or writing. Lessons for learning to learn how to play are unthinkable in today's concept of education. Yet, play serves a critical function for a child's learning. There is much evidence to suggest that it does not occur spontaneously in children who are deficit in some way. Since we have on hand a knowledge of the evolving order of milestones of play this perspective could be used to scrutinize experiences and opportunities that have been and are being provided for the child. The perspective, however, needs to be organized into a matrix which identifies the context in which play is evolved and supported.

THE CONTEXT

It is the proposition of this discussion that the play milieu or context permits the play behavior within the epochs to flourish or to perish. The literature is replete with explications of the term milieu or its synonyms, environment or culture environment. Milieu refers to the totality of the individual's surroundings. It is a matrix composed of the objects, the natural phenomena and the people as well as the internal structures of the individual. The definition developed for use in this chapter purports that the behavior of a playing child is the result of intimate interactions with the existing constituents of his surroundings. A dynamic interdependent relationship exists between (1) the *individual* as a *responding* element to (2) *external* and *internal factors* or group of factors which evoke a response from the individual.

Returning an event to its milieu and timeframe is critical to any examination of play. A particular play event derives meaning only as the context is understood in which it has occurred. The requisites of a milieu that nurtures play behavior, it is speculated, can be systematized into a model play environment. The first dimension of the model consists of two elements essential to elicit, guide and direct human functioning. These are divided into human and non-human components. Animals, plants and cultural artifacts such as toys are included in the non-human category. A second dimension critical for play analysis is the qualitative and the quantitative aspects of the behavior. The qualitative part specifies the conditions of play as: (1) opportunity to repeat actions; (2) opportunity to explore and to experiment within the environment; and (3) opportunity to imitate acts. The quantitative aspect refers to time available and time spent in play encounters with the human and the non-human elements.

The four elements—the human and non-human, the qualitative and quantitative—exist to that degree with is determined best by the child's particular level of play development. It is not sufficient to stipulate that each element must be in equal balance with the others in order that the milieu be effective. Instead the proposed classification of play is based on the dominant influence exerted by certain themes of play development extrapolated from the literature. The classifying principle that is used is that each epoch requires a different amalgamation of the above four elements. The significance of the play milieu lies in its potential for evoking, supporting, introducing and rewarding actions of play.

The mandates for a milieu that ensures play behavior are an initial but vital yardstick for completing a historical analysis of play. It provides, at least, elements for making comparisons about the play setting.

The milestones of play and a model of the milieu for play that have been identified constitute the underlying basis for gathering evidence about a child's play. Table 1 which follows provides a five-part guide to gathering play evidence: (1) general information (2) previous play experiences (3) actual play examination (4) play description (5) play prescription.

THE PLAY HISTORY INSTRUCTIONS

Taking a play history is critical for diagnostic purposes and ultimately for planning and implementing interventive measures. The quality as well as the quantity of the data obtained rests with the history taker's knowledge of play and its developmental nature. In addition interview techniques for extracting the desired information

TABLE 1
THE PLAY HISTORY

(1) *General Information*

Name: Birthdate: Sex:
Date: Informant(s):
Presenting Problem:

(2) *Previous Play Experiences*

A.   Solitary Play
B.   Play with others:
     mother   father   sisters   brothers   playmates
     other family members   pets
C.   Play with toys and materials (earliest preferences)
D.   Gross physical play
E.   Pretend and make-believe play
F.   Sports and games: group collaboration   group competition
G.   Creative interests: arts   crafts
H.   Hobbies, collections, other leisure time activities
I.   Recreation/social activities

(3) *Actual Play Examination*

A.   *With what* does the child play?
     Toys   materials   pets
B.   *How* does the child play with toys and other materials?
C.   What type of play is *avoided* or liked least?
D.   *With whom* does the child play?
     Self   parents   brothers   sisters   peers   others
E.   *How* does the child play with others?
F.   *What body postures* does the child use during play?
G.   *How long* does the child play with objects?   with people?
H.   *Where* does the child play?
     Home: indoors   outdoors
     Community: park   school   church   other areas
I.   *When* does the child play?
     Daily schedule for weekday and weekend

(4) *Play Description*

(5) *Play Prescription*

is a necessary prerequisite. At best, good history-taking is elusive. It is sharpened as knowledge about play is expanded and learned in depth and as the historian gains confidence in his craft. The play history outline is intended as a guide and not a plan of topics used to order the history-taking process. The actual gathering of data (the interview) and the recording of data are separate processes. The use of outlines has its drawbacks because the tendency to apply them too rigidly may sacrifice the presentation of individuals as alive human beings. Approaches to respondents and to recording of data may become too stereotyped. The play historian is cautioned not to sacrifice individualizing history at the price of fitting it to a fixed outline.

Elements of the Play History

Section 1, General Information, is included to ensure that identification of the child and informants is obtained. Each category of this section is self-explanatory.

Section 2, Previous Play Experiences, is designed to follow the sequential progression of play development. It highlights a principle of historical technique—using the past to understand the present. The proposed categories correlate to the changes in direction of the child's involvement with himself first, then with others and with objects in his environment.

It follows the milestones and the increasing complexity of the child's play actions. The categories solitary play, play with others, play with toys and materials, and gross physical play, designate, for instance, the expected arena of experiences for a child usually less than two or three years of age chronologically. The latter ones, hobbies and recreation activities aim at identifying the play of individuals in adolescence. To explain this another way, securing a history of play experiences of a five-year-old necessitates tracing his play subsumed under those categories which precede and include, pretend and make-believe play. In contrast, the search for play experiences of an adolescent requires that all categories preceding and including recreation and social activities, be covered sufficiently.

The data from this second section intend to identify the *form* of the child's play or to determine his play styles. They refer to the choice of materials selected in play and to the nature of the child's playfulness. Form of play or type of play parallels changes in development, but remains constant in its characteristics. For example, was the child active in his play? Or did he prefer sedentary play? Did he prefer to play alone more than the others? The *content* of play is a second and more variable element to gauge. It changes as it is that proportion of play which expresses the child's needs, his impulses and mirrors the life situations he has encountered.

A. Solitary play. One of the marks of play is its quality of self-initiatedness. Play is self-willed. Thus, securing data about the child's solitary play points to such a quality. Questions that answer how he played as an infant provide pertinent evidence. How did he play at six months of age as contrasted to when he was twelve months of age, 24 months of age, and so on? Did he require someone with him to initiate any actions? How did he engage in play alone? Noisily? Actively? Quietly? Did he play with a variety of toy objects or materials or did he limit himself only to one type of object? The search for identifying pleasureable elements in play is a critical and continuous part of evidence collecting.

B. Play with others. From solitary play the child moves to parallel play, then to associative play (sharing and involving others). One of the first tasks is to ascertain if the child's play involved others, and if so, how did he play with them. Who were they—his peers, his brothers and sisters, his parents, his neighbors? Early experiences involving mother is seen in peek-a-boo games. Questions about how he played with mother, with father, yields data about family attitudes regarding play. Actions with brothers and sisters are worth investigating as indicative of the availability of play models in forms other than parents or other adults.

Did the child play with children in the neighborhood and if so, how? Responses to these questions reveal information about prior opportunities for playing with others and may designate the physical space previously available to the child.

The category includes non-human objects such as pets. It is often a neglected consideration yet a significant one. When other children are not so readily available the opportunity to play with or to care for a pet offers a myriad of experiences. The child may relate better to a pet then to individuals. What kind of pet was it? Who took care of the pet? How did the child play with it? These are relevant lines of inquiry to furnish significant data about the interaction of object and context in the child's style of learning.

C. Nature of play with toys and materials preferred earliest. To obtain data about the early toy preferences of children the inquiry might include: What did he enjoy playing with as a baby? As a one-year-old? As a two-year-old? Information about what was available would be the intended yield. The play historian should not stop with mere identification of toys and objects. Corollary questions include: What did he do with them? The tendencies to prefer similar type objects or any obvious changes in preferences need to be noted. Playthings that afforded gross motor activity and sedentary activity need differentiation. Engagement in active versus passive play, or both, reveal helpful evidence about the child's earlier play style with non-human objects. Did he seek out transactions and explore on his own? Or, did he seem content and passively tolerant of situations around him? Did he interact with objects in stereotyped ways or did he vary his actions consistently as appropriate to the object in question?

The interviewer is cautioned to distinguish between a single mode of dealing with objects that changes as he moves from one phase of play to another, or a mode that remains the same despite changes and increase in chronological age. For example, a child's actions with toys at approximately 24 months of age were characterized by repeated casting of toys and mouthing of them. It was reported that when she was approximately 30 months her play with objects was described still as casting actions. In addition, she pulled, rolled and played with them in ways other than mouthing. Although these were actions not usually expected of a girl that age it was noted that her dealings with toys had progressed to other modes, as for example, touching and rolling.

D. Nature of gross physical play. There is need to obtain information regarding how the child has engaged in such physical feats as climbing, running, hopping, skipping, balancing, bicycling and so on. These actions provide the physical base for the development and enhancement of skilled performance in organized team sports, in manual manipulation of materials, in tasks demanding precise coordination and in recreational and even social activities in later years. Was the child involved in gross motor activities? Gross physical play is the arena for practicing and for learning one's physical powers and prowess.

What was the extent of gross play actions? A mere listing of them would not suffice because valuable data are obtaied from learning how the child actually performed gross physical tasks and the enjoyment derived from them. In addition, did the child demonstrate sufficient coordination or did he perform awkwardly and in which type of activity? Did he tend to prefer large-muscle activity over small-muscle activity, or did he prefer sedentary and quiet play?

E. Pretend and make-believe play. The change of play from sensorimotor to symbolic characteristics is a milestone in the genesis of play. It is indicative of a change in the child's cognitive repertoire. Engagement in symbolic play discloses a capacity to deal with representation of objects and situations? And this characterizes the mode of play designated make-believe and imaginative. Questions to determine if the child played in pretend manner and descriptions of that mode of play provide hopeful evidence of development. Finding out approximately when or at what age he began to do this furnishes pertinent data about the time when this milestone occurred. The kinds of themes expressed in his play tell about the situations he has encountered and has attempted to master. The child's use of imagination and the degree to which it is accepted and encouraged is another facet needing the continuous monitoring of a history.

The data for the final analysis are additionally enhanced by queries about who participated in pretend play? Did the child engage in this form of play alone? Did he have imaginary friends? If so, how did he play with them?

Other types of imaginative play might be seen in preferences for storytelling, reading story books, being interested in fairy tales. Examination of enjoyment in such forms and identification of preferences would be helpful.

Pretend play changes somewhat in the demands made by the child for costumes. At first he is content with a partial costume in dress-up play (a gun suffices as representation of cowboy); later, he requires the full get-up for any role that he reenacts.

F. Participation in sports and games. The first step in learning to play with others is to engage in actual collaboration with them. A child learns first to play *with* others before he learns to play against them. A historian needs to determine when a child begins to play with peers and how they played together? As the child moves out of the period designated symbolic play and into the one marked games with rules, he enters a phase of play characterized by numerous rule-bound behaviors. He and his "gang" go as far as making their own rules. Identification of the types of games he played alone and with others are important in the milestone sense to note. What were his responses when he lost a game? This supplies evidence regarding the preferences for certain types of games, that is, sedentary board games versus active playground sports versus "thinking" games and so on. Descriptions of the nature of the games add clarification.

G. Pursuit of creative interests. Involvement in the arts and crafts is particularly significant but often neglected as a natural avenue for specific skill learning. Using Erikson's framework of psychosocial development the period of acquiring a sense of industry to overcome a sense of inferiority requires reiteration. The school-aged youngster seeks to learn to do things well and to get along with people. Emphasis is placed on the process of doing things and of making things. Complete attention need not necessarily be on the end product, rather, on how to accomplish an end. With maturation of physical powers having occurred, the task is to practice them and to build competency and skill in handling a variety of materials. Opportunities for tool learning and tool using require identification by the play historian. What types of manual arts have been enjoyed and accomplished? What about creative art expression? Did the child enjoy tasks such as needlework, painting, and so on? These are examples only of a wide spectrum of media potentially available in the arts and the crafts.

From competent dealings with things in the milieu the child develops a feeling of efficacy according to White (1964). Establishing competency depends on a history of successful dealings with the human and the non-human environment. Effective interchange contributes positively to a developing self-identity. The history of successes must be accompanied with reward for the child, either intrinsically or extrinsically. Through use of tools and management of materials significant learning can occur. Specific rules and procedures become reinforced. Properties of materials are identified or particular likes and dislikes begin to be differentiated.

H. Pursuit of hobbies, collections or other leisure-time activities. As the child participates more and more in the serious nature of school work, the time he devotes to other activities need identification. Emersion in a hobby or hobbies provides data about the sources of pleasure available to the child and the development of any unique skill or talent. For instance, has the child had any collections? When children engage in collecting it begins for the sake of quantity only rather than quality. It matters not what it is; things get placed in pockets for the sheer pleasure of how much can be gathered. As the next step emerges, collections are made according to criteria of interest and quality. An array of hobbies and special interests are potentially available—movies, records, sports, musical instruments, gardens, to name only a few. Did the child do any of these? If so, did he do them alone, with someone else? Who in the family or without the family introduced and/or encouraged this?

I. Participation in recreation/social activities. Advent into the period of adolescence brings an increasing number of possible activities that represent both highly organized as well as unorganized ones, involving a peer group. Did he belong to any organized club, recreational or social group? What were the activities of the group or groups? What participation in such endeavors suggest important qualities regarding play with peers and time devoted to such activities? Are they socially acceptable?

The questions raised in each part of section 2 of the proposed Play History are not intended as a finite list. They suggest directions that the play historian might consider. Additional questions may be necessary depending on the nature of the evidence obtained and the requirement for individualizing each history of play.

THE PRESENT IN THE INTEREST OF THE PAST

Just as the present is misunderstood without knowledge of the past, so the picture is incomplete when the present is ignored. The immediate, perceptible here and now furnishes rich evidence for understanding both the past and present. The value of a past pattern increases tremendously when it can be confirmed by present observable evidence. Investigation progresses naturally when it is helped to separate what is best understood, for what is the most obscure.

Thus, the Actual Play Examination, Section 3, aims at obtaining evidence of play in the recent past-yesterday, last week. This evidence plus a description of play experiences from Section 2 corroborates as well as traces the antecedents leading to the actual play behavior. Discussion of each element follows.

A. With what does the child play? The child's current favorite playthings—toys, materials, objects—require identification. This reveals pertinent information about (1) their availability and non-availability, and (2) their appropriateness and inappropriateness to the child being examined. They reflect familial attitudes and values about play as well as the allowances made for engagement in "nonserious" and pleasurable activities. Underlining of educational toys and materials, vigorous sports and exercise are further reflections of specific parental learnings and interests. Acceptance and tolerance for the imaginative and dramatic dealings of the child's play or the use of creative and expressive types of materials (sand, clay, paints) indicate some play attitudes within a family.

An abundance of sedentary activities over active, large-muscle ones or vice versa are warning signs of imbalanced growth. Determining whether this differs from preferences six months to a year ago provides additional historical evidence. The nature of activities demanding passive versus active participation is of special significance, particularly if one type has predominated. For instance, unusually long hours devoted to television defines passive, dependent activity. The task of the historian in such instances is to ascertain whether television is the prime source for play. Lengthy hours viewing television should caution the investigator to probe further for more specific identification of the exact nature of the activity: How long does the child watch television? Does he focus absolutely on a given program or is it merely that the television is on and the child comes and goes, now watching and engaged in other actions? Further, a physically handicapped child needs to engage in more than just passive enjoyment from television. Active, physical participation is critical to his overall development. If other actions are reported there would be strong support that some sort of balance exists in the repertoire of materials available to the child.

Animals and family pets comprise a dimension of the play milieu oftentimes neglected or given too little importance. Similarly, experiences around growing plants and flowers need recognition. Participation in the preparation and the celebration of festive occasions, religious holidays, birthdays and other special occasions warrants identification and clarification by the play examiner.

B. How does the child play? Once materials, toys and other playthings are identified, a description of how the child manages them should follow. Detailed descriptions are especially significant in the final analysis of the play history. As play progresses the child's manner of dealing with a variety of toys and materials becomes increasingly differentiated and more complex. How he interacts with a variety of playthings, serves as a useful gauge for assessing the exact nature of his play actions in several domains: gross motor, fine motor, social imitation and participation and construction. Accounts of these actions help to establish the specific forms of play that the child utilizes.

The following illustration underscores the kind of evidence to seek:

> Amy is a severely physically handicapped five-and-one-half-year-old girl, diagnosed with cerebral palsy, mixed type. Mother reported that her favorite materials include balloons, books, and having stories read to her. Her actions with them were described as looking at the picture books and at the balloons, pointing grossly to the pictures and "scratching" on the balloon as well as *hitting* or *batting* at it using gross movement of either arm. She is especially delighted when her brothers and sisters play in a teasing way with her and when they show her the pictures in books.

C. What type of play is avoided or liked the least? In contrast to examining the favorite type of play, that which is avoided may be equally important. Patterns of avoidance of certain play actions have the likelihood of uncovering evidence in several areas: For example, preferences for fantasy play over gross physical activities; for gross actions over fine manual ones; for dealing with objects rather than with people; for engaging in solitary play rather than with play involving others.

Contrasts with what the child avoided or disliked six to twelve months ago help to make determinations if there are any unusual patterns emerging or patterns being reinforced that might be of potential concern. The changes in dislikes might be attributed to maturity in the child's interests in play, or having had varied exposure to many types of materials, people or toys.

D. With whom does the child play? The child himself assumes a critical position in the hierarchy of emerging play participation with others. The essence of play, it was stated earlier, involves spontaneity and self-initiatedness; thus, data concerning the quality of the child's solitary play are equally significant. When playing alone, does he reject toys or manage them only randomly or require someone else to initiate an activity? Does he demonstrate limited modes of interacting with people? All of these may be causes for concern and justify further delving into identifying the quality of the child's play.

Identification of the availability or the nonavailability of others for play demands special attention. Play with a variety of family members requires scrutiny by the history taker. These members might include parent substitutes, brothers, sisters, grandparents, cousins and so on. As the child develops he engages in play in increasing amounts of time with his peer group. The nature of and the availability of these groups receive gradual importance. What type of play does the family engage in together? Do these family activities occur weekly, monthly or only on special occasions?

The primary human contacts need to be sought: (1) play models or ideals, and (2) "playmates." Again, contrasting the information reported with whom the child played a year or more ago reveals critical evidence for the final story. Has the child's play changed because he has ascended the ladder of social participation in play? For example, has he moved from playing parallel to playing associatively?

E. How does the child play with others? The nature of the child's play with others requires detailed description. Does he act as if others are objects and uses them as such? Does he relate to them at all and if so in any particular or unusual way? Hiding and finding type play emerges first as the infant tests out the environment and its responses toward him.

When playful interchange with others takes on parallel qualities the child engages in play in different ways. He mimics and wants to do as others do; he plays alongside them. When social participation in play becomes associative in nature, the child begins to share toys and is a participant among others. When play interactions take on a cooperative quality, the child truly collaborates with others as in organized team sports.

Distinguishing the child's competencies in playing with others six to twelve months earlier warrants description. Changes in the social aspects of his play may indicate progress from one play phase to another. Lack of changes may represent equally significant evidence, and justifies further questioning along the lines of opportunity for playing with others and of the quality of the child's relationship with others.

F. What body postures does the child use during play? Child's play reflects and expresses his overall behavior. Taking into account the predominant postures he uses during play is an aspect sometimes

attributed too little value. For instance, it is worth examining
whether a five-year-old uses a variety of body postures which depend
upon the activity at hand. The postures to be identified at such a
time include lying on his back or abdomen, crawling, sitting,
kneeling, running, climbing, jumping, hopping, skipping and so on.

Evidence of a predominant posture such as sitting should stimulate
the historian to delve into subjects concerning where and how he sits
as well as what he does when he is sitting. This type of probing might
substitute evidence about the nature of the child's favorite playthings. That is, do they promote sedentary characteristics of play?

G. How long does the child play? The intended yield of this
question is to determine the child's length of attention when he
engages in pleasurable transactions. Hurlock, in an attempt to classify
play of children reports that during the babyhood period (birth to
three years) in her classification scheme the median time reported is
fifteen minutes for three-year-olds. Little actual recording of the
time infants spend per activity appears in the literature. Play of
three-year-olds according to Bott, is devoted to raw materials 29% of
the time, 25.3% to locomotion, 23.2% to patterns and 22.5% to
mechanical play. Increasing interest span with increasing age was
observed in eighty infants studies by Herring and Koch (1971).

The recorder must pay close attention to time spent per activity.
Does the child's span of attention depend on the activity at hand?
Has its duration changed within the past six to twelve months? Is it
different when he plays with others in contrast to when he plays
alone? Does it differ when he plays with objects and toys than with
people? Presented with a number of toy things does the child
incorporate them into a single activity? How quickly does he move
from one type of play to another? Is it random and undirected?
When confronted with a variety of objects does he focus his
attention on one object only? Or, does he become easily flustered,
and subsequently unable to engage in any type of play with toys?

H. Where does the child play? The primary intent of this query
and its corollary ones aims at identifying the physical space available
for play within the child's immediate and/or extended surroundings.
Specifications of elaborate and hygenic space for play are not the
primary focus. Indoors, outdoors, as well as recreational areas, parks,
school, church and others need identification. Further, is play space

limited, confining, or is it expansive thus, affording the child many opportunities? Is limited space or confinement imposed by others or by the actual availability of space per se?

I. When does the child play? Critical to the play examination and often given too little consideration is the question about how the child used his time. Scrutiny of a weekday schedule and a weekend schedule are essential.

A three-day sampling at least yields pertinent data relative to time spent in rest, meals, play and "work." An assessment of the child's occupation ought to reveal a large percentage of time devoted to the nonserious (for him) and self-satisfying task of play. Of course, these percentages change as the child advances into a student role in school and differences become more apparent in distinctions of "school work" from "leisure" time.

A Case Illustration

The actual reconstruction of a child's history of play constitutes a difficult yet crucial step. Since the facts do not speak for themselves, they must be methodically analyzed and interpreted. The yield is a diagnosis of play and finally a prescription for play which guides the plan for intervention.

The case of Sarah demonstrates actual use of the play history outline and of the procedure for analyzing and interpreting the play data. It is not the intent to present her case in its entirety, rather, to present only those salient elements which describe her physical status, her psychological-intellectual performance and her family milieu.

Sarah, a five-and-one-half-year-old girl, was brought to the clinic at the request of the school. According to her mother the problem is that "Sarah is too independent" and "she will not sit down and do the things her teacher wants her to do."

Her prenatal history was essentially unremarkable. She was the five pound, two-and-one half ounce product of a full-term pregnancy; there was no difficulty at birth. During the first three months of life, she vomited constantly following fluid intake. She remained at the same birthweight and was hospitalized for dehydration and anemia. Growth and weight gain were slow and Sarah was a poor eater. She was treated for anemia and there was no difficulty since that time.

TABLE 2
THE PLAY HISTORY

(1) *General Information*

    Name: Sarah L.   Birthdate: November 15, 1965   Sex: F.
    Date: May 7, 1971   Informant: Mother
    Presenting Problem: "She will not sit down and do the things her teacher
                        wants her to do" (according to mother).

(2) *Previous Play Experiences*

    A.   Solitary Play. Initiated her own activities and could be left to play by herself.
    B.   Play with others. Usually by herself, occasionally with brother, Jeff, who is younger. Rough-house play with father.
    C.   Play with toys and materials. Balls, dolls (informant could not really remember others).
    D.   Gross Physical Play. Running, climbing when she can; usually outside.
    E.   Pretend and make-believe play
    F.   Sports and Games
    G.   Creative interests
    H.   Hobbies, collections, other leisure time activities
    I.   Recreation/social activities

(3) *Actual Play Examination*

    A.   *With what* does the child play?
        Dolls, imaginary friends (Susu and Ray)—keeps under her pillow when in school; takes for walks; watches television (Flintstones; Hee Haw; Flipper).
    B.   *How* does the child play with toys and other materials?
        Pretend situations such as: school, doctor-nurse, house.
    C.   What type of play is *avoided* or liked least?
        Nothing in particular.
    D.   *With whom* does the child play?
        Elizabeth, a 4 year old neighbor; Jeff, a 3 year old brother (sometimes).
    E.   *How* does the child play with others?
        Shares, cooperates; doesn't fight too much.
    F.   *What* body postures does the child use during play?
        Varies according to what she is playing with.
    G.   *How long* does the child play with objects?
        At the most approximately 10 minutes; may change what she is doing and may return to it later.
    H.   *Where* does the child play?
        At home—indoors in bedroom, living room, also outdoors in front area.
        At friend's house close by; at school in playground.
    I.   *When* does the child play?
        Daily Schedule:
        8:00-9:30 a.m.—gets up; gets ready for school; watches television
        9:30-11:30 a.m.—attends school
            11:45 a.m.—lunch
        After lunch to 5:00 or 6:00 p.m.—plays with friend, Elizabeth; watches cartoons on television
        5:00 or 6:00 p.m.—dinner, then helps with dishes; bathes; watches television
        8:00-8:30 p.m.—bedtime
        Weekend Schedule does not vary too greatly. The only difference is an increase in time for play and in time for helping mother with household chores when Sarah felt like it.

On examination Sarah showed significant growth retardation—four S.D. below the mean in height and bone age of three years. Endocrine studies ruled out organic problems; the lack of growth is attributed to a combination of familial, nutritional and environmental influences. Height of the parents and grandparents ranged from 4 ft. 11 in. to 5 ft. 6 in. According to the nutritionist, her diet was marginal in calories and iron and low in vitamin C. A skull series was normal and findings of organ systems, extremities and skin are equally unremarkable. Her neuromuscular status was good.

Impression of the psychologist is that Sarah is not retarded. She scored an IQ of 87 on the Peabody Picture Vocabulary Test. Abilities in visual-motor integration and pre-school language ability were at a developmental level of 4.8 to 4.11 years. The lack of general information about her environment appears due to limited exposure and experience and not necessarily to an inability to learn.

Her performance in gross motor and fine motor skills, in self-help skills for eating, dressing and hygiene and grooming were assessed at the four to five year level. There were possible social-emotional difficulties. She was described psychiatrically as having a developmental deviation of early childhood, chronic, moderate with delayed development physically, some delay in communication and some delay socially. The family consists of both parents, Sarah and her younger brother. The father is not employed; her mother is.

Their home environment is untidy outside and in—though not unhealthy—and the family functions rather casually. The children appear to be under little supervision. There seems to be less stimulation in the home than would be optimal especially in experiences and tasks that would aid in enhancing Sarah's school performance. She is described as a "disadvantaged, ghetto child, only she is not living in a ghetto."

An actual play history of Sarah is shown in Table 2.

DATA ANALYSIS AND INTERPRETATION

A chart describing "The Use of a Play Milieu and Taxonomy for Diagnosis" (Table 3) guides the method of analyzing and interpreting the play data. Its formula derives from the major elements which measure a milieu for play. The chart consists of three categories: (1) the epochs of play; (2) the elements of the play milieu, and (3) the description of a child's actual play.

TABLE 3

CHART: THE USE OF A PLAY MILIEU AND TAXONOMY FOR DIAGNOSIS

Epochs	Elements	Description	
SENSORIMOTOR 0-2 years	Materials: Toys, objects for sensory experiences —see, mouth, touch, hear, smell—rattles, ball, nesting blocks, straddle toys, chimes, simple pictures, color cones, large blocks Action: Gross—stand/fall, walk, pull, sit on, climb, open/close Fine—touch, mouth, hold, throw/pick up, bang, shake, carry Motoric imitation of domestic actions People: Parents and immediate family Setting: Home—crib, playpen, floor, yard, immediate surroundings EMPHASIS: INDEPENDENT PLAY W/EXPLORATION HABITS EXPRESSED IN TRIAL AND ERROR.	Evidence: No Evidence:	Encouraged: Discouraged:
SYMBOLIC AND SIMPLE CONSTRUCTIVE 2-4 years	Materials: Toys, objects, raw materials (water, sand, clay, paints, crayons) for fine motor manipulation and simple combining and taking apart; Wheeled vehicles and adventure toys to practice gross motor actions. Action: Gross—climb, run, jump, balance, drag, dump, throw Fine—empty/fill; scribble/draw; squeeze/pull; combine/take apart; arrange in spatial dimensions Imagination w/storytelling, fantasy; objects represent events/things	Evidence: No Evidence:	Encouraged: Discouraged:

People: Parents, Peers, Other adults
Setting: Outdoors—playground; play equipment immediate neighborhood
    Indoors—home, "nursery"
EMPHASIS: PARALLEL & BEGINNING TO SHARE; SYMBOLIC PLAY EXPRESSED IN SIMPLE PRETENSE & SIMPLE CONSTRUCTIONAL USE OF MATERIALS

Encouraged:

DRAMATIC AND COMPLEX CONSTRUCTIVE AND PRE-GAME

Evidence:

Materials: Objects, toys, raw materials for fine motor actions and role-playing; large adventure toys for refining gross actions for speed and coordination; pets; non-selective collections
Action: Gross—"daredevil" feats of hopping, skipping, turning somersaults; dance
    Fine—combining materials and making products to do well, to use tools, to copy reality
    Dramatic role-playing—imitating reality in part/whole costumes, story telling
People: Peer group (2-5 members) "imaginary friends"
Setting: Parents, immediate family, other adults School, neighborhood and extended surroundings (excursions); upper space and off the ground
EMPHASIS: COOPERATIVE PLAY WITH PURPOSEFUL USE OF MATERIALS FOR CONSTRUCTIONS, DRAMATIZATION OF REALITY AND BUILDING HABITS OF SKILL AND TOOL USE.

No Evidence:

Discouraged:

Epochs	Elements	Description		
		Evidence:	*Encouraged:*	
		No Evidence:	*Discouraged:*	
GAMES 7-12 years	*Materials:* Games played w/rules dominoes, checkers, table-card games; ping pong; raw materials and tools for making complex products (weaving, woodwork, carving, needlework) Gross muscle sports—hopscotch, kite-flying, skating, basketball Books—puzzles, "things to do" biography, adventure, sports Selective collection or hobby Pet *Action:* Gross—refining and combining skills of jumping, hopping, running Fine—precision in using variety of tools, finer object manipulation and construction Making, following, breaking rules; competition and compromise w/peers *People:* Peer group of same sex; organized groups, e.g., scouts, parents, other adults *Setting:* Neighborhood, playground, school, home EMPHASIS: ENHANCEMENT OF CON-STRUCTIONAL AND SPORTS SKILLS AS EXPRESSED IN RULE BOUND BEHAVIOR, COMPETITION & APPRECIATION OF PROCESS COOPERATIVE PLAY.			

	Evidence:			Encouraged:
		No Evidence:		Discouraged:

RECREATION
12-16 years

Materials: Team games and sports and special interest groups for music, dancing, singing, discussing, Collections and hobbies; parties, books, table games

Action: Gross—team sports and individual precision sports (tennis, golf)

Fine—applying and practicing fine manipulative skills to develop craftsmanship, special talents

Organized group work

People: Peer group of same and opposite sex; parents and other adults

Setting: School; neighborhood and extended community; home

EMPHASIS: TEAM PARTICIPATION AND INDEPENDENT ACTION EXPRESSED IN ORGANIZED SPORTS, INTEREST GROUPS AND HOBBIES DURING LEISURE TIME.

HIGH RISK

OVER-ALL
STATUS

ACCEPTABLE

The epochs of play defined earlier provide the major divisions within which play elements are identified. The elements selected to describe play in each period are : (1) materials; (2) action; (3) people; and (4) setting. There are changing emphasis of play actions as development progresses. This requires a different amalgamation of the four play elements in each play epoch. Thus, to describe the milestones of each play period the following are specified: (a) the composite parts of each major element, and (b) the primary play actions which differentiate one epoch from the next.

The description of the actual play is subdivided into sections—evidence and no evidence, and play actions encouraged and discouraged. It is in these sections that the data recorded on the play history outline becomes charted (Table 4). Actual data reporting the materials, people and the setting specific to each epoch are recorded in the section designated evidence. Missing information of materials, people, setting appropriate to a given play epoch are noted accordingly as no evidence. Play events or actions that are fostered, reinforced, applauded and emphasized are entered as encouraged. On the other hand, play events and actions that remain neglected, stifled, deemphasized, limited and precarious are marked in the discouraged section of the chart.

Charting the play evidence in this way reveals the outstanding and subtle assets and deficits of the child's play. The persons within a play environment are viewed as play models or as playmates and play peers. The play models are persons whom a child emulates or persons from whom a child receives encouragement, support and reward. In the case of Sarah the available play models are her mother and father primarily. There are no grandparents or other immediate family members available to her. Playful interaction with her mother or father was generally infrequent. What did exist was usually in the form of "roughhouse" type play with her father, and this occurred only occasionally. Despite the presence of her parents, it is noted throughout that there was limited play participation with them and with other significant persons in her milieu. Opportunities for imitating the acts of others were unstructured and erratic. There were some, but not many, occasions for Sarah to learn from her parents, especially her mother, such actions as using tools, ways of combining materials, receiving instruction and storytelling.

Further data analysis indicates a lack or limitation of opportunities, objects and materials serviceable for practicing skills and learning new skills of a constructional nature. These are best introduced and rehearsed in interaction with a careful selection and variety of objects and materials. Those which nurture actions of building, scribbling and drawing, coloring and those which teach properties of size, shape, color, texture, weight are essential during the epochs of simple constructive play and of complex constructive play. They provide the prerequisite experiences for reading, writing, counting and learning spatial properties. Sarah neither dislikes nor avoids any particular media; rather, she enjoys any type of materials presented to her. The problem is that they have not been readily available nor abundant for her use.

Examination of the data shows that Sarah's imagination and fantasy are not stifled. Her parent's acceptance, recognition and encouragement of these actions are strong positive aspects of her play. Her parents support and talk with her about her imaginary friends and recognize this as a transitional, but important phase of "growing up."

Acquisition of Sarah's imaginative qualities might be traced to such antecedents as (1) animal and cartoon shows viewed on television; (2) her parents' high value of a child's capacity to make-believe, and (3) her only mode of expression since there was a lack of materials and objects for providing other avenues of play. Her pretend-play mirrors some of the situations she has encountered at home, at school and possibly during visits to the doctor. She has had definite vicarious experiences to develop her fantasies with animals.

Relating her imaginative, role-playing behaviors to the developmental scheme of play indicates that Sarah's actions are well into the epoch of dramatic play. The evidence suggests further that Sarah possesses the capacity to play alone and to initiate her own activity. From an early age it was found that she was expected to play by herself and was left alone to deal with her surroundings without much guidance, selectivity or challenge. Her play actions with others included modes of sharing and cooperating now, indicating that her social participation in play has progressed. According to the developmental play scheme she has surpassed the first two modes, playing alone and playing alongside others. She has ascended to the mode of associative play, a pattern denoted by the inclusion of others, sharing and taking turns. However, her play group is limited to two—herself and one girlfriend. Thus, although Sarah has moved from solitary play to play involving others, it is not

TABLE 4
CHART: THE USE OF A PLAY MILIEU AND TAXONOMY FOR DIAGNOSIS

Epochs	Elements	Description
SENSORIMOTOR 0-2 years	*Materials:* Toys, objects for sensory experiences —see, mouth, touch, hear, smell—rattles, ball, nesting blocks, straddle toys, chimes, simple pictures, color cones, large blocks *Action:* Gross—stand/fall, walk, pull, sit on, climb, open/close Fine—touch, mouth, hold, throw/pick up, bang, shake, carry Motoric imitation of domestic actions *People:* Parents and immediate family *Setting:* Home—crib, playpen, floor, yard, immediate surroundings EMPHASIS: INDEPENDENT PLAY W/EXPLORATION HABITS EXPRESSED IN TRIAL AND ERROR.	*Encouraged:* Gross actions of climbing, pulling, opening, closing and rough housing *Evidence:* Ball, child's book and comic books, dolls Occasional rough housing with father Occasionally watching mother bake cookies Usually left alone to play and initiate own activities Outdoors available *Discouraged:* Parent-child play of consistent and repeated nature Repetitive, exploratory use of toys *No Evidence:* Variety of toys and materials for sensory experiences and for repetitive trial and error Opportunity to watch mother do domestic chores Actual mother-child play interaction
SYMBOLIC AND SIMPLE CONSTRUCTIVE 2-4 years	*Materials:* Toys, objects, raw materials (water, sand, clay, paints, crayons) for fine motor manipulation and simple combining and taking apart; Wheeled vehicles and adventure toys to practice gross motor actions. *Action:* Gross—climb, run, jump, balance, drag, dump, throw Fine—empty/fill; scribble/draw; squeeze/pull; combine/take apart; arrange in spatial dimensions	*Encouraged:* Climbing, running applauded Outdoor large muscle action Independent play either alone or with girl friend Making believe in relation to animals *Evidence:* Ball, tricycle, simple rope swing, doll, toy stove Best friend Elizabeth (4 years) Occasionally plays with brother Sometimes read stories from child's book, but Sarah did not keep still and left disinterested Watch animal stories on T.V. *Discouraged:* Actual play involving Sarah and her mother *No Evidence:* Variety of toys and raw materials for fine motor

	Imagination w/storytelling, fantasy; objects represent events/things *People:* Parents, Peers, Other adults *Setting:* Outdoors—playground; play equipment immediate neighborhood Indoors—home, "nursery" EMPHASIS: PARALLEL AND BEGINNING TO SHARE; SYMBOLIC PLAY EXPRESSED IN SIMPLE PRETENSE AND SIMPLE CONSTRUCTIONAL USE OF MATERIALS.	manipulation or for experimenting with them Opportunities to watch mother with materials and doing household tasks	or father Being shown use of play materials by mother, especially, or father
DRAMATIC AND COMPLEX CONSTRUCTIVE AND PRE-GAME	*Materials:* Objects, toys, raw materials for fine motor actions and role-playing; large adventure toys for refining gross actions for speed and coordination; pets; non-selective collections *Actions:* Gross—"daredevil" feats of hopping, skipping, turning somersaults; dance Fine—combining materials and making products to do well, to use tools, to copy reality Dramatic role-playing—imitating reality in part/whole costumes, story telling *People:* Peer group (2-5 members) "imaginary friends" Parents, immediate family, other adults *Setting:* School, neighborhood and extended surroundings (excursions); upper space and off the ground EMPHASIS: COOPERATIVE PLAY WITH PURPOSEFUL USE OF MATERIALS FOR CONSTRUCTIONS, DRAMATIZATION OF REALITY AND BUILDING HABITS OF SKILL AND TOOL USE.	*Evidence:* school, house, doctor-nurse Using gross actions of jumping, turning somersaults Play with 2 imaginary friends Some play, kitchen toys Has best friend to play with in sharing way Watching television (animal and cartoon shows) Animals—dogs, parrot *No Evidence:* Use of costumes for role-playing Availability of objects and raw materials for making things and for learning to use tools and implements Opportunities to take excursions and to expand her surroundings Music, Books and Pictures	*Encouraged:* in gross muscle actions Begin imaginative and keeping imaginary friends Saving Sarah's painting done in school *Discouraged:* Story telling because Sarah was not interested Repeating and experimenting with sampling of materials to combine together, to take apart Opportunity to watch parents and other adults

Epochs	Elements	Description		
		Evidence:		Encouraged:
GAMES 7-12 years	Materials: Games played w/rules dominoes, checkers, table-card games, ping pong; raw materials and tools for making complex products (weaving, woodwork, carving, needlework)			
	Gross muscle sports—hopscotch, kite-flying, skating, basketball			
	Books—puzzles, "things to do," biography, adventure, sports			
	Selective collection or hobby			
	Pet			
	Action: Gross—refining and combining skills of jumping, hopping, running	No Evidence:		Discouraged:
	Fine—precision in using variety of tools, finer object manipulation and construction			
	Making, following, breaking rules; competition and compromise w/peers			
	People: Peer group of same sex; organized groups, e.g., scouts, parents, other adults			
	Setting: Neighborhood, playground, school, home			
	EMPHASIS: ENHANCEMENT OF CONSTRUCTIONAL AND SPORTS SKILLS AS EXPRESSED IN RULE BOUND BEHAVIOR, COMPETITION AND APPRECIATION OF PROCESS COOPERATIVE PLAY.			
RECREATION 12-16 years	Materials: Team games and sports and special interest groups for music, dnacing, singing, discussing. Collections and hobbies; parties, books, table games	Evidence:		Encouraged:

Action: Gross—team sports and individual precision sports (tennis, golf)
Fine—applying and practicing fine manipulative skills to develop craftsmanship, special talents
Organized group work
People: Peer group of same and opposite sex; parents and other adults
Setting: School, neighborhood and extended community, home
EMPHASIS: TEAM PARTICIPATION AND INDEPENDENT ACTION EXPRESSED IN ORGANIZED SPORTS, INTEREST GROUPS AND HOBBIES DURING LEISURE TIME.

No Evidence:

Discouraged:

Availability and use of materials and objects for
Fine motor manipulation and construction—especially for color, shape, weight, size, etc.
Opportunity to sample and use various tools with materials and exposure to her real surroundings
Channeling practice of gross muscle actions
Opportunity and approval of imitative actions, especially of parents
Opportunity for engaging in play with parents, especially mother.

Encouragement of fantasy and imagination in play
Recognition of Sarah's paintings by keeping them

OVER-ALL STATUS

HIGH RISK

ACCEPTABLE

surprising that she has difficulty with instruction and learning from demonstration. And, while her imagination may be thriving, skills essential for school performance are still in a latent state and in school she is barely surviving.

A child's mobility and space for play are closely interrelated. Physical handicaps of any nature should alert the play historian about the degree of a child's actual mobility. Whether materials need to be brought to him and whether the child assumes only one body posture for prolonged periods of time are critical in the final analysis. Since Sarah is not physically impaired, this element is not a primary concern here. The absence of a physical handicap directs the historian to another level of questioning—to determine if a child has unusual and repetitive postural preferences such as rocking, head banging, twirling which would be legitimate warning signs for other possible disturbances. No evidence of this was found in Sarah's behavior.

Actual play setting, physical space and time allotted for play appear adequate in Sarah's situation. The missing ingredients are (1) in objects and materials for practicing fine motor actions, for making and naming products, for building in space, for sorting, counting and matching; (2) persons to serve as play models who can show her how to use certain materials and implements, guide her and structure her actions; (3) avenues for channeling and guiding gross physical actions still in need of practice.

Just what the data mean in light of what is known about development through play brings us closer to a diagnosis of Sarah's play. She plays in an imaginary, pretend manner and has done so for a number of months prior to obtaining the history. The pattern antecedent to this one is sensorimotor in quality. Conclusion is made that her play extends beyond pure sensorimotor transactions with her environment. She engages in both: (1) play in a strict sensorimotor fashion—physical and active manipulation of objects and of her own body, and (2) play in a symbolic manner. For Sarah objects can represent other things and events; situations can be reenacted as she has experienced them ans as she has interpreted them. She is able to take the role of others; she is the teacher, the nurse or the mother when she is playing. However, she has not yet required the complete paraphernalia in her dramatic reproductions of each role; this is another stage in the development of pretend and imaginative play.

The Play Diagnosis

The synthesis and interpretation of the play evidence form the basis of the play diagnosis.

Sarah's overall status of play is concluded to be at high risk. The deficiencies fall in the realms of (1) availability and use of materials and objects for fine motor manipulation and construction; (2) opportunity to sample and use various tools with materials and exposure to her real surroundings; (3) channeling practice of gross muscle actions; (4) opportunity and approval of imitative actions, especially of and with her parents; and (5) opportunity for engaging in play with parents, especially with her mother. The healthy and acceptable dimensions of Sarah's play lie in (1) self-initiated actions and intrinsic pleasure derived from them; (2) social participation in play characterized by associative qualities; (3) parental encouragement of fantasy and imagination in play, and (4) parental recognition of her paintings from school.

In the main, Sarah's play actions characterized those expected primarily in the epoch of dramatic and complex constructive and pre-game play (4-7 years) and she is now five-and-one-half years of age. The exceptions are found in the segments dealing with constructional use of materials due to limited availability of them and encouragement for using them.

Play Prescription

Child's play constitutes a chain of events spanning the years. To ensure continuity and to assist Sarah in making the transition to the succeeding epoch of games active measures for intervention are indicated.

Materials and objects suitable for evoking and nurturing "pre-school" type skills have not been abundant nor the major focus of her play actions. Play enrichment must focus on experiences with materials and objects for learning such properties as weight, size, texture, shape. There is need to bombard her with opportunities to manipulate and use such materials and media as scissors and paper, crayon and paper, paints, simple puzzles, form-boards, yarn and dull needle, simple sewing, cards, clay and play dough, simple cooking.

Hartley and Goldenson (1957) stress the need for practice, rehearsal and copyist play rather than inventing and designing during this period. Visits to real places and finding out how things work are experiences to be induced and monitored by her environment. Conquering upper space by using stilts, trapeze bars, rope ladders so that they are highly enjoyed are next goals of space mastery. Interpreting music through dance is an additional dimension that her environment should offer.

Sarah's play prescription must also involve her parents. Selected guidance of her mother and father would focus on materials and objects, demonstration and instruction regarding "how to" play with Sarah. It is important to Sarah and the family that the younger brother be included as a vital part of this instruction too.

The legitimacy of understanding play behavior and interventing in the deficit play behavior children should need little underscoring. It is seen that gathering a history of play monitors the state of play, diagnoses a state of learning and provides ultimately a prescription for play. For Sarah and for deficit children like her, play cannot be assumed as a spontaneously emerging behavior. Their play deficits express learning deficits. One behavior monitors the other. It is not enough that play should occur by mere happenstance or by fortuitous matching of persons and toys to a child. Selective play prescriptions or designs are a necessity rather than a baby-sitting luxury for those children who neither play well nor learn well.

REFERENCES

BARZUN, J. and H. GRAFF (1957) The Modern Researcher. New York: Harcourt, Brace & World.

BLOCH, M. (1953) The Historian's Craft. New York: Vintage.

COLLINGWOOD, R. G. (1970) The Idea of History. New York: Oxford Univ. Press.

ERIKSON, E. (1963) Childhood and Society. New York: Norton.

FLOREY, L. (1968) A Developmental Classification of Play. Thesis, University of Southern California (unpublished).

GESELL, A. (1940) The First Five Years of Life. New York: Harper & Bros.

HARTLEY, R. and M. GOLDENSON (1957) The Complete Book of Children's Play. New York: Crowell.

HERRON, R. E. and B. SUTTON-SMITH (1971) Child's Play. New York: John Wiley.

LOWREY, L. (1950) Psychiatry for Social Workers. New York: Columbia.

MEAD, G. H. (1934) Mind, Self and Society. Chicago: Univ. of Chicago Press.

MILLAR, S. (1958) The Psychology of Play. Baltimore: Penguin.

MILLER, D. L. (1970) Gods and Games. New York: World.

PIAGET, J. (1962) Play, Dreams and Imitation in Childhood. (C. Cattegno and F. M. Hodgson, trans.) New York: Norton.

WHITE, R. W. (1964) "Motivation reconsidered: the concept of competence," pp. 164-191 in C. B. Stendler (ed.) Readings in Child Behavior & Development. New York: Harcourt, Brace & World.

CHAPTER 6

A PLAY SCALE

Susan H. Knox

The way a child plays provides data about his development, learning, and ability to cope with the world. When the observation is structured the information may be collected systematically and any planned intervention becomes more predictable and measurable. This section develops and applies such a technique. The strategy consists of adapting an observational model originally postulated by Erik Erikson. The adapted model provides the basis for constructing a play scale from which a play quotient is derived (see Figure 1).

The adaptation consisted of altering part B, the criteria for description of play, and D, the assessment of behavior. By these changes the play scale structured the observation and a developmental frame of reference guided the interpretation (see Figure 2).

CHARACTERISTICS OF THE SCALE

The adapted model required certain organizational devices to ensure the accuracy of the play observation description. A play scale was constructed based on descriptions of normal play behavior ages 0-6 years (Knox, 1968). The task required the scale to describe play in terms of yearly increments and in four dimensions of Space management; Material management; Imitation; and Participation. The four dimensions were extrapolated from a literature review and

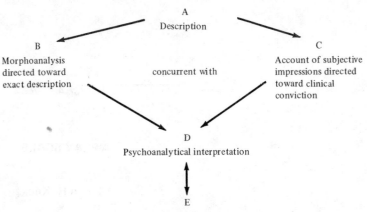

Erikson (1940) explains his model briefly:

> A gives a common-sense description of what happens before the observer's eyes; B and C demonstrate two concurrent tendencies in the observer's mental activity; B is directed toward a future exact description in areas which can be explored and measured under other than psychiatric conditions; C toward the clinicians age-old right and duty to allow himself to be led by subjective factors. The reader should visualize the relations of B and C, and their intervention between A and D.

Figure 1: ERIK ERIKSON'S MODEL FOR PLAY INTERPRETATION

coincided approximately with the areas of division shown by many play theorists. They met the four criteria for dimensions of scales: observability, measurability, definability, and literature consensus.

1. *Space management* is defined as the way a child learns to manage his body and the space around him, through the processes of experimentation and exploration. The bases for the repertoire of activity are the basic postural mechanisms (lying, sitting, walking, etc.), and progresses in the following manner:

(a) experimentation with what his own body is capable of doing through gross physical activity;

(b) exploration of immediate space and time through expansion of bodily activity;

(c) exploration of space outside the limits of immediate time and space through remembrance of past events and anticipation of future events.

2. *Material management* defines the manner in which the child handles materials and the purposes for which he uses materials. It includes ways in which the child learns control and use of material surroundings. The progression of material management is as follows:

(a) exploration of self and objects through oral and tactical senses with the emphasis on the sensation itself;

(b) expansion of the tactical senses through manipulation and construction, the emphasis being on process;

(c) refinement of skills through fine manipulation and construction with emphasis on the result;

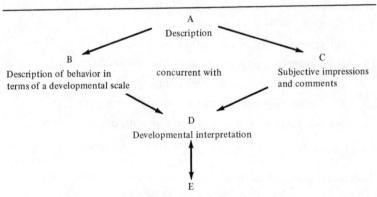

A−Play behavior to be analyzed−represents behavior during "free play" periods within a pre-school setting.

B−description of behavior−in terms of a developmental scale delineating four areas of play behavior:
   1. Space management
   2. Material management
   3. Imitation
   4. Participation

C−Subjective impressions and comments−general descriptions of play behavior and comments covering areas or types of behavior either not noted no the scale or amplification of any area.

D−Interpretation−in terms of the developmental sequence of play behavior, noting overall level of behavior, areas of advanced or regressed play, and areas of special interest.

E−Confirmation, speculation−in terms of any additional evidence obtained about the subject outside of that offered by the behavioral item [Knox, 1968].

Figure 2: ADAPTED MODEL FOR OBSERVATION OF PLAY BEHAVIOR

(d) emphasis on reasoning and the permanence of products.

3. *Imitation* is defined as the way a child gains an understanding of the social world around him, and learns how to express and control his feelings through the process of observation of parents, peers, and others. It includes mimicking the actions and speech of others, imitation of present, past and anticipated future events, and dramatization of events and feelings. Through imitation, the child learns control of self and expands this understanding to balancing the control between the self and the environment.

4. *Participation* defines the amount and manner of interaction with persons in the environment and the degree of independence and cooperation demonstrated in play activities. Participation develops in the following manner:

(a) egocentricity and attention demand;

(b) interaction with one person, the mother figure;

(c) interest in others, primarily through observation;

(d) association but not true interaction with peers;

(e) cooperation and true interaction with others.

Utilizing the previously described levels and dimensions of play, the scale was constructed spreading the yearly increments across the horizontal axis and running the four dimensions up the vertical axis. The body of the graph contains descriptions of play behavior during these intervals. The child's play is scored by the fit between the descriptions and the observed behavior. Space for comments is also provided. On the reverse side of the form is a Personal Data Form which contains such information as name, age, etc., and the results of any other testing. The exact form of the proposed scale is presented in Tables 1-4.

INTERPRETATION

The play scale is interpreted in accordance with the developmental principles of play. The age level at which a child plays and the dimensions manifested in his play aids in evaluation since they show the habitual performance of the child. The scale tends to be utilized in two general ways.

TABLE 1
PLAY SCALE

	0-1 years	1-2 years
SPACE MANAGEMENT	*Gross motor activity:* reaches, plays with hands and feet, moves to continue pleasant sensations *Territory:* crib, playpen, house *Exploration:* of self and objects within reach *Comments:*	*Gross motor activity:* stands up, sits down, bends, walks, climbs, low objects, broad movement *Territory:* home, immediate surroundings *Exploration:* of all unfamiliar things, oblivious to hazards *Comments:*
MATERIAL MANAGEMENT	*Manipulation:* handles, mouths toys, brings 2 objects together, picks up *Construction:* not evident yet *Interest:* people *Purpose:* sensation or function *Attention:* follows objects with eyes *Comments:*	*Manipulation:* throws, picks up, inserts, pulls, carries, pounds, bangs, gross grasp *Construction:* combines 2 objects, towers, takes apart, puts together *Interest:* movement and moving objects *Purpose:* experiments in movement and process *Attention:* rapid shifts *Comments:*
IMITATION	*Imitation:* of expressions, emotions, hugs toys *Imagination and Dramatization:* not evident *Music:* attends to sounds *Books:* near end of first year, pats, strokes *Comments:*	*Imitation:* of present events, adults, mimics actions, domestic mimicry (telephone, sweeping) *Imagination and Dramatization:* not evident yet *Music:* sways, listens *Books:* handles, points to pictures *Comments:*
PARTICIPATION	*Type:* solitary–up to 30 minutes, enjoys company, being picked up, swung up *Cooperation:* demands personal attention. 7-10 mos.–initiates games rather than follows *Language:* enjoys noise, attends, babbles *Comments:*	*Type:* solitary, onlooker, hide and seek with adults *Cooperation:* offers toys, but possessive, persistent, helps put toys away *Language:* enjoys noise, jabbers during play *Comments:*

TABLE 2
PLAY SCALE

	2-3 years	3-4 years
SPACE MANAGEMENT	*Gross motor activity:* involvement of whole body, climbs, jumps, throws *Territory:* outside, short excursions *Exploration:* "age of discovery" *Comments:*	*Gross motor activity:* jumps, runs, climbs, love for vehicles *Territory:* home, immediate neighborhood *Exploration:* interest in new experiences, places, animals, nature *Comments:*
MATERIAL MANAGEMENT	*Manipulation:* feels, pats, pounds, dumps, squeezes, fills, pushes, pulls *Construction:* builds with blocks, puzzles (4-5 pieces) *Interest:* little things, moving parts, mess *Purpose:* process rather than result *Attention:* intense interest, quiet play up to 15 minutes *Comments:*	*Manipulation:* small muscle activity, hammers, sorts, inserts small objects, cuts *Construction:* combines playthings, takes apart, simple products and designs evident *Interest:* anything new *Purpose:* results rather than process *Attention:* longer span (around 30 minutes) *Comments:*
IMITATION	*Imitation:* domestic (house, dolls as babies), of animals *Imagination:* starts with imaginary friends *Dramatization:* not evident *Music:* movement, actions *Books:* looks, touches, likes familiar stories, fills in words and phrases *Comments:*	*Imitation:* continues but more complex *Imagination:* very important, assumes roles, pretends *Dramatization:* mirrors, experiences *Music:* sings simple songs, instruments *Books:* likes new books, information books, pictures important *Comments:*
PARTICIPATION	*Type:* parallel, plays in company up to 1-2 hours *Cooperation:* little social give and take, much snatch and grab, independent, initiates own play, does not ask for help, helps put toys away, likes a place of his own *Language:* talkative *Comments:*	*Type:* associative, groups of 2-3, shifting, enjoys companions *Cooperation:* limited, some turn taking, asks for things, puts toys away with supervision, takes out emotions on toys *Language:* interest in words and meanings *Comments:*

TABLE 3
PLAY SCALE

	4-5 years	5-6 years
SPACE MANAGEMENT	*Gross motor activity:* marked rise, climbs, clambers, tests of strength, exaggeration, daredevil *Territory:* neighborhood *Exploration:* anticipates trips, likes change of pace *Comments:*	*Gross motor activity:* more sedate, good muscle control and balance, hops, skips, somersaults, climbs, skates, hoists *Territory:* up off the ground *Exploration:* plans and enjoys excursions and trips *Comments:*
MATERIAL MANAGEMENT	*Manipulation:* yanks, pulls, force and speed evident *Construction:* puzzles (10 pieces), products and designs evident, builds complex structures *Interest:* pride in work, complicated ideas *Purpose:* exaggeration *Attention:* amuses self up to 1 hour *Comments:*	*Manipulation:* combination of materials, use of tools to make things *Construction:* recognizable products, draws and arranges designs, likes small construction *Interest:* miniature things, making something useful, permanence of products *Purpose:* reality *Attention:* concentration for prolonged periods of time *Comments:*
IMITATION	*Imitation:* of adults, homemaking, dress up, reality important *Imagination:* prominent, oriented *Dramatization:* "shows off" *Music:* sings, dances, good rhythm *Books:* listens better, no longer needs physical contact with book *Comments:*	*Imitation:* same, costumes important *Imagination:* continues *Dramatization:* acts out stories, puppets, familiar things, here and now *Music:* knows melodies and tunes *Books:* must be credible, repetition of the familiar *Comments:*
PARTICIPATION	*Type:* cooperative, groups of 2-3, favorite companions, some solitary play *Cooperation:* takes turns, puts toys away without supervision *Language:* very talkative, fabricates, brags, threats, clowns *Comments:*	*Type:* cooperative, groups of 2-5, friendships becoming stronger, group games *Cooperation:* limited social give and take, rivalry *Language:* interested in here and now, how, why, what for *Comments:*

TABLE 4
PERSONAL DATA FORM

Initials _____ Date of observation_____

Sex _____ Time and place of observation _____

Examiner's initials _____ School or hospital _____

Additional comments on behavior observed: (include such information as a general description of the behavior, lack of any dimensions, and any unusual behavior)

The following to be filled after the observations are recorded:

Mean ages for the dimensions:

   Space management _____ Imitation _____

   Material management _____ Participation _____

Play age: (mean of all dimensions) _____

Date of birth _____ Diagnosis _____

Results of other testing:

---

1. *Determination of a "play age."* Since the scale is divided in terms of age levels, an overall level of everyday play behavior is determined by computing the mean value of the dimensions manifested. For example, a child whose space management is 3, material management is 2, imitation is 1, and participation is 2, has a play age of 2. The play quotient acts as a statement of balance among the four dimensions. It is useful in conjuction with other testing procedures in evaluating individual performance. Comparison of overall play behavior with other developmental testing procedures both confirms and supplements the information on a child's developmental status.

2. *A profile of the play behavior is shown by the scale.* For normal growth and development, it is important to maintain a balance among the four dimensions. Analysis of the profile and of each dimension separately shows trends of behavior, areas of ability or disability, gaps in behavior, stereotyped or unusual behavior. This kind of information helps the speculation about why a particular child develops competency within his environment or fails to do so.

APPLICATION

The play scale has been applied to mentally retarded children and to children with multiple handicaps. In the original study, the scale was tested with 12 four-year-old children in a pre-school program for the mentally retarded (Knox, 1968). All the children were ambulatory and free from obvious physical handicaps which would limit their activity, and all were from approximately the same social and cultural background. They were observed individually during group free play periods, both outdoors and indoors. Each observational period lasted for approximately 15 to 30 minutes, and each child was observed four or more times (twice outdoors and twice indoors). The observations were made during the scheduled play periods so as to obtain as natural a sample as possible. These periods were:

Morning:	outside play	9:00-9:30 and 10:30-11:00
	inside play	9:30-10:00 or 10:30
Afternoon:	outside play	12:30-1:00
	inside play	1:30-1:45* and 2:15-2:30

*This period of time was designated for play with such toys as puzzles, blocks, beads, and the like.

During these periods (with the exception noted above), the children were free to choose whatever toys they desired and could play in any way they wished. The teachers interfered with play only when it was necessary to discipline or when a child approached them for help or conversation. Also, if a child appeared to be wandering aimlessly for a long time (5 to 10 minutes) the teacher suggested that he find a toy. The observer was non-participant.

The observations were recorded on the rating scale described. Each dimension was marked at least once by placing a "+" mark before those statements which best described the behavior and a "−" when the behavior was absent. If the opportunity to observe a particular dimension did not arise, an "NA" was put before the dimension. Forcing a response to each dimension in this way increased the reliability of the observations. Items of special interest were also underlined (e.g., if the child engaged in any one type of behavior excessively). Space was provided under each dimension for any comments by the observer, and this might include such things as stereotyped behavior, absence of any form of play, and any interfering factors. Space was also provided on the reverse side for a general description of the play observed and any further comments.

The basic hypothesis that the play behavior of the retarded reflected their developmental level was supported by the study. An important element in the play of the normal child is a balance among the various dimensions. The retarded children showed a relative balance but at a level approximately two years lower than would be expected of normal four-year-olds. Analysis of the scale with other testing and with classroom performance showed that many of the children demonstrated isolated skills when called for in classroom activities which were not apparent during free play. This led to the proposition that the retarded child does not use, in everyday activity, many of the skills that he may possess. Since learning is accomplished through repetition and practice of abilities, then possible failure to learn may result from failure to assimilate past experiences and abilities into everyday behavior.

Investigation of the observed dimensions and factors showed the following trends:

Space Management

The type of gross motor activity demonstrated by these children did not differ greatly from normal physical activity. The majority of the children played at about the two-year level, being active and generally participating in play that called for whole body involvement, such as running, climbing, etc. Although the type of activity did not differ greatly, the time element involved played an important part. The majority of the children spent a great deal of time, not in play activities, but in watching others play. Some possible explanations for this hesitancy to engage in physical activity could be fear of getting hurt, lack of skill or experience in the play activity, or lack of energy or drive for physical activity. Further investigation is necessary to clarify these explanations. Territory could not be assessed because of the setting in which the observations took place. Further observation, perhaps in the home setting, or information obtained by the parents would help to establish this factor. Exploration was also difficult to assess since the majority of the children showed littel interest in new experiences or new toys. Upon encouragement, many did try activities, but seldom did they continue after encouragement was removed. This factor suggests a possible lack of curiosity among this group of children, a point which, again, needs further investigation.

The questions which emerged from analysis of dimension were:

(1) What are the underlying factors involved in the hesitancy of the retarded child to participate in active physical play?

(2) Is there a lack of curiosity among retarded children that affects their investigation and assimilation of new experiences?

(3) Can the mentally retarded child structure his free time in a way conducive to learning? Should his play be structured for him?

Material Management

Most of the children studied, manipulated materials at about a two-year-old level as demonstrated by gross manipulation, pounding, pulling, etc. There was also a certain amount of stereotyped manipulation, such as twirling and banging objects. Wheel toys were great favorites as were push-pull toys. With unstructured material such as clay, the children again manipulated it and generally did not form products. There was comparatively little spontaneous construction activity. A few of the children took apart simple toys and put them back together and a very few did puzzles. Interest was greatest for moving objects and toys (one- to two-year level), and least for new experiences or toys (three- to four-year level). The major purpose of play was movement and the process of doing something. Only three subjects showed any interest in products, which would normally be expected at the three- to four-year level. The factor of attention showed that most of the children watched things intently but did not generally appear to learn much from observation. Only one child was considered hyperactive and had to be physically restrained and watched constantly. The major trend shown by looking at material management shows that this group of children favored toys and play items that they could handle and manipulate, rather than those that called for a definite purpose.

Two questions emerging from analysis of this dimension are:

(1) How much repetition is necessary for the retarded to learn behavior? When does it get caught up in compulsive repetition?

(2) Does the retarded child favor unstructured material and toys and avoid those toys which lead to prescribed activity?

Imitation

The most outstanding trend noted in imitative play was the lack of imaginative and dramatic play. These would normally become evident at the two- to three-year level. Only one child showed beginning imaginative play and two showed dramatic play, notably, "showing off." Imitative play was demonstrated on about a two-year level. About half the children mimicked the actions of others and imitated isolated domestic activities. Only one child showed imitation of a domestic sequence (e.g., giving a doll a bath). Many of the children seemed to have difficulty remembering and relating past experiences, and this may possibly explain the small amount of imitation. However, immediate imitation or mimicking was particularly noticeable. For example, if one child did an activity, many of the other children would do exactly the same thing, particularly it, by doing so, they could obtain the attention of the teacher or of their peers.

The factor of music showed that all the children enjoyed music and moved, clapped, and/or sang sounds and words to simple songs. Since this interest normally takes place at around three to four years of age, it is possible that music may be quite an effective tool in facilitating the learning of these children.

The opportunity to observe behavior with books was seldom presented. In one class, the teacher read simple books aloud to the class, but during free play, the children seldom approached books. An exception to this was one child who would sit and look at picture books, jabbering to himself.

Questions that arise from this discussion include:

(1) Does the retarded child have a lack of imagination that hinders spontaneous play?

(2) Does the retarded child learn through observation and imitation? Is he able to remember experiences and apply them to new situations?

(3) What role does parental or sibling encouragement play in imitative play?

(4) What roles can music and books play in the behavioral adaptation of the mentally retarded child?

Participation

The majority of the children played alone most of the time, a trend evident in the normal one- to three-year- old. There was a great amount of onlooker play, as was there a lot of wandering. The children seemed to prefer being in a group, but their play seldom included others. At times, a group of children would be involved in the same type of activity (e.g., playing in the kitchen area) but the play was still individual. This trend, called parallel play, is true for normal pre-school children also and does not necessarily show abnormal behavior; although this group showed a lower level of participation than normal children of the same age. Only one child seemed to have a favorite companion, with whom he would talk and play. However, many of the children had favorite persons to pester, notably, the younger children or those with physical handicaps. The cooperation factor showed a great deal of snatching and grabbing activity, common in the normal two-year-old.

An interesting situation to note was the relative passivitiy of the children whose toys were taken away. The child might cry, but generally he did not attempt to retrieve the toy. Most of the children helped to put toys away, but it was felt by the investigator that this was partially a result of the pre-school training in which they were all engaged. A few of the children put toys away without supervision. Language ability showed that nine of the children could talk and express their needs and three had no speech or speech limited to one or two words. All the children appeared to understand directions, although they did not always obey.

Questions in this area are:

(1) What are the factors involved in the apparent desire of the retarded child to play along? How does the fact that he appears to enjoy being in a group enter into this?

(2) Does the retarded child show a passivity towards upsetting influences? Does this affect the manner in which he plays?

Since the time of formal application of the play scale with the mentally retarded child, it has been used as an assessment tool for pre-school children in a rehabilitation center for physically and psychosocially handicapped. The structure of the center allows for multiple opportunities to observe the child at play, and for close contact with most of the parents. Direct observation of the child's play behavior as well as analysis of the home environment are deemed important in gaining an understanding of the child's level of functioning. In direct observation, the scale is used as a guide to determining age appropriateness of play as well as quality and quantity. In determining whether the home environment is conducive to play and supports a balance in the major tasks of play, the scale is used as a general guide for observation and for interviews. In order to describe the use of the play scale in this setting the following case is described.

Bill—Bill was a two-and-a-half-year-old boy brought to the hospital for "failure to thrive" (below the third percentile in height and weight). When he was first seen by the author, he was sitting in the corner of the crib, his hands clasped, legs stretched out in front of him, and he was watching all that was going on. If someone approached him or handed him a toy, he would cry, push them away and wring his hands together. He seemed afraid of people, toys, and even of moving his own body. If he were put in any other position, he would return to sitting and when he became tired, he would put his head down between his legs and sleep.

Because of his fear of anything new, our initial approach was cautious. The first few times he was seen in the bed or held near the bed, giving him an opportunity to become adjusted to persons. Slowly, different toys were presented to him and often left so he could explore them on his own. As he became more trusting, he was taken into the therapy room where a number of toys were available. During this time, his spontaneous behavior, skills and abilities were assessed through the use of the play scale and other developmental tests.

Bill's gross motor play was limited to the few body positions he could assume and to what he was able to do with his hands. His territory was limited to the crib or to the spot on the floor where he was placed and exploration was only of objects within reach. If something was beyond his reach, he made no attempt to move towards it. In material management, Bill refused and seemed afraid of all toys except for a few in his crib. He particularly liked spinning a small wheel that was attached to the crib side. The type of manipulation that he showed was around the one-year level with fingering of hands and objects evident. In the area of imitation, he watched peers and adults intently and mimicked actions and expressions of those who interacted with him directly. Imagination and dramatization were not evident. In participation, his play was generally solitary and tentative, but he was beginning to interact with adults through simple games such as pat-a-cake. He watched everyone intently, listened attentively to sounds, but his language was limited to clucking and a few vowel sounds.

In summarizing Bill's spontaneous behavior, his fear of the unknown and of exploration was striking. All areas of play were around the one-year level and he seemed to have had little or no exposure to areas outside a crib, to toys, or to persons other than his immediate family. His reaction to new experiences was to retreat to the safest place he knew, the corner of the crib, to sit quietly.

Analysis of Bill's home added to further understanding about his behavior. He lived with his mother and two older children. His older sister attended school, and the brother, who was not in school, was reported to be nonverbal and hyperactive. His mother worked part of the day, so he and the brother were cared for by a sitter. When visited, the home and the children were spotlessly clean and the house was well furnished. Bill shared a room with the other children. His mother stated that he spent most of his time in the crib, where he was easier to care for and keep clean. Very few toys and play objects were evident and the mother reported that she could not keep toys around the house because the older boy tore them up. Because Bill was in his crib most of the time, he had little exposure to persons other than his brother. In summary, the home, although clean and well kept, was deficient in providing opportunities for play development. The environment offered little change for Bill to experiment or explore his surroundings. Exposure to play objects was very limited and has seldom given the chance to observe or interact with others. His major model to imitate was his brother whose hyperactive and destructiveness caused him to retreat and protect himself.

Since the striking factor in Bill was his fear of new experiences and his inability to explore, provisions for security and safety were essential preconditions to encourage his exploration. Therefore our first approaches were within the safety of his crib, until he gained a sense of trust with a few persons. At the same time he was observing peers and their activities. Gradually his territory was expanded in the company of those he trusted, to include the ward, the therapy room, and eventually the rest of the building and outside. The novelty of different toys was introduced slowly and time was allowed on his own to experiment, explore, and repeat. Within play experiences, he was taught specific skills such as crawling and walking. Games and interaction with peers and adults encouraged social responses. A mirror was especially effective with Bill and he soon came often to the therapy room specifically to sit in front of the mirror and practice expressions and actions, such as smiling, winking, and playing pat-a-cake. Bill's mother was included early in order to help her understand his behavior, teach her ways of encouraging play, and offer suggestions of activities to encourage exploration. Treatment proved very effective with Bill and within five months he was walking and actively exploring his environment with his total body and by manipulation. He also became quite socially responsive and verbalizations increased markedly. At the time of discharge, Bill's mother seemed to understand not only how to deal more effectively with him but was applying some of the same principles about play management to his brother. Both boys were recommended to a pre-school setting to further opportunities for play exploration to be expanded.

IMPLICATIONS

The evaluative implication drawn from the use of the play scale, as shown in the above discussion and case, is that the investigation of play behavior from a developmental viewpoint is useful in measuring the everyday behavior levels of children. It often yields information which cannot be obtained or analyzed with more conventional forms of assessment. It not only points out assets or skills, but also areas of deficit, and helps show the child's current ability to function successfully within the environment. It particularly points out the child who cannot play, whose play is stereotyped, repetitive, or non-functional, whose environment does not permit play, or whose play has become distorted due to physical and/or emotional problems. Comparison of the scores on this scale with those shown on a developmental scale that demonstrates abilities is necessary to evaluate effectively the total picture of the child's behavior. This type of comparison would allow for effective intervention based on the everyday behavior and on the abilities shown by the child. Such intervention would seek to incorporate the child's abilities into his everyday repertory, thus making learning more effective.

Recommendations for further use of this scale with different populations offer the following suggestions to increase the precision of the instrument.

(1) Revision of the behavioral descriptions to increase universal understanding.

(2) Application of the scale to a population of normal children of varying ages to determine normative data.

(3) Application of the scale to other diagnostic groups to determine overall applicability.

(4) Performance of the observations under varying conditions (e.g., home setting) to increase applicability.

(5) Use of more than one observer and statistical comparison of their results to increase reliability.

Application of the play scale as an evaluative tool suggests areas for further exploration.

(1) The mentally retarded child does not seem to incorporate many of his abilities into his everyday repertoire of behavior. He also demonstrates a hesitancy to initiate or to participate in new or unfamiliar experiences. What effect does this failure to incorporate and assimilate abilities and past experiences and hesitancy towards new experiences have on learning? Certain underlying factors such as curiosity, motivation, and imagination are evidenced in play of the normal child. These factors lead towards exploration and in turn growth and learning. Analysis of the play of the retarded showed these factors to be absent or distorted. Can play be structured in a way so as to stimulate curiosity, motivation, and imagination?

(2) Other children, because of physical, emotional, or environmental factors show developmental lags or distortions in their play. Since a balance in play dimensions is necessary to develop competence, what are the ways of helping the child achieve this balance? As with the retarded, inability and distortion in play seem to be traced to basic exploratory forces. A disability or a poor environment can often stifle exploration (as illustrated by Bill). What are the incentives conducive to developing exploration?

Nurturing Exploration

The behavior that does not occur spontaneously in children takes careful nurturing. The timing and manner of intervention need to be arrived at through skillful assessment. The trick or the art lies in creating environments conducive to play, providing certain preconditions to play, and applauding the incorporating skills into the everyday behavioral repertory. Environmental provisions can be structured in order to facilitate intrinsic motivation upon which exploration and experimentation depends. The environment must be so contained that repetition necessary to assimilate skills can occur.

Since the development of competence depends on motivation to explore and experiment, this in turn flourishes when there is some kind of satisfactory interaction with the environment. While no one can "make" a child play, one can remake the situation to provide necessary preconditions and incentives to encourage exploration. The following five guidelines are suggested as preconditions for exploration.

1. *Freedom from stress.* It is important to consider factors that inhibit the exploratory behavior of play. These include such things as hunger, anxiety, physical and emotional stresses such as pain, isolation, and fear. A child who is worried about his own safety is not likely to explore, nor is a child who knows that play may bring pain. Koestler (1964) states,

> play can only arise at an evolutionary level or in such special situations, where the organism has been partially liberated from the tyranny of "primary needs" in the traditional sense and can afford to "take time off" to play.

2. *Reinstallation of a mothering figure.* There needs to be one central person who can successfully balance love and playfulness and provide expectations. This central figure is essential to the development of a sense of security from which to operate. She can provide appropriate responses for successful experiences and encourage further exploration. Smith feels that a mothering figure is essential in developing a sense of well-being, stimulating interplay with the environment, and affecting the child's readiness for exploration (Smith, 1969). Ideally, this person should be the mother or guardian, and professional help should be directed toward helping the significant person assume this role. Sometimes, involvement of the mother is not feasible or practical and this role must be taken over by another. It is the responsibility of health professionals trained in child development and in play phenomena to serve in this role and to train others working with the child, including the mother. It is not good practice to turn such a sensitive and critical job over to a lay person, a hospital aid or to an unskilled mother and expect the play process to prosper.

3. *Opportunities for self-initiated activity.* In order for learning to

take place and for intrinsic motivation to develop, the child should be given opportunities for uninterrupted and undirected repetition and experimentation (Miller, 1968; Smith, 1969; White, 1967). It is not known just how much repetition is necessary for a deficit child to assimilate a task and certainly all children learn at different rates. There needs to be ample time for the child, at his own pace, to repeat, and change activities. Self-initiation is the much cherished building block in the learning to learn process. Until the child gains satisfaction from or realizes the purpose of an activity, he does not appear to incorporate it into his everyday repertoire and extend the learning into future situations.

4. *Something to imitate.* Theorists stress the importance of having humans, adults and peers, to imitate in enabling the child to adjust to his environment and to his society. In addition, animals, toys, and mirrors can be effective in encouraging imitation. Imitation should be looked at developmentally as a prime stimulation for catching the next behavior. It should be close enough to the existing behavior physically and mentally for the child to be able to imitate and should not be so complex that he would be afraid to try.

5. *Provision of novelty.* This, perhaps, is the area which needs to be analyzed more carefully. Novelty and a variety of experiences are necessary to incite curiosity and exploration. On the other hand, an environment which provides too much variety may overwhelm or frighten a child. Also too intense stimulation of any type will serve to focus the attention on that particular thing and not allow for general learning to take place. White (1967) proposes arrangements which use periods of less intense motivation for the development of competence:

> Strong motivation reinforces learning in a narrow sphere, whereas moderate motivation is more conducive to an exploratory and experimental attitude which leads to competent interactions in general without reference to an immediate pressing need.

There is a fine balance in designing novelty. It is highly dependent on the developmental level of the child and is deeply interrelated with the other factors. If the child has a secure relationship with the mother figure and is allowed to go at his own pace, he is better able to handle a variety of experiences. He also needs to experience success in order to advance. New experiences should be close enough to his present level of functioning to encourage further exploration and not to cause a child to retreat.

The art of the matter consists of a trained appreciation of the intricately intertwining of such factors as: familiarity, repetition, imitation, novelty, and the freedom from stress. Optimal settings for play are those which can provide these factors and also maintain a balance in the play experiences available. Within this type of setting, the optimistic conclusion is that much can be done in treating the child, training hospital staff, and counseling and training parents.

SUMMARY

This chapter presented a model for observation and assessment of play behavior. The model provides the means to measure the age appropriateness of play behavior as well as the means of detecting any play behavior imbalances. Application of the scale for evaluation of play was described with mentally retarded children and with a child with environmental failure to thrive. Implications were discussed with suggestions for further exploration. The findings of the play scale were considered in the context of competence behavior and this confrontation evoked suggestions for the environmental nurturing of play.

REFERENCES

ERIKSON, E. H. (1940) "Studies in the interpretation of play," Genetic Psychology Monographs 23: 557-671.

KNOX, S. H. (1968) "Observation and assessment of the everyday play behavior of the mentally retarded child." Master's Theses, University of Southern California.

KOESTLER, A. (1964) The Act of Creation. New York: Dell.

MILLER, S. (1968) The Psychology of Play. Baltimore: Penguin.

SMITH, M. B. (1969) Social Psychology and Human Values. Aldine.

WHITE, R. W. (1967) "Motivation reconsidered: the concept of competence." Sourcebook in Abnormal Psychology. Boston: Houghton Mifflin.

CHAPTER 7

A PLAY SKILLS INVENTORY

Janith Hurff

A child leaving the first decade of life, and moving along the developmental itinerary toward adolescence is at a critical, but usually ignored, behavioral intersection. We know less about this age than we ought. A possible explanation might be that the higher visibility and more dramatic nature of infancy and adolescence cause these ages to enjoy a kind of scrutiny not at all common to the ten-year-old period. In this instance, by a ten-year-old, we mean a hypothetical conceptualization of those behaviors usually included in the eight to twelve-year-old range.

Common sense tells us that the second decade of life is committed to the adolescent struggle for the coherence that the real-life tasks of adulthood require. It is less obvious, however, that much of the success of the adolescent venture depends upon learnings accumulated in the middle childhood level. The intent of this chapter is to say that the ten-year-old period is a critical point for monitoring abilities and offers a relatively unexploited opportunity for intervention. A means for monitoring the gross deficits of middle childhood play is proposed in this chapter.

Havighurst (1952) has described the behavioral readiness of this period as the function of three levels. A child, says Havighurst, is free to explore the alternatives of adolescence when (1) he has physically moved into the world of games which give practice to his neuromuscular controls; (2) he has psychologically developed his mental processes which include symbolization, conceptualization, and communication; (3) he has socially expanded his life space from home into peer groups. To the Havighurst levels we would add a fourth dimension in the interest of the occupational behavioral itinerary that is well en route by this age. Family membership has already required the child to learn what is expected of him in the roles assigned by family events and chores. In school he is already well into the student role and struggling for competency with the intellectual tools of reading, writing, reasoning, and problem-solving.

Erikson (1963) emphasizes the tool-learning requirements of middle childhood in his description of this age as being a struggle between industry and inferiority. It is a time, says Erikson, when the child must forget past hopes and wishes and tame his exuberant imagination by harnessing it to the laws of objects. The child at this time moves along the developmental itinerary toward becoming a worker and potential provider and learns that recognition can be gained by producing things. The sense of industry develops as the laws of the tool world of skills and tasks are explored and practiced. When these technological fundamentals are in place, then they are readily available for adolescent use. Their very presence influences favorably the struggle to learn and to achieve the economic, technical, and social roles which are demanded by the wider society beyond home and school.

What are the consequences for the ten-year-old child if the laws of objects are not adequately learned? Nature, Erikson reminds us, provided the relatively emotional quiet of latency just so that the basic skills or tools could be practiced. He warns that if this biological task is not served, adolescence will fail in its struggle for coherence. The wish to learn and the will to learn will proceed with difficulty. The incremental learning that nurtures a sense of worth and identity will be blocked. Thus the acquisition of physical, intellectual and social skills could be decimated by the violence of frustration or defeated by the apathy that results from feelings of inferiority.

THE CONSTRAINTS OF ASSESSMENT

Logically, it would seem a good idea to be able to inventory the skills of a ten-year-old and thus assess the readiness to move into adolescence. This very simplistic statement should alert us to the hazards standing between the wish and its realization. When any commonplace task, which ought to have been done, has not been done, it is usually because of many difficulties hidden beneath the obvious. It is true that we have on hand some monitoring devices. There are the traditional achievement tests that check out school ability, such as the I.Q. tests, and other formal checks upon mental ability. A steady stream of feedback on a child's behavior flows from the home, the school, and the street. The peer group is a notorious and realistic evaluator of its members through its methods of acceptance and rejection. Medicine has served the classical function of protecting the health of the child through its collectively trained judgment to detect pathology in the developmental process.

Yet there are children who by age ten have not learned an ordinary skill like bicycling while all their peers have, or who may perform well with a guitar while they cannot pitch sufficiently to be tolerated in the street ball games. Why a child learns some things easily, other things not at all, or learns some complex things while failing the simpler things remains a mystery. Generally, such unusual patterns of learning are explained as the awkwardness of growth, and we must depend upon further growth over time to smooth out the performance. The truth lies more in the middle, that we do not have, but should have some gross overview system for monitoring the incrementally acquired skills of childhood. The overview should have some power to discriminate between the awkwardness natural to partially learned skills and the poor habits which result from the institutionalization of inadequately learned skills.

This study accepts the premise that the multiple dimensions of developmental behavior have precluded any generalized perspective. The complexities of the tempo, variations, and phased interaction have so far defied the traditional test battery approach. There are no comprehensive theories of either development or play to support testable hypotheses that might check out the skill readiness of a ten-year-old child and predict the safe passage of the adolescent phase of the competency itinerary. The strategy of this study is to push aside a trained concern for the dependabilities inherent in traditional testing methodology and exploit the potential that play has to express the empirical world of childhood.

THE AREAS INVENTORIED

The four general abilities selected arbitrarily to describe both development and play are sensation, motor, perception, and intellect. Sensation is defined as the ability to detect and identify stimulus change. Motor ability is defined as physical strength, endurance, speed, flexibility, and motor accuracy. Perception is the ability to attend selectively to a group of stimuli and to ·recognize patterns. Intellect is defined as the ability of the child to pull past learnings from his memory bank, select the best solution for the task, adapt his actions to meet the task and then reflect upon the outcome of his action.

The abilities are seen as developmental sequences which are both hierarchical and interactive. They are hierarchical in the sense that sensation must precede perception and perception must precede intellect development. They are prepotent, meaning that loss or disruption of the lower hierarchy will prevent or warp the functioning of the higher level of developmental skills. They are interactive or dynamic in the sense that each affects the others through time and cannot be conceived of exclusively in lineal sequential terms.

The basic or primary learnings require time and much practice to develop and extension into many settings before they are acquired. More complex organization skills depend upon these basic abilities. Sensation, motor, and perception skills are the critical prerequisites for advanced academic learning. Readiness implies that the child has adequately learned the foundation skills.

DESCRIPTION OF THE INVENTORY

The multiple interactions that development and experience have built into the repertory of a ten-year-old child require the inventory to stretch across a fairly extensive continuum. The play inventory was constructed of twenty tests, chosen to assess a child's performance level in each of four abilities. Some test one area directly, others test several areas simultaneously. The battery of play situations was designed to identify minimal performance. While the activities were selected for their appropriateness for a specific age level, they had to appeal to the capable as well as to the less able player.

The inventory is composed of popular playground games and commercial indoor and outdoor games as well as achievement tests selected from physical fitness and perceptual motor programs. It was pilot tested for gross refinement. The test was administered to a sample of twenty-one normal children, aged ten. The eleven boys and ten girls who completed the battery were an incidental sample selected from a limited population of a small, moderately affluent community. Names of potential subjects were secured from local elementary school teachers, youth leaders, and recreations personnel. The tests are organized and presented under the four areas of sensation, motor, perception, and intellect; scoring sheets and miscellaneous materials for administering the battery are in Tables 1-6, and Figures 1-7.

REFERENCES

ERIKSON, E. H. (1963) Childhood and Society (2nd ed.). New York: Norton.
HAVIGHURST, R. J. (1952) Developmental Tasks and Education. New York: Longmans, Green.

TABLE 1
PLAY TESTS

I. SENSATION

Test No. & Title	Purpose	Method	Scoring	Time
1. Tactile Ability	To check the ability to detect sensory awareness of varying tactile stimuli.	The blindfolded child is requested to run his fingers along a "roadway," a track constructed using 18 varying textures mounted to resemble a road. Textures include sandpaper, flock, punched holes, wax bumps, fine mesh, lace, netting, etc. The subject indicates a change of texture as he experiences it.	Each correct detection scores one point. Possible score is 18/18. Passing score is 10 or more.	Less than 5 minutes
2. Color Discrimination Ability	To check the ability to identify visual stimuli, and detect stimuli change.	A picture representing prime colors with various paired color hues of these prime colors is presented. A psychedelic poster is suggested. The subject identifies one color, then attempts to match it to its color mate within the picture.	Each correct detection scores one point. Possible score is 22/22. Passing score is 15 or more.	2 minutes
3. Auditory Ability	To assess the ability to identify auditory stimuli change.	A xylophone is used to present one tone followed by a second tone one-half tone higher or lower. The subject indicates if the second tone is identical to the first, higher or lower. Any tone comparison repeated on request.	Each correct decision scored one point. Possible score is 4/4. Passing score was 2 or more correct.	2 minutes

II. MOTOR

4. Physical Fitness Tests	To assess minimum muscular fitness (strength and flexibility)	Six fairly simple tests were administered to the subject. All challenges had to be executed per instructions. Lack of minimum physical fitness implied the subject ill prepared to face normal living demands, such as coping with physical or emotional emergencies. See Figure 1 for six tests.	Check "+" if executed as per instructions, "–" if any part was not performed, i.e., time requirement or positioning.	5 minutes for all six. 10 sec. holds for 3, 4, 5.

Test	Objective	Procedure	Scoring	Time
5. Body Roll	To check motor control, motor planning, and motor accuracy.	Must roll lengthwise across a 30-40 foot floor to a designated target. 3 trials are given to accomplish this.	"+" excellent roll, "x" satisfactory, "—" failure.	less than 10 minutes.
6. Gross Motor Corodination (Commercial "Pitch Back" Used)	To assess gross motor planning and control.	2 in. square marked off in center. Mark chalk line at 8 ft. and '0'. Given 3 trials at both distances to acquaint subject with action at these points. Requested to throw softball 10 times at target area and catch on return.	½ point each successful throw and ½ for each catch. Passing score is 5 points at each distance (out of possible 10).	less than 5 minutes.
7. Stick Static Test (Balance)	To check the body's ability to adjust to external forces while maintaining a desired position.	Requested to stand on heavy, stable block (3 in. x 2 in.) to maintain balance for 60 seconds. Stand with the ball of one foot placed crosswise of block, highest score is recorded.	The best of three tries for each foot. Passing score is 5 seconds.	10 minutes.
8. Dynamic Balance Beam	To check body coordination, motor planning, motor control, and the ability to correct self in space while moving.	Use beam not less than 2 in. wide and 6 ft. long. Balance while walking length only once. If balance is lost is asked to remount and continue. Mistakes and performance quality noted. Walk backward once. Walk sideways once.	"+" excellent, "x" satisfactory, and "—" failure. Passing is: forward allowing one error, backward 2 mistakes, sideways 2.	10 minutes.
9. Circle Hopping Test	To assess the ability of the body to adjust to external forces while participating in a desired action.	Mark ten 2 in. circles on floor or ground. See diagram. Leap into 1 in. circle with either foot, maintain balance on ball of foot for 5 seconds. Continue through all ten circles, alternating feet.	For accuracy and time. 5 points for each 5 seconds hold per circle. 50 is perfect score, 25 is passing.	5 minutes.

II. MOTOR (continued)

Test No. & Title	Purpose	Method	Scoring	Time
10. Fine Motor Coordination. Use commercial Game "OPERATION" (Milton-Bradley)	To test fine motor coordination and dexterity.	Requires the use of tweezers to position small plastic body parts into varied indentations on a cardboard frame (human form). Buzzer and light activated when error is made.	Five errors permitted per each part. Perfect score is 12. Passing is 6 or more; one score for each part.	limit of 5 minutes.

III. PERCEPTION

Test No. & Title	Purpose	Method	Scoring	Time
11. Visual Perception Test	To test the ability to recognize patterns selective attention, and check rate of search.	Place picture with many hidden objects outlined within context. When each of 13 hidden outlines is recognized and identified, it is checked off by examiner. See Figure 2 for picture.	1 point for each correct detection. Perfect score is 13/13. Passing score is 6 or more.	5 minutes deadline.
12. Space Dot Test	To check visual ability to recognize patterns, attend to stimuli, and reproduce visual patterns.	Use a cardboard divided into 3 sections, each with identical dot pattern with different line designs. Subject must reproduce one of the designs on a dotted test sheet. Figure 3: illustration and scoring.	Credit given for each correct movement from one pattern point to another. Perfect score 18/18. Passing 13 and up. Figure 3: example of scoring.	5 minutes limit.
13. Spatial Stick Test	Tests spatial patterning, the ability to estimate visual spatial distance and spatial memory.	A stick pattern is arranged with ice cream sticks to be studied for 5-10 second periods. Star of David was used, to be recreated from memory.	1 point for each correctly placed stick. Possible score 24/24. Passing score 20/24.	5 minutes limit.

14. Rhythm Reproduction Task	To check ability to reproduce auditory stimuli and sound patterns.	4 or more rhythm patterns are tapped out. Following each presentation the subject is asked to repeat the rhythm message. Check sense of timing, reproduction of sound pattern, and short term memory retention. See Figure 4 for patterns.	1 point for each correct repetition of rhythm. Possible score 4/4. Passing 3.	no time limit, takes 2 or 3 minutes.
15. Walking Reading Task	To test the ability to perform when confronted with	Reading material suitable for the subject's reading skill is used. He is asked to read while sitting, walking, and finally, while walking and being confronted with distractions. The examiner may converse while subject attempts to maintain his concentration.	Rated "+" satisfactory, "—" failure.	5 minutes or less.

IV. INTELLECT

16. Conceptualization (transformation)	To test ability to focus on a cognitive process called transformation. This is a process where one stage changes into another.	8 small cards representing pictorial stages of birds in flight were used. Each card depicted a sequential stage of wing flapping. The numbered cards are shuffled and arranged by subject to display the correct movement sequence. See Figure 5 for cards and scoring.	Perfect score is 7. 1 error is 4. Passing score is 2 and up. After cards are arranged, turn them over. Numbers on back in sequence score.	less than 5 minutes needed.
17. Conceptualization (ordering)	To assess ability to synthesize classification and order, hence enabling structuring of relationships.	10 cardboard rockets were drawn with each increasing in length by 1/8 in., shuffled and presented randomly to subject to be arranged in straight line in some kind of order. Next 10 strips of paper of varying widths were presented for ordering in same order as rockets. Task was completed via visual judgment. See Figure 6 for picture.	Each rocket numbered in own proper sequence scored 1. Perfect score 10/10. Same for paper strips. Passing is 7 for each.	less than 5 minutes needed.
18. Conceptualization (egocentricity)	To test ability to shift between own viewpoint and that of another which cannot be directly experienced.	A small detailed wooden house is placed before the subject. A dog figurine is set in various positions around the house. 4 cards each depicting a vew of the 4 sides of the house are shuffled. The subject must select the view as seen by the dog at varied positions. See Figure 7 for diagrams.	Each correct scored 1. Perfect is 4. Passing is 1 or more.	3 minutes or less needed.

IV. INTELLECT (continued)

Test No. & Title	Purpose	Method	Scoring	Time
19. "CLUE"	To check decision making skill and problem solving abilities.	Group of 4 players are brought into an informal game setting to play board game "Clue" (Parker Brothers). The examiner's observation focuses on the subject's skill in recognizing the problem, his retention and memory, the ability to eliminate incorrect clues, alternatives tested, relationships formed, deductive thinking and many social skills.	The play behavior and decision making skills are observed and recorded following dismissal of the group. "+" is excellent, "x" is better than satisfactory, "-" for satisfactory but weakness noted, "F" for failing.	1 hour for one complete game.
20. Group Lego Block Construction	To observe the individual's social interaction in pursuit of a group goal.	An abstract design formed from Lego blocks is placed in the center of the table. 4 participants, with an equal number of duplicate Lego parts matching those of the center model are instructed to work together to build an identical model. Complete freedom is allowed in their group organization.	A rating of "+" for excellent, "" for satisfactory, and "-" for failure.	15 to 20 minutes to complete.

TABLE 2
PLAY INVENTORY SCORING SHEET

Test	*Acceptable*	*Unacceptable (high risk)*
		Performance Categories

Test	*Acceptable*	*Unacceptable (high risk)*
1. Tactile Ability	10-18	0-9
2. Color Discrimination Ability	15-22	0-14
3. Auditory Ability	2-4	0-1
4. Physical Fitness Tests	+ (requires all executed as instruced)	– (if any missed)
5. Barsch Body Roll (Spatial Ability)	+ if at least one try completed	– if none completed
6. Gross Motor Coordination	5-10	0-4
7. Bass Stick Static Test (Balance)	5 seconds or less	more than 5 seconds
8. Dynamic Balance (Walking a Beam)	satisfactory: one error forward, 2 errors sideways, 2 errors backward	
9. Bass Circle Hopping Test	50-100	0-49
10. Fine Motor Coordination	6-12	0-5
11. Visual Perception Test	6-13	0-5
12. Space Dot Test	13-18	0-12
13. Spatial Stick Test	20-24	0-23
14. Rhythm Reproduction	3-4	0-2
15. Walking Reading Task	Reads correctly under all conditions (sitting, walking, being interrupted)	incorrect reading
16. Conceptualization (Transformation)	2-7	0-1
17. Conceptualization (Ordering)	7-10	0-6
18. Conceptualization (Egocentricity)	1-4	0
19. Decision-Making and Problem-Solving ("CLUE")	Acceptability based on printed rules of the game	Not acceptable based on inability to follow rules
20. Social Interaction (Group Lego Block Construction)	Working together to achieve goal	Working in isolation or continuous interruption of group's goals

TABLE 3
PLAY INVENTORY PROFILE ANALYSIS SHEET

Date _____ Name _____

Age _____ Sex _____ File No. _____

Critical Ability Areas	Performance Categories		
	Raw Score	Acceptable	Unacceptable
I. SENSATION			
1. Tactile Ability			
2. Color Discrimination Ability			
3. Auditory Ability			
II. MOTOR			
4. Krause Weber Physical Test			
5. Barsch Body Roll (Spatial Ability)			
6. Gross Motor Coordination			
7. Bass Stick Static Test (Balance)			
8. Dynamic Balance (Beam)			
9. Bass Circle Hopping Test			
10. Fine Motor Coordination			
III. PERCEPTION			
11. Visual Perception Test			
12. Space Dot Test			
13. Spatial Stick Test			
14. Rhythm Reproduction			
15. Walking Reading Task			
IV. INTELLECT			
16. Conceptualization (Transformation)			
17. Conceptualization (Ordering)			
18. Conceptualization (Egocentricity)			
19. Decision Making/Problem Solving ("Clue")			
20. Social Interaction (Group Lego Block Construction)			

Directions for 6 Tests

(1) Subject lies flat on his back, hands behind head. Examiner holds feet on the floor and the subject must roll up into a sitting position. Child does this one time.

(2) Same position as previously but the subject's knees are bent. Same requirements demanded as in test (1). Failure in test (1) and (2) indicates dangerously weak abdominal muscles. This suggests that the youngster is unable to lift his own weight which he must do to live, work, and play normally.

(3) Subject lies on his back, legs outstretched, hands behind head. He is instructed to raise his feet, keeping legs straight to the count of ten seconds. This is done one time. Failure in this shows deficiency in hip flexors used in running, jumping, and standing erect. These muscles are vital for defense, offense and physical survival.

(4) Subject lies on his stomach and arches back, hands and feet are held together and lifted off the floor assuming a bow fashion. This is held for 10 seconds. This is done once.

(5) Child lies prone with legs outstretched, hands behind back. He raises his legs keeping knees straight for 10 seconds. This is done one time. Failure in test (4) and (5) indicates that motor ability is underdeveloped.

(6) This is a floor touch task. The child bends from his hips, knees straight, feet together, finger tips to the floor for a count of 3 seconds. This is done one time. Failure in test (6) may indicate emotional imbalance plus muscular inadequacy. Individual under emotional stress tend to tighten their muscles. If muscles are maintained in a tightened condition for a prolonged period of time, they shorten.

Figure 1: TEST 4—PHYSICAL FITNESS

Figure 2: TEST 11 VISUAL PERCEPTION TEST (This is a portion of the test picture. Four figures are visable: bear, beaver, bobcat, and an Indian)

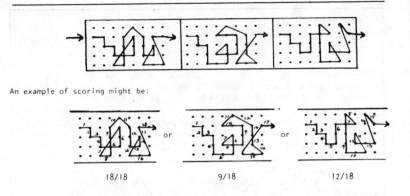

An example of scoring might be:

18/18   9/18   12/18

Figure 3: TEST 12—SPACE DOT TEST

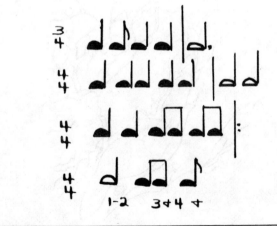

Figure 4: TEST 14—RHYTHM

Score: Each card carries a number on its back denoting its position sequence. All cards are turned over following completion of the test. The sequence pattern is recorded. Adjacent numbers in chronological sequence are given a point score. A perfect score is 7. However, one error would register 4. A passing score is 2 or more. Score example:
1 7 2 3 4 6 5 8 = 2/7
1 2 3 4 6 5 7 8 = 4/7

Figure 5: TEST 16—CONCEPTUALIZATION (Transformation)

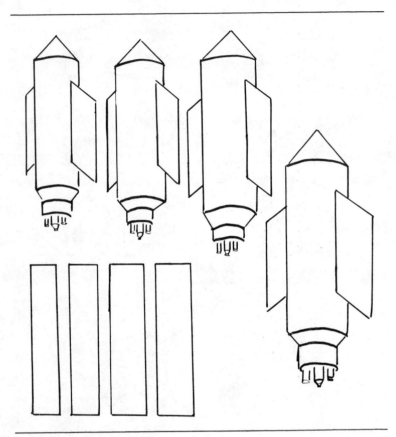

Figure 6: TEST 17—ORDERING

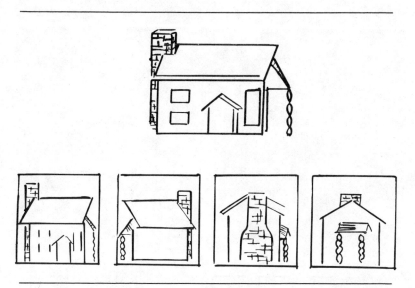

Figure 7: TEST 18—CONCEPTUALIZATION (Egocentricity)

CHAPTER 8

OCCUPATIONAL CHOICE: DECISION-MAKING PLAY

Phillip D. Shannon

INTRODUCTION

A distinguishing feature that separates man from lower animals is his capacity to choose. At no other point in development is the capacity to choose wisely more crucial than during the adolescent years, for it is during this period that the individual is seriously involved in the process of choosing an occupation.

Because work is so much a part of our daily lives, and because adjustment to work has such a profound influence on adjustment to life itself, the adolescent's choice of an occupation is one of life's most important decisions, deserving of our most intelligent consideration.

In preparation for the task of occupational choice there must be opportunities to project occupational interests, fantasies or daydreams into occupational roles, there must be opportunities for discovering one's assets and limitations and there must be opportunities for learning and practicing decision-making skills. The nonserious world of play may be viewed as an exploratory, experimental, safe environment for simulating work roles, for self-discovery and for developing competence in decision-making in preparation for occupational choice and the serious world of work.

To understand the relationship of play to each of these requisite experiences or occupational choice skills, this chapter will identify the nature of the occupational choice process, and describe the qualities inherent in the environment of choice that limit or expand the individual maneuverability in the choice process. The significance of play and its influence on occupational choice skill development is explored as a prelude to clinical data based on a skill inventory administered to five emotionally disturbed, adolescent servicemen, whose inability to choose an occupation could be linked to deficits in the quantity and quality of their play experiences.

For the multitude of deficient children in our society, occupational choice play as a concern of parents, teachers, play leaders, counselors and health care professionals, is essential to the deficient child's needs for achievement, competence and mastery.

It is hoped that the material that follows will enrich the understanding of concerned adults.

OCCUPATIONAL CHOICE

Theodore Sorensen, in his book *Decision-Making In The White House* (1963), hypothesized that decision-making is infinitely more difficult today compared to a generation ago. Mr. Sorensen's hypothesis might also be appropriately applied to the adolescent in contemporary society. Not only has the opportunity for choice greatly increased, but the options available have also increased. Occupational choice for the adolescent a generation ago was a basically simple matter—there was little if any choice to make. The adolescent was expected to move into his father's occupation. Today this is not the case. Few adolescents perform the work of their fathers' and instead seek work from the multitude of jobs available to them in twentieth-century America. As such, occupational choice has become a matter of increasing complexity in our society.

The choice of an occupation is not a single decision made at a particular point in time, but is instead a developmental process that involves decision-making over a span of years with regard to one's interests, capacities and reality.

Occupational choice is defined by Ginzberg and associates (1956) as a process involving fantasy choices, tentative choices and realistic choices. They describe the period of fantasy choices (prior to age eleven) as being characterized by choices based only on interests. In play the child projects himself into occupational roles such as doctor, carpenter, teacher, policeman, fireman. These choices change frequently and are made exclusive of reality factors such as capacities and limitations.

The period of tentative choices (ages eleven to seventeen) is described as the phase where realism begins to influence choice. At the beginning of this period interests continue to dominate choice. Later, capacities are assessed and values are weighed in the choice process. This period terminates at approzimately age seventeen or when the individual is finishing high school, at which time he must reconsider his interests, capacities, limitations and values in contemplating his vocational future.

The period of realistic choices (from age seventeen) is divided into three stages: exploration, crystallization and specification. The first concerns job opportunities within a wide range of choices, that is, the individual tries to match what is available with what he wants or sees himself as capable of doing. The second involves a narrowing of the choice field where the individual moves toward the choice of a specific occupation. The third stage specifies that occupation, that is, a job is chosen.

Essential to the task of occupational choice are those learnings found in play that serve as the basis for choice. These learnings, as well as the child's maneuverability in the choice process, are limited or expanded by environmental opportunity. Each warrants further discussion.

THE ENVIRONMENT OF CHOICE

The Act of Choosing

The choice of an occupation is certainly subject to environmental influence. Not only does the environment specify the alternatives for choice, but it significantly affects how one chooses.

For example, the alternatives available to the adolescent in search of an occupation are determined by the availability of occupational information. Because this information is not always readily available, his alternatives for choice are frequently restricted to what he sees others doing, to what he reads in magazines or to what he sees on television and in the movies.

The related elements of time and commitments cannot be

underestimated as to their influence on the occupational choice process. For example, in the final year of high school occupational choice becomes a matter of increasing concern to the adolescent, for his impending graduation forces him into a decision with respect to his occupational future. If he has failed to plan for his employability the situation becomes tense and complex. Within a relatively short period of time, which increases the risk factor in terms of making the best possible decision, he must choose with regard to his future role as a worker. He may find that his alternatives are severely limited. He may, for example, lack the necessary qualifications for college and thereby be forced into an unskilled occupation, when in actuality he sees himself as capable of moving into one of the skilled occupations.

On the other hand, if he has been pursuing a particular course of study in high school in preparation for a specific occupation, he will approach this critical period already having made a series of decisions or commitments in support of his occupational objective. It is probable, based on the principle of irreversibility, that choice at this stage will be based on these previous commitments, for choices are commitments to action and are irrevocable without the loss of prior investment.

The degree to which commitments are environmentally influenced is determined in part by time, in part by the extent to which there has been opportunity to become skilled in decision-making, or the extent to which one is able to commit himself, and in part by the degree of freedom in the choice process. The parent who has committed his son to becoming a lawyer, for example, has restricted or deprived his son of his right to choose and the son's commitments will be based on parental expectations versus free choice.

In choosing an occupation numerous essentials must be considered. For example, the adolescent whose aspirations lean toward engineering must concern himself with the difficult task of choosing an engineering specialty. The *Occupational Outlook Handbook* lists ten specialties in engineering, each with numerous subspecialties and each must be explored with regard to such essentials as salary, advancement opportunities, working conditions, employment opportunities, training requirements (to include cost and time) and, of course, motivation or intrinsic values.

Next he must itemize his capacities and limitations. In this example, intelligence, mathematical and mechanical abilities and financial capabilities are important considerations for the aspiring engineer. When his inventory is complete environmental influences such as parental wishes or parental indifference, peer group expectations, the influence of relatives and teachers, college entrance requirements, overcrowded colleges and universities, military service requirements and not to be forgotten, the quality of play experiences are but a few of the environmental forces that may act to influence the occupational choice process and may, in fact, determine how the adolescent is to choose.

The Basis for Choice

The resources available to the adolescent significantly affect the occupational choice process. Leading the list of resources that includes the obvious need for occupational information, is experience in two dimensions.

First, the youngster who lacks actual experimentation with the work role by participating in chores at home or by engaging in part-time employment, or whose environment has not provided him with the kinds of play experiences that encourage self-discovery and experimentation with work roles via simulated play experiences, is ill-prepared for the task of choosing an occupation. It is probable that his choice will be based on interest only without consideration for capacity and reality factors.

Second, it is equally true that the adolescent who lacks experience in decision-making is deficient in his capacity to choose. Crystallization failure in the third stage of vocational development may have a great deal to do with deficiencies in decision-making skills. As such, it is crucial that decision-making skills be developed, nurtured and protected in childhood for the inevitability of choice in adolescence.

The development of decision-making skills is dependent upon the following environmental conditions:

(1) there must be opportunities for choice, that is, for risk-taking, trial and error and commitments;

(2) these opportunities must be in keeping with the child's physical and mental capabilities;

(3) the alternatives for choice must be specified, that is, the child must be aware of the alternatives in order to choose;

(4) these opportunities should be sequential in nature and progress from simple to complex decision-making activity based on prior experience and previous commitments.

In other words, there must be lessons in choice at home, at school and on the playground in the interest of developing the child's capacity to choose.

It has been suggested by Weisselberg and Cowley (1969) that the decision-making process involves choice under four major conditions: certainty; uncertainty; conflict; and risk. For the deficient children in our society it is likely that few choices are made under conditions of certainty, but are instead made under conditions of uncertainty, conflict and risk. If this is true, and I believe that it is, it can only mean that the deficient or dysfunctional have been poorly prepared for choice; if they are poorly prepared for choice, they are poorly prepared for the future. If we are to help dysfunctional children and adolescents we must begin to provide the kinds of experiences that contribute to the development of individual capacities. We must offer them opportunities for self-discovery, for the development of decision-making skills and for work-role experimentation. These requisite experiences are found in the socially oriented environment of the family, the task-oriented environment of the school, but most important, in the play environment of the child.

THE SIGNIFICANCE OF PLAY

The contributions of play to the development of occupational choice skills are numerous. In play the child learns to cope with his environment and with himself. It is in play that the child's habits and attitudes are molded into an orientation toward life, congruent with his value orientation. Play provides for the development of the child's physical and intellectual capacities and is thereby a major force in shaping self-concept. Play is the arena in which the child discovers his creative potential and has opportunities to learn and practice organizational and leadership skills. Play teaches discipline, responsibility and citizenship. Cooperation, competition, loyalty and a respect for others are learned in the play milieu.

Play encourages risk-taking, trial and error and commitment, essential to the development of problem-solving or decision-making skills. Play also provides for identification with the worker role through the simulated experiences of role-playing and daydreaming. Most important, the repetitive nature of play lends itself well to the child's expressive needs and to the development of self-confidence and competence; it is in the exploratory, experimental play milieu that the child's human achievement endeavors are tried and rehearsed in the interest of task mastery.

The development of occupational choice skills in play cannot be reduced to magical phenomena, but must be viewed as within the influence of those responsible for the socialization of the child. Central in the child's environment are parents, teachers and peers, whose influence on the development of occupational choice skills is directly related to the quantity and quality of play experiences provided.

It is primarily, but not exclusively from his peers for example, that the child learns the kinds of social behaviors necessary for adaptation in the adult world. In group play with other children the mechanisms of acceptance and rejection teach self-control and press the child to the mold of social conformity. It is in play with others that the child learns that some behaviors are rewarded while others are not. He learns, for instance, that sharing, cooperativeness, honesty and sportsmanship (which will be discussed in greater detail later) are qualities that are praised, while stinginess, stubbornness, cheating and being a "bad loser" are behaviors that are not reinforced. As a measure of social competence, the ability to get along with others in play is implicitly fundamental.

At home and at school there should be opportunities to learn the relative merits of competition and sportsmanship via games, contests, recreational and athletic activities. Like most learnings, competitive and sportsmanship behaviors are learned in activities that progress from the simple to the complex. Games of chance like Bingo, Old Maid, and Fish, or games where the roll of the dice determines the action to be taken as well as the "winners" and "losers," are of the first type and must precede involvement in more complex games such as checkers, where winning or losing is contingent upon decision-making strategies and individual competence.

Games like Scrabble, racing toy cars, tug of war, and London Bridge is falling down should precede the more highly competitive activity of spelling bees, foot races and organized athletics, where individual capacity rather than chance has more to do with achievement or failure. Games of chance are less likely to threaten the ego integrity of the loser, whereas games requiring special skills inflict a greater wound upon the loser's self-esteem.

Likewise, team competition does more to preserve self-esteem than individual competition. Misery loves company, and with a little help from his friends the child can manage to accept defeat as a collective versus an individual failure.

Sapora and Mitchell (1961) indicate that perhaps the greatest value of competitive team activity is that it teaches such sportsmanship behaviors as unselfishness, honesty, responsibility, courtesy and tolerance which lead to the development of such civic behaviors as loyalty, cooperation, obedience and service. Sportsmanship behaviors may well serve as prototype behaviors for social adaptation in adulthood.

To parents and teachers falls the responsibility for providing the kinds of play activity that arouses the imagination. Experimental, creative, problem-solving activity should be basic ingredients in the play milieu. While some of the commercial toys such as erector sets and tinker toys are particularly good in this regard, commercial toys all too often fail to excite the imagination. We forget the values of such everyday playthings as scissors, paper, glue, pots and pans, sand and water, boxes and string and sticks and rocks, scraps of materials and all the kinds of household-backyard things with which the child can experiment, problem-solve and create.

He should be encouraged to scribble, to draw, to experiment with paints and colors, forms and shapes, to try one thing, then another, to take a chance on mixing red and blue to see if he gets green and, if he gets purple instead he can try and try again until he solves the mystery of the color wheel.

He should have opportunities to develop manipulation and construction skills. To be able to operate a wind-up toy, the bed of a toy dump truck—to be able to take things apart and put them back together again—to be able to steer a tricycle or scooter—all are the kinds of experiences that encourage object manipulation, self-awareness and mastery and add to the child's repertoire of skills.

The magic of building, fabricating or constructing is critical to achievement in later years, for in such activities as nailing pieces of wood together into some desired shape or form, modeling animals or objects out of clay, building model cars and airplanes, the child projects a part of himself into the activity and its success or failure is his success or failure. In such activities he must plan and organize; he must make decisions and risk their consequences; he must employ and test his manipulation skills.

Activities that develop coordination and build physical tolerance rank high on the list of essential play experiences. In addition to athletic and some recreational activities, bicycle riding, swinging, tree climbing, rope swinging, jump rope, hop scotch, stilt walking and skating are vital considerations for the play milieu.

There must also be provisions in the play milieu for the kinds of toys and games that encourage work role experimentation. The role-playing aspects of dress-up, cops and robbers, cowboys and Indians, as well as play with toy cars and trucks, doctor kits and carpenter sets greatly contribute to the child's exploration of the worker role.

The child must have opportunities to project himself into occupational roles via movies, television and reading; there must be time for storytelling and he must have time to daydream about the future and his future role as a worker.

Before the miracle of television, children all over the nation were fascinated with a Saturday morning radio program called "Let's Pretend." For many, the dramatization of fairy tales on radio was the essence in storytelling. For most children, the pretense experience of being the handsome prince, the poor woodcutter or the clever merchant was as close as they could come to identifying with the worker role. Cartoons on television have replaced the "Let's Pretend" of radio and as such, storytelling nowadays is limited to those children whose parents and teachers realize its value.

The value of daydreams with regard to work-role exploration cannot be overlooked. To use a personal example, I was discussing the writing of this chapter one day with my ten-year-old son, and after I had explained my proposal that play had a great deal to do with the simulation of work roles he suggested that I include something about daydreaming. When I inquired as to what he meant, his reply was: "well, many times when I'm in my room and everything is quiet, I imagine that I'm a mountain climber, or a spaceman, or a racing car driver or a famous athlete, and then I fall asleep." It became apparent that my son's daydreams (and I would suspect the same with other children) are an important vehicle for work-role simulation. In the process of daydreaming the child actually projects himself into the adult work world and imagines what it would be like "to be" or "to become."

In instances where overcrowded living conditions limit children's opportunities for solitude, such as in the case of ghetto and institutionalized children, not only are they denied their right to daydream, but they are deprived of their need to experience "being" or "becoming" via the imaginative world of daydreams.

Play must also provide opportunities to learn the decision-making strategies involved in such indoor games as aggravation and card playing, and in such outdoor games as marbles, hide and seek, kick the can and war.

To use another personal example, it has been fascinating to watch my son and my seven-year-old daughter play Casino, which is a card game involving some degree of decision-making. In playing with their father they have observed that the majority of his plays have frequent payoffs, and they began to imitate these moves or strategies once they were identified. Then, in the process of developing their own strategies they have begun to experiment and take risks in protest of their father's superior skill. Their efforts have resulted in their getting payoffs equal to their father's; needless to say, their father no longer plays Casino for the odds of winning have become too great.

To use still another personal example of learning decision-making strategies in play, I can recall playing the game of war when I was a growing youngster during the second world war. I had seen the movie "Sahara Desert" with Humphrey Bogart and was so taken by it that when I returned home, I began digging trenches in the field behind our house exactly like those I had seen in the movie. Before long I was joined by some of my neighborhood friends and in a matter of a couple of weeks or so, we had dug trenches and foxholes over an entire city block area. Command posts as deep as ten feet were camouflaged and candles lighted our underground passageways from one command post to another. Soon the kids on the next block began to construct a fortress of their own. When it was completed, the battle plans were drawn up and the war began. Everyone (over fifty children) had a role to play (work-role simulation) and everyone played it for real. Every conceivable strategy was developed to protect ourselves against sabotage, air attack, nighttime invasion and so on. Our own invasion plans were elaborate and complex and although we were too young to realize it at the time, we were learning and practicing decision-making in a simulated war that lasted several weeks.

Had it not been for the arrival of heavy equipment on the scene to level the area for a housing development our interest would have extended beyond the several weeks' period. As a final action we had decided to "cave in" all the trenches and foxholes to protect the heavy equipment from disaster, all except one, a ten-foot-deep command post that was so well camouflaged that even the heavy equipment operator could not see it until it was too late.

Finally, there must be an extension of the play milieu to the out-of-doors type activities such as camping and fishing and exploration of the non-human environment, where the opportunity to come to grips with the environment and become its master is essential to the development of autonomy. The non-human environment has much value "as a link to one's past and as a reminder of the continuity of one's identity."

If the development of occupational choice skills is dependent upon experiential opportunities and repetition, then the value of play as activity in which the repetition of experience in inherent cannot be underestimated any more than the roles of parents, teachers and peers can be underestimated as to their responsibility for and influence on the quality of the play milieu.

For the deficient children in our institutions—the mentally retarded, the emotionally disturbed, the physically handicapped and the delinquent—and for the deficient children not in our institutions—the school drop-out and the ghetto child—it is imperative that we provide the kinds of experiences that will contribute to the development of individual capacities. Play, as the arena in which individual capacities are discovered and developed should be viewed as a necessary requisite for the deficient child's adaptation as a productive human being.

The play experiences of the child can be grouped into three major skill categories essential to occupational choice; self-discovery skills, decision-making skills and work-role experimentation skills. To understand the relationship of play to each of these requisite experiences a skill inventory was developed and administered to five emotionally disturbed, adolescent servicemen, whose inability to choose an occupation could be linked to deficits in the quantity and quality of their play experiences. Each of these cases will be presented subsequent to an explanation of the skill inventory.

AN INVENTORY OF OCCUPATIONAL CHOICE SKILLS

In the process of developing an inventory for rating occupational choice skills, a total of 77 play-chore activities were selected for evaluation. Each of these activities was selected on the basis of their universality; that is, it was assumed that these activities were the ones most likely within the experiential realm of most children and adolescents. This assumption was made fully realizing that cultural differences and environmental limitations would significantly affect responses to the inventory. A low score nevertheless, would be indicative of a play deprivation and thereby not adversely affect the integrity of the inventory.

In regard to the kinds of activities selected for evaluation it should be mentioned that the crafts were excluded from the original 77 activities. The primary reason for doing this was because the patients with whom the skill inventory would be used had already been involved in craft activities as a part of their occupational therapy treatment program. Had the crafts been included in the inventory their responses would necessarily be biased based on their recent experiences. The intent of the inventory was to evaluate the quality of play experiences from a historical perspective, that is, prior to their hospitalization. The possibility that the patients had been involved with crafts prior to hospitalization was considered; even so, their exclusion from the inventory seemed to be the better approach.

It should also be pointed out that although 58 of the original 77 activities were eliminated, the values of these activities as well as others is still inherent and useful to the development of occupational choice skills.

And finally, although the inventory was developed for use with the emotionally disturbed in late adolescence, similar inventories could be devised to rate occupational choice skill development with pre-school, elementary, and high school-age children. These inventories could be useful for identifying play deficiencies and for their guidance value when considering play enrichment programs.

To return to the matter at hand, each of the 77 activities was rated by six registered occupational therapists as to their self-discovery, decision-making and work-role experimentation values. Each of these components in each activity was assigned a rating value on a scale from one to seven. By dividing the number of raters (six) into the total points earned by each component, a value point for each component in each activity was determined. For example, the self-discovery component of erector set play received the following rating on the seven point scale:

1	2	3	4	5	6	7
				11	1	111

Two raters valued the self-discovery component of erector set play at five points, one at six and three at seven. Totaled, the amount of points earned was 37. Divided by six (the number of raters), the self-discovery component of erector set play received a 6.2 value point. This, then, was the method by which each of the 77 activities was rated for their self-discovery, decision-making and work-role experimentation values.

These rating values not only varied from one activity to another, but variations within a single activity were also evident. For example, some activities (such as painting) were rated high by all raters in all three components; other activities (such as playing with toy tools) were rated high for their work-role experimentation values and low for their self-discovery and decision-making values. As such, it became obvious that some activities would have to be eliminated from the proposed inventory based on low value ratings for all three components, while others could be retained based on high value ratings for a single component, two components or all three.

The decision as to which of the activities should be retained was dependent upon the next step, which was to decide upon a weighing system for rating each of the components with some measure of equality. Because the work-role experimentation component in each activity was usually, but not always rated at a lower value than the self-discovery and decision-making components, it was not possible to equally weigh the components by simply selecting the highest rated 20 activities for each component; their total values would be respectively unequal. The alternative method chosen was to select an unequal number of activities from those with the highest value ratings per each component, and whose total value points would be relatively equal.

Because some activities received high value ratings in more than one component, all but 29 of the original 77 activities could be eliminated with the resulting number of activities and their value points for each component as follows: self-discovery—14 activities; 81.4 value points; decision-making—14 activities; 80.8 value points; work-role experimentation—17 activities; 81.0 value points. This method, then, in which unequal numbers of activities were used to arrive at an almost equal number of value points (the difference being negligible), proved to be the most satisfactory method for accomplishing the parallel objectives of determining which activities should be retained and for weighing the self-discovery, decision-making and work-role experimentation component values of each of the activities with a measure of equality.

It was then possible to construct a skill inventory for rating these components or occupational choice skills of five emotionally disturbed, adolescent servicemen. The inventory (Table 1) measures the degree to which each serviceman had participated in the 29 activities listed, and in so doing, determined the degree to which self-discovery, decision-making and work-role experimentation skills had been developed. Because norms were not established the inventory is limited to a measurement of the relationship of each of the three components to each other, not to other individuals. For example, a 50.6 rating for self-discovery, a 27.8 rating for decision-making and a 38.9 rating for work-role experimentation says nothing as to whether these scores are sufficient in terms of occupational choice skill development. What can be concluded is that as compared to self-discovery skills, further decision-making and work-role experimentation skill development is indicated based on the lower scores of these two components. Certainly the establishment of norms is a task for further study.

The rating scale (Table 2) is used to determine the total number of value points earned per each component. For example, if erector set play is checked as sometimes, the 6.2 value point for self-discovery is circled; the 6.3 value point for decision-making is circled; the 5.3 value point for work-role experimentation is circled. If play with tinker toys is checked as sometimes, a 5.7 value point is earned for decision-making. If play with toy cars and trucks is checked as often, a 10.6 value point is earned for work-role experimentation on the basis that an activity that is engaged in often as compared to sometimes is deserving of twice the value points. The assumption is made that the individual participated in that activity more to the exclusion of others. If never is checked no value points are earned. When all of the value points are totaled for each component, the sum becomes the score or degree to which occupational choice skills have been developed.

The case illustrations that follow will perhaps provide a clearer understanding of the inventory, its usefulness in identifying occupational choice skill deficiencies and its guidance value when constructing activity programs that will foster the development of occupational choice skills. Each of these cases concerns adolescent servicemen whose emotional instability requires that they be separated from the service, and whose occupational futures are uncertain based on occupational choice skill deficiencies.

TABLE 1

INVENTORY OF OCCUPATIONAL CHOICE SKILLS

Name: _____ Age: _____ Date: _____

Instructions:

As best as you can recall, check the frequency of your participation in the activities listed below.

Sometimes – if you have participated in the activity once in a while or only on a few occasions.

Often – if you have participated in the activity a great deal.

Never – if you have never participated in the activity.

Activity	Sometimes	Often	Never
1. Erector Set			
2. Tinker Toys			
3. Toy Cars and Trukcs			
4. Household Odds and Ends			
5. Toy Tools			
6. Dress-Up			
7. Cops and Robbers			
8. Races			
9. Contests			
10. Model Building			
11. Photography			
12. Cards			
13. Scrabble			
14. Painting			
15. Sketching			
16. Drawing			
17. Dramatics			
18. Play Musical Instruments			
19. Writing			
20. Inventions			
21. Experiments			
22. Football			
23. Basketball			
24. Baseball			
25. Track Events			
26. Skiing			
27. Hunting			
28. Care for Pets			
29. Care for Sister(s) and/or Brother(s)			

TABLE 2
RATING SCALE OCCUPATIONAL CHOICE SKILLS

Instructions:

For each activity checked, circle the appropriate value point in the columns labeled S (sometimes) or O (often). Total the scores for each component to determine the total value points earned.

Activity	RATING	Self Discovery Component Value Point	Decision Making Component Value Point	Work Role Experimentation Component Value Point
1. Erector Set	S	6.2	6.3	5.3
	O	12.4	12.6	10.6
2. Tinker Toys	S	–	5.7	–
	O	–	11.4	–
3. Toy Cars and Trucks	S	–	–	5.3
	O	–	–	10.6
4. Household Odds & Ends	S	–	5.3	–
	O	–	10.6	–
5. Toy Tools	S	–	–	5.8
	O	–	–	11.6
6. Dress-Up	S	–	–	5.5
	O	–	–	11.0
7. Cops and Robbers	S	–	–	5.5
	O	–	–	11.0
8. Races	S	–	–	3.8
	O	–	–	7.6
9. Contests	S	5.7	–	–
	O	11.4	–	–
10. Model Building	S	–	–	4.3
	O	–	–	8.6
11. Photography	S	6.0	6.2	–
	O	12.0	12.4	–
12. Cards	S	–	5.3	–
	O	–	10.6	–
13. Scrabble	S	–	5.7	–
	O	–	11.4	–
14. Painting	S	5.7	5.5	4.2
	O	11.4	11.0	8.4
15. Sketching	S	5.7	5.3	4.0
	O	11.4	10.6	8.0
16. Drawing	S	5.7	5.5	4.0
	O	11.4	11.0	8.0
17. Dramatics	S	5.8	5.3	6.0
	O	11.6	10.6	12.0

TABLE 2 (continued)

18. Play Musical Instruments	S	5.8	–	–
	O	11.6	–	–
19. Writing	S	–	6.0	4.8
	O	–	12.0	9.6
20. Inventions	S	6.2	6.5	5.0
	O	12.4	13.0	10.0
21. Experiments	S	5.8	6.5	5.5
	O	11.6	13.0	11.0
22. Football	S	5.7	–	–
	O	11.4	–	–
23. Basketball	S	5.7	–	–
	O	11.4	–	–
24. Baseball	S	5.7	–	–
	O	11.4	–	–
25. Track Events	S	5.7	–	–
	O	11.4	–	–
26. Skiing	S	–	–	3.8
	O	–	–	7.6
27. Hunting	S	–	–	4.0
	O	–	–	8.0
28. Care for Pets	S	–	–	4.2
	O	–	–	8.4
29. Care for Sister(s)	S	–	5.7	–
and/or Brother (s)	O	–	11.4	–
TOTAL		–	–	–

OCCUPATIONAL CHOICE AND THE DEFICIENT:
SOME CASE ILLUSTRATIONS

Although each of these cases concerns the dysfunctional adolescent in the military service, the assumption that their dysfunction is a result of their military service experience is a false assumption. They are instead typical of dysfunctional adolescents everywhere, whether they be in school, out of school, in institutions or on the street.

Case Illustration One. This first case involves an 18-year-old soldier who entered the service six months after his high school graduation. Not only was he unemployed during this six-month period, but he never held a part-time job or participated in chores at home to any great extent. His entry into the service was on impulse, and it was here that he encountered his first real work experience. In addition to completing basic training (two months) and advanced infantry training (two months), he had, due to the manpower needs of the service and not to his own inefficiency, worked as a combat engineer, a military policeman, a switchboard operator and a company clerk prior to his entry into the psychiatric unit of a military hospital. Here it was discovered that he had a history of drug abuse that included smoking marijuana and taking hallucinatory drugs which were considered primary in contributing to his depression. Pending separation from the service as a result of his emotional instability, his occupational plans, as before service entry are undetermined.

An inventory of his occupational choice skills produced the following scores: self-discovery skills—87.2 value points; decision-making skills—86.8 value points; work-role experimentation skills—100.7 value points. Compared to other cases that will be described these scores are relatively high. However, as previously mentioned, these scores do not reflect his standing on a scale of norms, only the relationship of these components to each other. In this case, self-discovery and decision-making skills score lower than work-role experimentation skills indicating the need for skill development in these two areas.

In a follow-up interview with the patient (which is always essential) it was discovered that his occupational interests span a wide range of occupational fields, and it became apparent that his present level of vocational development coincides with the period or stage of fantasy choices, where occupational aspirations are based entirely on interests without consideration for capacity and reality factors. In other words, this patient has not yet arrived at the second stage of vocational development or the period of tentative choices, where interests, capacities and environmental limitations are assessed in the process of choosing an occupation.

In addition, this case clearly illustrates the first of two deviations in the occupational choice process, that is, this patient significantly lags behind the majority of his contemporaries in the task of choosing an occupation as contrasted with the second deviation, or the inability to select from a wide range of occupational oppor-tunities a job that will prove emotionally satisfying based on interests, capacities and reality factors. In the case of the second deviation this patient has not as yet determined what jobs are potentially emotionally satisfying, that is, he has not as yet weighed his interests against his capacities and environmental limitations, and his deviation is therefore of the first type.

If the patient is to succeed in choosing satisfying work as opposed to forced entry into the labor market as a matter of necessity, which increases the risk of job dissatisfaction, several measures will need to be taken.

First, in terms of occupational choice skill development the patient must be involved in the kinds of play experiences that will stimulate self-discovery and decision-making activity. Photography and painting, high in value points in each component and within the avocational interests of the patient, may prove particularly useful in developing both self-discovery and decision-making skills. However, one of the basic rules for developing decision-making skills, you will recall, is that there must be a progression in decision-making activity from the simple to the complex. The crafts are particularly suited to low level decision-making activity, while the arts involve a higher level of decision-making. Therefore, in the case of this patient it will be important that he follow this sequence of the crafts to the arts in the interest of developing competence in decision-making.

A well-rounded activity program to include recreational and athletic activities (for their self-discovery values), and games (for their decision-making values) as well as the arts and crafts are important for this patient and his choice of an occupation.

Second, in choosing an occupation one must be consciously aware of his capacities and limitations. As such, it is essential that this patient itemize his assets and liabilities in terms of his occupational future. The following is his self-inventory.

> *Assets.* Honest, open-minded, relatively intelligent, generally patient, firm of beliefs and convictions, but willing to realize others' opinions and respect such, conscientious, have insight, familiarity with many ethnic and cultural groups, mature for my age, true of heart, clean of speech, polite and generally mannerly, peaceful and passive.

> *Liabilities.* Undecided about future, former "doper," somewhat of a procrastinator, insecure, unemphasized lack of personality knowledge, feelings of stagnation and of going nowhere, general self-dissatisfaction due to above faults.

With few exceptions, what was generally described by the patient were his character traits (not to be minimized) as opposed to his abilities, skills or competencies. What he needs is tangible proof of his capabilities, that is, he needs the kinds of experiences that will identify for him what he can or cannot do, for in order to know what he is good for, as Friedenberg says (1963), he must first of all know what he is good at.

Third, when his assets and liabilities are identified via experiential opportunities, he must consider his occupational aspirations and begin a program of job exploration. He must investigate books and catalogues in search of occupational opportunities and information in the interest of determining tentative occupational choices.

Finally, referral to a vocational counselor may be indicated for assistance in narrowing the choice field, job choice and employment.

Such a program would better prepare this patient for the choice of a satisfying occupation and for his future adult role as a worker.

Case Illustration Two. This case involves an 18-year-old soldier who enlisted in the service because he found civilian life boring. Prior to service entry he had lived on a farm in an isolated area of a small community. He had worked on the farm most of his life and rarely went into town or had visitors. He left school after ten and one half years to work full-time as a farmer which he continued to do until service entry. Although trained as a medic in the service he had not worked in this specialty, and eight months after his enlistment (or after he had completed his training) he had a schizophrenic break and was admitted to the psychiatric service of a military hospital. Pending separation from the service his occupational plans are indecisive.

An inventory of his occupational choice skills produced the following scores: self-discovery skills—126.6 value points; decision-making skills—83.8 value points; work-role experimentation skills—80.8 value points. Based on the significant difference in scores the patient's needs are obvious.

This patient's indecisiveness (as discovered in an interview with him) as to his occupational future—farming versus something in the health care professions, probably x-ray technology—places him somewhere in between the second and third stages of vocational development. He is involved in a struggle between what he can do (farming) and what he wants to do (x-ray technology). Thus far he has considered interest and capacity and has tentatively chosen medicine over farming. He has narrowed the choice field in medicine to x-ray technology which puts him close to the period of realistic choices where he must consider ability. He has demonstrated the skills needed for farming, therefore, the question is: "is x-ray technology what he really wants and can he become qualified?"

A minimum of two years' training is required to complete a course of instruction in x-ray technology. Entry requirements specify a high school diploma. Course work, primarily the sciences, includes anatomy, physiology, physics and chemistry. In high school the patient's grade average was a "D+." His best subjects were math, shop, art and physical education. All factors considered, there is a fair possibility that he can achieve this occupational objective.

The fact that he completed his training as a medic in the service demonstrates that he can apply himself to academic material when needed. Also, this training which includes some of the same course work as would be required for x-ray technology is an indicator of his ability to deal with scientific subject matter, and his knowledge of the subject matter would serve as an asset to him in an x-ray technology course of instruction. Because he received his highest high school grades in math (algebra and geometry) it is possible that he could manage chemistry and physics.

In terms of his deficits, a daily activity program should consist of the following. First, referral for educational assistance is primary for two reasons: (a) to complete the requirements for a General Education Diploma, which is the equivalent of a high school diploma and, (b) to take basic course work in the sciences to test or strengthen already existing capacities. A third objective would focus on the development of good study habits.

Second, a portion of each day must include time for play. Time must be provided for the purpose of developing decision-making skills necessary for job choice commitment in the third stage of vocational development. For this patient painting will be used subsequent to simple card games and basic woodworking, all of which are within the patient's interests. In addition to the decision-making possibilities inherent in some woodworking projects, the use of tools and machinery would be important for developing or strengthening the mechanical skills needed for x-ray technology.

Third, actual work experience in the hospital radiology laboratory will be required for crystallization of job choice. If the patient should decide against x-ray technology, further work role experimentation will become necessary.

Case Illustration Three. This case involves a 19-year-old soldier who was drafted into the service two years after his high school graduation. In this two-year interim he had worked as a plumber's helper, a drug store helper, an office clerk and as a construction laborer, each of which were to his dissatisfaction. He had worked as a carpenter's helper in the service, also to his dissatisfaction. Seven months after service entry he developed a depression and was admitted to a military hospital for psychiatric treatment. Here it was learned that he had been involved with marijuana and LSD both before and after service entry, or for a period of two-and-one-half years. Although he has not taken drugs since his hospitalization, he continues to experience frequent hallucinatory episodes (flashbacks) which only increase his depressive feelings to the point of his becoming a suicidal risk. Primary concern: "when I grow up I don't know what I want to be."

An inventory of his occupational choice skills produced the following scores: self-discovery skills—22.8 value points; decision-making skills—16.7 value points; work-role experimentation—38.4 value points.

In discussing his occupational future it became apparent that this patient, like the first patient presented, is at the first stage of vocational development or the interest stage. A striking dissimilarity exists between the two, however. While the first patient is actively exploring his occupational interests in discussions with other people, this patient has no interests at all and is literally at the daydreaming stage where he imagines himself in such occupational roles as policeman and social worker. The confusion that surrounds his choice of an occupation is pitifully sad. He views his future as hopeless and his existence as meaningless and empty.

It is crucial to this patient's occupational future that his activity program provide for a versatility of experience, which he did not have as a growing child. In his case, two levels of learning should be considered.

First, there will need to be involvement in low level decision-making and self-discovery activity. In other words, he must have the opportunity to discover and develop low level manipulation and construction skills, decision-making capacities and creative potential. In such structured activity as leatherwork and the semi-structured activity of gardening these capacities can be tested. Making a leather wallet for example involves the cutting out of the pieces and their assembly (construction and manipulation); transferring (from a template) and working the design on the wallet, making the leather lacing holes and lacing itself (manipulation); choosing the design, color of lacing and color of stain (low level decision-making). The quality of his choices and the quality of his work are early determinants of creative potential.

At the same time his participation in a gardening project should be considered, not only for its decision-making and creative values, but for its value in reaffirming his relationship to the non-human environment. He will need involvement in activity designed to test physical capacity and activity in which he can at first compete only with himself. Swimming is an example here. On the ward he will need encouragement to play simple card and table games such as Hearts and Monopoly for their low level decision-making, but high level self-esteem values.

As he gains increments of self-awareness and self-esteem he must move to a higher level of decision-making and self-discovery activity that will demand more from him in terms of planning and organizational skills, manipulation and construction skills and problem-solving. Working with clay, for example, can be an activity of this type where the quality of the project is influenced less by structure and more by the individual's skill in forming and shaping the clay into an end product. Choice becomes more complex in that the form the clay will take must be predetermined, which involves a greater degree of risk-taking, and the choice of design and color will serve as a measure of his creativity on a higher plane.

His physical activity will need to be extended to include competition with others in the interest of developing sportsmanship behaviors. And, he will require the stimulation of higher level decision-making games on the ward.

When this sequence of activity is completed, it is anticipated that he will be able to approach the period of tentative choices and eventually the period of realistic choices in the vocational development hierarchy with a measure of self-confidence, and with the hope of successful achievement.

Case Illustration Four. This case involves a 20-year-old soldier who was drafted into the service one-and-one-half years after leaving high school at the eleventh grade level. In this 18-month interval he managed to get married (eight-month marriage), produce a child and work at 15 different jobs all involving manual labor. He was never fired from a job; he kept moving from job to job seeking some unknown satisfaction. Like the second patient described, this patient also grew up on a farm where he worked more than he played. He had very few toys, games or friends, having assumed the role of worker quite early in life. In the service he was trained as an artillery computer operator, serving in this capacity in the Republic of Viet Nam where he began experimenting with drugs that included the use of marijuana, LSD and heroin. Shortly before his rotation back to the United States he felt himself withdrawing deeper and deeper into a fantasy world. He became confused and disoriented and one day after his arrival in the states, psychiatric help was indicated. Like the last patient he too continues to experience hallucinatory episodes to the point where they are almost continuous. Occupational aspirations: unknown.

An inventory of his occupational choice skills produced the following scores: self-discovery skills—52.5 value points; decision-making skills—39.9 value points; work-role experimentation skills—73.0 value points.

In reviewing this patient's activity history it is painfully evident that his history is one of failure—failure to complete school, failure in marriage, failure in work, failure in life. He has no interests, no goals. He is far behind his contemporaries in the process of choosing an occupation. At this crucial time in his life when he must plan for his employability he has little hope of success.

Based on his history of failure, activities in which he can achieve a measure of success and self-worth are primary. Like the preceding patient, he too will require a versatility of experience based on his play deprivation. Like the preceding patient he is equally confused as to occupational aspirations; like the patient that follows, he commits himself to action only to make new commitments in a different direction. Not only must his program emphasize self-discovery activities in which capacities are tested, but it must also provide for those kinds of experiences in which the relationship between commitment and responsibility is learned.

Almost any craft activity involves commitments to oneself with regard to the specific way in which the project will be completed, commitments for which the individual is singularly responsible. Commitments to oneself must precede commitments to others. Team competition is excellent for teaching the relationship of commitment to responsibility in that it demands cooperation and loyalty from its participants. As opposed to short-term commitments characteristic of single-game competition, participation in tournaments represents prolonged commitments and prolonged responsibilities. These are the kinds of learnings in which the patient must be involved.

As a consequence of his inability to commit himself to work (15 jobs), actual work experience in a closely supervised setting where work skill deficiencies can be identified and treated (in the interest of sustained employment), should be considered subsequent to self-discovery and decision-making activity that will prepare him for the task of occupational choice.

Finally, he should be encouraged to complete the requirements for his high school diploma to enlarge the scope of occupational opportunities, and to improve his odds for employability.

Case Illustration Five. Following his high school graduation, this 20-year-old soldier enlisted in the National Guard and at the same time enrolled himself in a university to study engineering. At the end of his first year in college his grades were failing, his attendance at National Guard meetings was sporadic and he was subsequently activated for full-time military duty. Within days after his activation he went AWOL, living in an abandoned house in an isolated area near his home town. He had used drugs prior to his activation and had taken LSD over 500 times. When he began to realize that drugs were destroying him (his thinking processes), he decided to terminate his eight-month absence from the service and seek help in a military hospital. He continues to experience frequent hallucinatory episodes as a result of his prolonged drug use, which also has him in a deep depression. Occupational choice: Uncertain.

An inventory of his occupational choice skills produced the following scores: self-discovery skills—98.3 value points; decision-making skills—87.2 value points; work-role experimentation skills—98.9 value points.

During high school the patient had worked as a life guard and in college as an office clerk. Neither job was particularly satisfying. He has not abandoned his original occupational objective (engineering), although he is considering other alternatives such as becoming a social worker or an artist. At the period of tentative choices, he must commit himself to action.

Similar to, but unlike the last patient, this patient characterizes the drop-out who, in this case dropped out of school, out of the National Guard, out of the service and out of life. Like the last patient he will need opportunities for learning the equation: commitment = responsibility. In committing himself to life, he will need to learn and practice sportsmanship and civic behaviors via games, recreational and athletic activities. He must learn new methods of problem-solving, that is, he must explore alternative solutions to problems and he must risk choice and its consequences in favor of avoidance and escape. He can develop his decision-making strategies in play, or in simple games that lead to more complex games such as cribbage where each action, each move involves considerable risk. Eventually he must risk the choice of an occupation and his assimilation into adult society.

The Dysfunctional Adolescent

Collectively these cases might be used to describe the dysfunctional adolescent in contemporary society.

The dysfunctional adolescent deviates from his peers in the process of choosing an occupation. He has been poorly prepared for choice as a result of early play deprivations and is particularly deficient in his ability to make commitments to action. He has a poor record of academic achievement and his work experience, if any, have been unsatisfactory.

He is uncertain of who he is and where he is going. He "turns on" with drugs in a vain effort to discover himself and his place in a world in which he feels alienated. He is confused, indecisive, insecure, disorganized and afraid. He risks his future to chance and passively awaits its outcome with pessimism and despair.

Certainly the future of dysfunctional children and adolescents is clearly dependent upon early experiences and the present, and what concerned adults can do to ensure that they have as equal an opportunity as their healthy contemporaries in meeting the future with optimism and hope.

STRATEGIES FOR ENRICHMENT OF THE PLAY MILIEU

The proposition of this study says that the concern for the future of deficient children and adolescents extends to the play milieu, where the essential learnings for adaptation in the adult world are dependent upon the quantity and quality of the child's play experiences.

As parents of deficient children we tend to protect them from the ominous pressures, threats and responsibilities of the real world. We maintain them in a prolonged state of dysfunction which to them becomes a form of adaptation.

For the handicapped, retarded and emotionally disturbed children in our public, private and special schools there appears to be a greater emphasis on training and control, and a lesser emphasis on learning the skills for living. For some reason it seems more important to clutter the child's head with a conglomerate of useless facts that will soon be forgotten, than to teach him the kinds of behaviors that will lead to social competence. When school funds are cut it is the "extracurricular activities" that are the first to go, and with them a most valuable opportunity for learning the rules for social adjustment.

In our medical institutions and special treatment centers for the deficient there is a greater concern for the physical or emotional disability, and a less concern for the social development needs. We encourage dependency in our hospitals, and forget that the deficient child's needs are the same as those of the normal child with one exception—his needs are greater as a result of disability and early deprivation in the maturation process. More than an ordinary child he needs to explore, to experiment, to discover, to achieve, to master. For the deficient child, play is the prelude to competence and adaptation.

As adults concerned with the quality of the play milieu, three primary strategies are suggested as guides to action.

Strategy One: Analysis of the Play Milieu for its Learning Potential

In demonstrating a concern for deficient children we must first inspect the play environment for its learning potential. The major elements are: (1) the play space; (2) a versatility of experience; and (3) regimentation.

The Play Scene. For most children in our society play begins in the crib, progresses to the backyard and extends to the neighborhoos, school, parks and recreation centers. For the institutionalized child where the space is limited to the dimensions of a hospital ward, play becomes sedentary, regimented and stifling. Whereas the normal youngster has the opportunity to explore and master the environment, the institutionalized play is restricted to an exploration of the inner boundaries of a ward. For any disabled child the quality of his play experiences is limited by the quantity of his play space. The extension of the play space into the out-of-doors and into the community is action in the transforming of behavior to competence and mastery.

A versatility of experience. Day after day an institutionalized child is expected to respond to the same activities and what is more, he is expected in the process to accumulate life satisfaction. Probably more than most children, he requires the stimulation and excitement of new experiences. His play, as with any child needs to be varied and balanced to include opportunities for developing his physical and mental capacities.

Regimentation. Most often an institutionalized child is subjected to highly structured activities that emphasize control versus free expression. It is necessary for growth that regimentation is minimized so that a child may discover his creative potential.

Strategy Two: Examination Learnings in the Play Milieu

An appraisal of the child's learnings in the play milieu in an ongoing process that is essential to the safeguard of the play environment. Some of the important learnings that need to be monitored are encapsulated in the answers to the following:

(1) Is he learning how to play by himself as well as with others?

(2) Is he learning the social equation of give and take in his play with other children?

(3) In competition with others is he learning to lose gracefully?

(4) Is he learning how to be a follower as well as a leader?

(5) Is he learning to respect the rights of others?

(6) Is he learning to control anger and to express his frustration in acceptable ways?

(7) Is he learning to exercise good judgment in situations where the rules are not specified?

(8) Is he learning the meaning of responsibility?

(9) Is he learning how to solve problems by taking risks and by trial and error?

(10) Is he learning how to express himself in creative activity?

(11) Is he learning how to take things apart and put them back together again?

(12) Is he learning the limits of his physical capacities?

(13) Is he learning about the worker role in chores, in daydreams and in role-playing experiences?

(14) Is he learning to become self-sufficient?

(15) Is he learning to be resourceful?

(16) Is he learning perserverance?

(17) Is he learning the habit of being thorough?

(18) Is he learning to concentrate for increasingly longer periods of time?

(19) Is he learning to cope with his environment?

White (1971) writes, "To be competent means to be sufficient or adequate to meet the demands of a situation or task." Competence for the deficient child is dependent upon the quality of his play experiences, and upon the quantity of his learnings therein.

Strategy Three: Contributions of Adults to Play Enrichment

According to Sapora (and Mitchell, 1961), the learnings expected of the child in play are contingent upon his readiness to learn, the repetition of experience and the degree of satisfaction achieved. In other words, no one can be coerced into learning a task or behavior for which he is not yet ready of capable of learning. To learn, it is necessary to practice what is learned or it is quickly forgotten. And, there must be an element of satisfaction from the learning or it will not be integrated.

With these basic rules in mind, efforts to improve the quality of the play milieu should be guided by the following:

(1) Consider the child's capabilities. Over stimulation is as discouraging as under stimulation.

(2) Consider the child's interests, for his learning is contingent upon his attitude.

(3) Interests change and with them, so too should the nature of the play experiences provided.

(4) Consider the child's need to play and replay certain experiences. Rehearsal or reinforcement is the key to learning.

The deficient child is both like and unlike his healthy contemporaries. He is similar in that he faces identical tasks in development; he is dissimilar in that he is less well-equipped to meet these tasks effectively. In play, the deficient child discovers his human potential and becomes his own navigator in the safe passage through the future. The right of every individual to a sufficient and meaningful play life is as basic as his claim to life itself.

REFERENCES

FRIEDENBERG, E. Z. (1963) The Vanishing Adolescent. New York: Dell.

☞ GINZBERG, E., S. W. GINZBERG, S. AXELRAD, and J. L. HERMA (1956) Occupational Choice: An Approach to a General Theory. New York: Columbia Univ. Press.

REILLY, M. (1971) Work Potential Continuum. Paper presented at a workshop on prevocational evaluation, Ann Arbor, February.

SAPORA, A. V. and E. D. MITCHELL (1961) The Theory of Play and Recreation. New York: Ronald Press.

SHANNON, P. D. and J. R. SNORTUM (1965) "An activity group's role in intensive psychotherapy." American J. of Occupational Therapy 19 (6).

SORENSEN, T. C. (1963) Decision-making in the White House. New York: Columbia Univ. Press.

U.S. Department of Labor (1960-71) Occupational Outlook Handbook. Washington, D.C.: Bureau of Labor Statistics.

WEISSELBERG, R. C. and J. G. COWLEY (1969) The Executive Strategist. New York: McGraw-Hill.

WHITE, R. W. (1971) "The urge towards competence." American J. of Occupational Therapy 25 (6).

ZIMBARDO, P. G. (1969) The Cognitive Control of Motivation. New York: Scott, Foresman.

LIST OF CONTRIBUTORS

LIST OF CONTRIBUTORS

Janith Hurff, MA, OTR
Occupational Therapy Staff
University Affiliated & Training Project
Children's Hospital
Los Angeles, California

Susan Knox, MA, OTR
Occupational Therapy
Children's Hospital Rehabilitation Center
Los Angeles, California

Shirley Michelman, MA, OTR
Assistant Supervisor, Rehabilitation Services
Neuropsychiatric Institute
University of California at Los Angeles
Center for the Health Services

Mary Reilly, Ed.D., OTR
Professor and Graduate Coordinator
Occupational Therapy
University of Southern California
Los Angeles, California

Phillip Shannon, MA, OTR, Maj. USA, AMSC
Chief, Occupational Therapy
Valley Forge General Hospital
Phoenixville, Pennsylvania

Nancy Takata, MA, OTR
Clinical Associate Professor, USC
Director for Training in Occupational Therapy
University Affiliated Program
Children's Hospital
Los Angeles, California